LOCAL GOVERNMENTS IN UGANDA
Democracy, Accountability and Civic Engagement

Adonis & Abbey Publishers Ltd

St James House
13 Kensington Square,
London, W8 5HD
United Kingdom

Website: http://www.adonis-abbey.com
E-mail Address: editor@adonis-abbey.com

Nigeria:
Suites C4 – C6 J-Plus Plaza
Asokoro, Abuja, Nigeria
Tel: +234 (0) 7058078841/08052035034

Copyright 2019 © ACODE

British Library Cataloguing-in-Publication Data
A catalogue record for this book is available from the British Library

ISBN: 978-1-906704-35-3

LOCAL GOVERNMENTS IN UGANDA
Democracy, Accountability and Civil Engagement

Edited By

Arthur Bainomugisha, Kiran Cunningham, Lillian Muyomba- Tamale & Wilson Winstons Muhwezi,

ADONIS & ABBEY
PUBLISHERS LTD

ACKNOWLEDGEMENT

The Editors gratefully acknowledge the assistance that has made this book volume possible. We are grateful for support from the development partners who supported the research that produced the book chapters. In a special way, we would like to thank the Hewlett Foundation whose support to ACODE's Centre for Budget and Economic Governance (CBEG) enabled much of the research carried out by the authors. ACODE is also grateful to the Democratic Governance Facility (DGF) contributing partners: The Netherlands, Norway, Sweden, United Kingdom (UK), and the European Union (EU). The DFID through Practical Action (Lima) also supported the research on local content which is the focus of one of the book chapters.

We are also appreciative to the Think Tank Imitative (TTI) which provides core funding to ACODE that made it possible to explore a wide range of issues on governance within Uganda while at the same time making the staff and research associates committed to scholarship.

Special thanks go to Professor David Francis and Professor Kenneth Omeje who until recently were based at the Bradford University's John and Elnora Ferguson Centre for African Studies (JEFCAS) for their technical and professional assistance in preparing this volume for publication. Profound debt is owed to the ACODE technical team who worked in concert with the Bradford team to prepare and transform this volume into a publishable form.

Notes on the contributors

Wilson Winstons Muhwezi is a Director of Research at Advocates Coalition for Development and Environment and Professor of Behavioural Sciences and Mental Health at Makerere University College of Health Sciences. He was jointly awarded a PhD degree by Karolisnka Institutet and Makerere University in 2007. He is a social worker with expertise in community-based work, public policy, advocacy, evaluation and mentorship. His competencies straddle design of curricula, managing vulnerability, building resilience; and research in mental health, psychosocial functioning, natural resource use and local governance. He has run workshops and trainings in research approaches, data management and analysis, scientific writing and public policy analysis. He has taught and examined students in several global universities. What sets him apart from professionals in his field is his niche associated with involvement in matters straddling social and health sciences. His publications include book chapters and numerous scholarly articles published in well-regarded international journals.

Kiran Cunningham is Professor of Anthropology at Kalamazoo College (USA) and a Research Associate at Advocates Coalition for Development and Environment (Uganda). She received her PhD degree in Anthropology at the University of Kentucky in 1992. She is an applied anthropologist with expertise in action research, community-based research, gender analysis, community development, institution-building, deliberative democracy, transformative learning, and international & intercultural education. She has worked in collaboration with a wide variety of organizations and institutions to design and implement action research projects in areas such as land use, local governance, youth needs and services, and women's economic empowerment. She has designed workshops and trainings for numerous groups and organizations in leadership development; gender analysis, transformative learning, and mind set change. She uses participatory research methods to bring the full range of stakeholders into the change process. Her publications include two books and numerous journal articles.

Arthur Bainomugisha is the Executive Director, Advocates Coalition for Development and Environment, a leading public policy research think-tank in Eastern and Southern Africa. He was a Technical Advisor for Uganda Peace Support Team on South Sudan and was involved in brokering a peace agreement between SPLA (IO) and Government of Uganda after war broke out in December 2013. He lectures Peace and Conflict in the Department of Religion and Peace Studies at Makerere University College of Humanities and Social Sciences. He was a Civil Society Fellow at the International Peace Institute (IPI), a New York-based public policy think-tank. He has authored several publications, book chapters and articles in Peace, Security, Natural Resources and Governance. A holder of a PhD and Master's degrees in Peace and Conflict Studies from University of Bradford (UK), Bainomugisha has a Diploma in National Security from Galilee Institute (Israel) and a Bachelor of Mass Communication degree from Makerere University.

George Bogere is a Research Fellow at ACODE. He holds an MA Economics Degree from Makerere University before joining ACODE in January 2011, George was a Researcher at Makerere Institute of Social Research (MISR) - Makerere University for over five years. George is interested in Economic Growth and Development, Decentralization, Governance and Service Delivery, as well as Natural Resources Management particularly land.

Naomi Asimo is a teacher, trainer and researcher currently working with ACODE as a research officer. Over the last 7 years she has worked broadly within one of her areas of research interest - local governance - with specialty in performance monitoring for political accountability; civic engagement and project implementation. Her other areas of interest include public administration and public health. Naomi has engaged in numerous qualitative research and capacity-building initiatives for policy advocacy mainly geared towards strengthening the capacity of local communities and governments for better governance. She has empirical experience and keen interest in Civic Engagement Action Plans, a unique approach for communities to engage government on service delivery and promote accountability. She has published under ACODE's series on Local Governance. She is presently rounding up her Master's degree programme in Public Administration at Uganda Management Institute. She also holds a Bachelor's degree in Education from Makerere University, Kampala.

Phoebe Atukunda is a Research Officer at Advocates Coalition for Development and Environment (ACODE) - one of the leading public policy research think tanks in Eastern and Southern Africa. Phoebe is in charge of ACODE's Information and Communication Technology innovations namely the Local Government SMS Platform that facilitates communication between citizens and their elected local leaders on matters of public service delivery, accountability and governance; A Citizen Monitor -Mobile Application which is used to strengthen the demand side of accountability in Uganda; and the online Citizen Budget Database that provides national budget data to citizens. Phoebe holds a Master's degree in Business Administration and a Bachelor of Science degree in Computer Science both from Makerere University, Kampala. Phoebe has also contributed to ACODE's research work and published in ACODE's policy research series.

Sabastiano Rwengabo is a Research Fellow at the Advocates Coalition for Development and Environment (ACODE), where he researches on the Governance of Oil and Gas Wealth in Uganda and East Africa. A Uganda and Singapore-trained Political Scientist, Rwengabo holds a Doctor of Philosophy (PhD) degree from the National University of Singapore (NUS). He was a President's Graduate Fellow at NUS where he taught undergraduate courses in International Relations, International Security, and Civil - Military Relations before re-joining the Social Sciences community in Africa in 2015. Rwengabo has research interests and publication record in Civil - Military Relations, International Politics/Security, Regionalism and regional security measures under the African Union (AU), Urban Security, Democratization, Nation-Building, and Governance of Strategic Resources.

Lillain Muyomba-Tamale is a governance specialist with over 15 years of experience in decentralization, local governance and human rights. Currently, Lillian is a Research Fellow at the Advocates Coalition for Development and Environment (ACODE). Lillian is also a Project Manager of the Local Governments Councils' Scorecard Initiative (LGCSCI) – one of ACODE's flagship projects on monitoring the performance of elected leaders. She holds a Master's degree in Human Rights and a Bachelor's degree in Social Work and Social Administration (SWSA) both from Makerere University, Kampala. Lillian is a published researcher in the field of local governance, political accountability and public service delivery with several publications in the ACODE policy research series. Lillian is a co-author of the sixth Local Government Scorecard Report that won ACODE the position of the best policy research think tank in Uganda with the University of Pennsylvania's Global Go-To Think Tanks ranking Report of 2016.

Eugene Gerald Ssemakula is a researcher who for the past 12 years has undertaken various social research assignments with interests in Monitoring and Evaluation, Local Governance, financing and accountability. His other works in the field of decentralisation include: Process/Formative Evaluation of Decentralisation Policy; Local Economic Development Policy; Profiling the Nature of Conflicts Affecting Local Service Delivery and Development of Strategic Interventions. He is currently a research officer with the Advocates Coalition for Development and Environment where for the past 8 years he has conducted annual capacity-building and assessment of political leaders under the Local Government Councils' Scorecard initiative. Eugene's training background is Social Work and Social Administration from Makerere University.

Jonas Mbabazi is a Research Officer with Advocates Coalition for Development and Environment (ACODE), a Policy Research and Advocacy Think Tank in Uganda. He has been a policy and governance analyst with over 10 years of consistent contributions in developing and analysing policies of government agencies and multinational organizations. He is adept at Policy Research, Advocacy and Capacity-building of Local Councils. He has widely published policy research papers, policy briefs and opinion articles on decentralization and local governance in Uganda. He is passionate about governance ideals. Well-versed in good governance and performance management of public institutions, conflict management, research, policy formulation and analysis. He has extensive hands-on experience in projects' design and evaluations, qualitative and quantitative research from working with multiple organizations and agencies. He is a passionate Social Work and Social Administration graduate of Makerere University, currently pursuing a Master of Arts degree in Peace and Conflict Studies.

Paloma Campillo is completing her BA degree at Kalamazoo College (USA) in Anthropology and Sociology, majoring in Anthropology &

Sociology with a concentration in Public Policy. She was an intern for ACODE in 2017, where provided research support to the Centre for Budget and Economic Governance, and the Local Government Councils Scorecard Initiative. She has additionally worked as an intern for the Mexican American Legal Defence and Education Fund, focusing on the legislative and litigative challenges faced by the Latino community in the United States.

Gerald Byarugaba is an Economist, Policy Analyst and Researcher with special interest in the area of Natural Resource Governance in the Great Lakes Region. His areas of speciality include Petroleum Policy and Resource Management and Monitoring and Evaluation. He has worked as Research Associate at ACODE and National Coordinator, Civil Society Coalition on Oil and as in Uganda (CSCO). Gerald holds a Post-Graduate Diploma in Monitoring and Evaluation from Uganda Management Institute, and is currently at an advanced stage of completing a Master of Management Studies degree in Monitoring and Evaluation. He holds a Bachelor of Arts degree in Economics from Kyambogo University, Kampala-Uganda. He is a 2014 Fellow of the PETRAD 8-Weeks course in Petroleum Policy and Resource Management and has undertaken much professional training in Natural Resource Governance. For the past seven years, Gerald has been involved in research, advocacy and capacity building to strengthen civil society and citizen engagement with government and private sector to ensure sustainable of Oil, Gas and Mineral Resources in Uganda.

Table of Contents

Chapter Nine

Wilson Winstons Muhwezi, Arthur Bainomugisha, Kiran Cunningham &
Lillian Tamale-Muyomba

List of Figures

List of Tables

List of abbreviations

ACODE	Advocate Coalition for Development and Environment
ACE	Autonomous Community Engagement
ALCs	Area Land Committees
BUKITAREPA	Bunyoro-Kitara Reparations Agency
CAO	Chief Administrative Officers
CBEG	Centre for Budget and Economic Governance
CBOs	Community-Based Organizations
CE	Civil Engagement
CEAP	Civil Engagement Action Plan
CEDAW	Convention on the Elimination of all forms of Discrimination against Women
CEMs	Civic Engagement Meetings
CRC	Citizens Report Card
CRED	Civic Response on Environment and Development
CSC	Community Score Card
CSCO	Civil Society Coalition on Oil and Gas
CSO	Civil society Organization
DEC	District Executive Committee
DLBs	District Land Boards
DTS	Fiscal Decentralisation Strategy
FGD	Focus Group Discussion
FMD	Foot and Mouth Disease
FOWODE	Forum for Women in Development
FY	Fiscal Year
GDP	Gross Domestic Product
GWED-G	Gulu Women's Economic Development and Globalisation
HPM	Hand Pump Mechanic
IDPs	Internally Displace Persons
IMF	International Monetary Fund
IT	Information Technology
LCE	Induced Community Engagement
ICSID	International Centre for the Settlement of Investment Disputes
LGs	Local Governments
LGCs	Local Government Councils

LGCSCI	Local Government Councils Scorecard Initiative
LGFC	Local Government Finance Commission
LGHT	Local Government Hotel Tax
LRA	Lord Resistance Army
LST	Local Service Tax
MDAs	Ministries, Departments and Agencies
MDG	Millennium Development Goal
MIGA	Multilateral Investment Guarantee Agency
MoLHUD	Ministry of Lands, Housing and Urban Development
MTEF	Medium Term Expenditure Framework
NGO	Non-Governmental Organization
NPPAs	National Priority Programme Areas
NRA	National Resistance Army
NRM	National Resistance Movement
NRM/A	National resistance Movement/Army
NUDIPU	National Union of Disabled Persons in Uganda
NUSAF	Northern Uganda Social Action Fund
OPM	Office of the Prime Minister
PAPs	Project Affected Persons
PRDP	Peace, Recovery and Development Pan
PWDs	Persons with Disabilities
RDC	Resident District Commissioner
RC	Resistance Council
SCE	State-centric community engagement
SDG	Sustainable Development Goal
SWGs	Sector Working Groups
UGX	Uganda Shillings
UHT	Ultra-Heat Treated
ULGA	Uganda Local Governments' Association
UNDP	United Nations Development Programme
UNICEF	United Nations Children's Fund
UNRA	Ugandan National Roads Authority
UPC	Ugandan People's Congress
USA	United States of America
UPE	Universal Primary Education
USAID	United States Agency for International Development
USD	United States Dollar

Map of Uganda

Map of Uganda

Source: Uganda Map, https://www.mapsofworld.com/uganda/, 11 July 2018.

Map of Africa

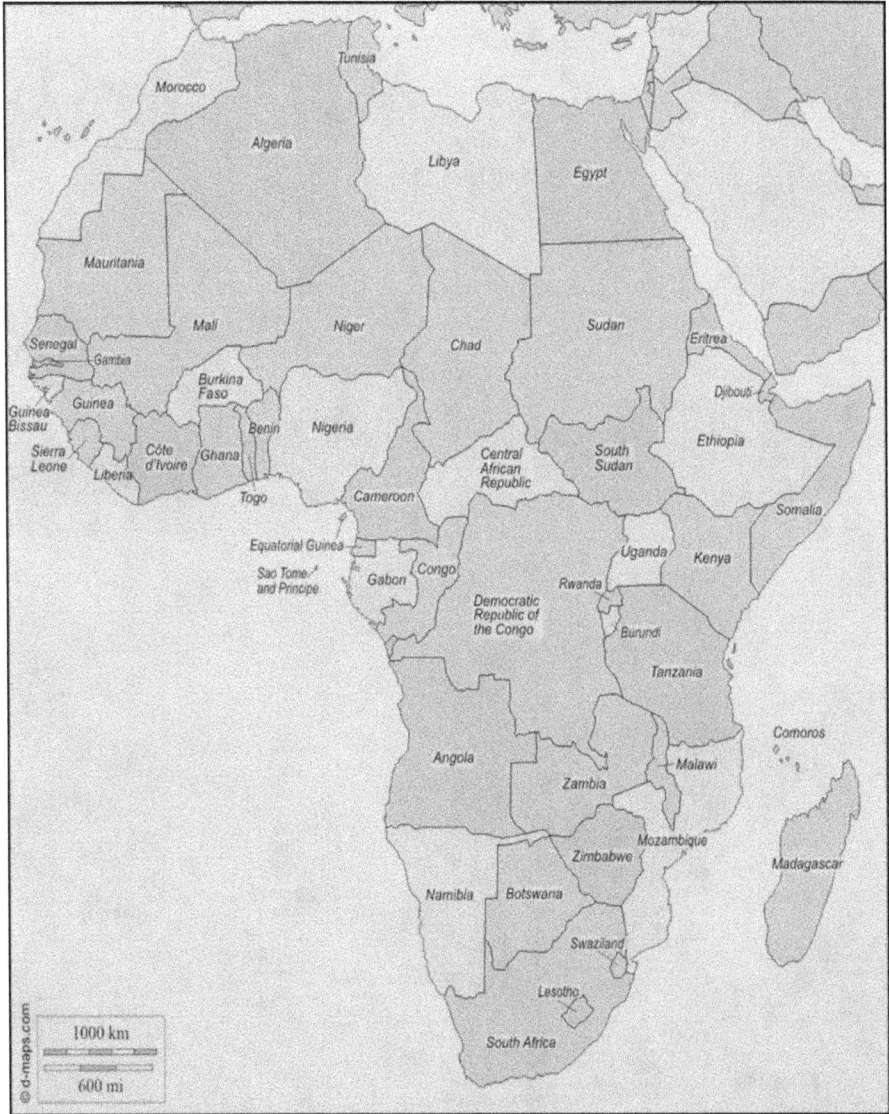

Source:
D-maps.com, Map Africa, http://www.d-maps.com/carte.php?num_car=25459&lang=en

CHAPTER ONE

Introduction to Local Governance and Democratic Accountability

Arthur Bainomugisha, Wilson Winstons Muhwezi and
Kiran Cunningham

Introduction

Several scholars have noted that the concept of decentralization is sometimes imbued with various and often contradictory meanings and interpretations. For example, distinction is often made between vertical and horizontal decentralization. Horizontal decentralization is where power is distributed among political institutions across the same level of government, while vertical decentralization distributes power to political institutions between two or more levels of Government (Lambright, 2011). Scholars distinguish between different types of vertical decentralization to include deconcentration and devolution (Regan, 1995; Crook and Manor, 1998). Deconcentration or administrative decentralization merely shifts representatives of central government ministries to branch offices at the local level. In the case of deconcentration, there are limited changes in the distribution of power. Local administrators can make few decisions without consulting the Central Government Ministries. In this case, the Central Government maintains full discretionary power over the decisions of local administrators. Fiscal decentralization is aimed at the transfer of limited influence over the budgetary and financial decisions to lower levels. On the other hand, devolution shifts full decision-making and financial authority to local levels and is often referred to as democratic or political decentralization. Decentralization has also been defined in two ways. Firstly, it refers to the physical dispersal of operations to local offices. Secondly, it refers to the delegation and devolution of authority to lower levels of administration or government. Local democracy which is consistent with decentralization fits in with the needs of daily life

(Danny, Hambleton and Hoggett, 1994). Citizens can finally change the course of events by participating in the management of their own affairs (Buijtenhuijs and Thiriot, 1995). In the same vein, decentralization has been defined as the transfer of power to different subnational levels of government by the Central Government (Oxhorn and Selee, 2004; Lambright, 2011).

In spite of the complexity of the concept of decentralization, all definitions emphasize that decentralization is the vehicle that takes government closer to the people where citizens are not mere spectators but key actors and shapers of their destiny. After many years of mismanagement of state affairs, coupled with poor or absence of public services and suffering in Uganda, citizens spoke through the Constitutional Commission in 1992. After five years of intensive consultations by the Constitutional Commission about the nature and form of government that should govern in Uganda, the Commission Report declared that:

> People want a form of government that is fully democratic and all-embracing in terms of participation and benefit. It should be one where the leaders put the interests of the people above their own. Such a form should make leaders at every level fully accountable to the people who elect them (Report of the Uganda Constitutional Commission, 1992).

The adoption of the decentralization in Uganda in 1992 has been hailed by scholars and technocrats as one of the best far reaching local government reform program in the developing world (Steiner, 2006). Decentralization policy was expected to contribute to development by empowering citizens and institutions at every level of society including; public, private and civic institutions; improving access to basic services; increasing people's participation in decision making; assisting in developing peoples capacities; and enhancing governments responsiveness, transparency and political accountability (Saito, 2000). From a status of a highly centralized and a near collapsed state in 1985 to a vibrant democratizing society, Uganda fully embraced the decentralisation policy to improve its governance. A critical analysis of the socio-economic and political achievements recorded under decentralization over a period of more than two decades of implementation reveals a combination of significant progress, somewhat stagnation, some reversals and policy challenges in critical areas that require reforms (Bainomugisha et al., 2014). However, what is not in doubt is that Uganda has steadily been able to maintain sustained socio-economic and political development. Democratic decentralization coupled with sound macroeconomic stability, post-conflict reconstruction of northern Uganda and consistent donor inflows and investment response to pro-market reforms largely accounted for a sustained period of high economic growth during the 1990s and the first decade of the 21st century. According to the World Bank, Uganda's recorded real Gross Domestic Product (GDP) growth averaged 7 percent per year in the 1990s and 2000s, making Uganda one of the fastest growing countries in Africa (The World Bank, 2017).

Introduced in the late 1980s by the National Resistance Movement (NRM) Government, decentralization sought to address governance failures of the past decades and improve the quality of service delivery to the citizens. The promise and the expectations of decentralization are captured in a statement by Sam Njuba, the then Minister of Constitutional Affairs, while opening a workshop for local government executives:

> The policy thrust of the Local Government Reforms is to promote active citizen participation in the national development process, to integrate and invigorate the local planning process, and to optimize resources utilization at the local level. The ultimate goal of the reforms is the provision of an appropriate institutional framework, which ensures public participation in Governmental process and facilitates greater public service delivery system (Lubanga and Villadsen, 1996).

From the onset, the adoption of decentralization program had to be seen as a fundamental change in as far as the organization of social, political and economic life of Uganda was structured and this was based on a number of indicators (Kanyeihamba, 2002). First, it was during this period that Ugandans either individually or in groups, in meditation or meetings were preoccupied with the economic development of their country by engaging in debates and discussions in respect to the making of the new constitutions and protection of human rights and democracy. Second, it was during this period that the relevance for protection of human rights became prominent and a hallmark of the NRM Administration. Third, the citizenry, the media and NGOs and other civil society organizations paid particular attention and campaigned openly and freely against any alleged abuse or violation of civil liberties at all levels of government.

Political Economy and Political History of Uganda: The Rationale for Decentralization

The rationale for the adoption of decentralization in Uganda was mainly a political imperative driven by the desire to improve efficiency and effectiveness in service delivery, national development and to deepen democratization. At the forefront of the National Resistance Movement (NRM) Ten Point Program was the promise to restore democratic rule and return of power to the people who had been disenfranchised by the successive post-independence Governments in Uganda (Kanyeihamba, 2002). The independence Constitution was violently abrogated in 1966 by the Uganda Peoples' Congress (UPC) Government led by President Milton Obote which was later on replaced by the Republican Constitution in 1967. The Republican Constitution also commonly referred to as a Pigeon Hole Constitution (it is called a pigeon hole constitution because members of parliament were told to pick their copies from their pigeon holes without debating the constitution) was crafted by a handful of wise men who subdued the entire country to respect it without question. In 1969 the Government of Milton Obote declared Uganda a one party state and embarked on the move to undermine opposition parties. In 1971, the army under Idi Amin who was the army commander took advantage of the political tensions to capture power and institute a reign of terror which characterised Ugandan politics up to 1979 when he was overthrown by the Tanzanian army barked by Ugandan exiles. The aftermath of the fall of Idi Amin was total breakdown, violence, anarchy and political uncertainty. The 1980 general elections that returned Milton Obote to power with his Uganda Peoples' Congress did not help the situation. The opposition disputed the election results with the majority of them opting to launch armed rebellions against the government of the second Obote presidency. President Museveni's National Resistance Army (NRA) captured political power after five years of a bush war (1981-1986).

When the National Resistance Movement (NRM) came to power in 1986, it inherited a near collapsed state. The economy was in shambles, the infrastructure such as roads, industries, telephones and the railway was in a state of disrepair (Mugyenyi, 2001). People lacked basic goods including soap, sugar and salt. These commodities under the Obote II government were being rationed and one had to be closely linked to a political heavyweight to get a coupon in order to access these essential commodities.

Ironically, in comparison to other African countries, Uganda's economy at independence in 1962 was in excellent form. It was one of the economies in Black Africa (Eric, 2013). Given the economic mismanagement and the political turmoil that characterized the first Obote government, the economy became the first casualty (Mugyenyi, 2001). Economic mismanagement was one of the reasons given by Amin for overthrowing the Obote I Government. Obote's first government adopted and preached socialism and a move *to the left* while at the same time cabinet ministers and political elites and security operatives were busy grabbing national assets for themselves. *This was the kind of move to the left, while I take everything on the right'* (Kanyeihamba, 2002).

The second Obote government, which succeeded the Military Commission, did not help improve the economy in spite of the massive donor support the government received after the 1979 liberation war. In order to win international recognition and the badly needed foreign exchange, the Obote 11 Government accepted all the conditionalities imposed by donor countries and the International Monetary Fund (IMF). A study that was commissioned by Sweden revealed that such money did not benefit the common people who would have to bear the burden of paying it back (Mugyenyi, 2001).

Besides poor economic policies prescribed by the IMF and economic mismanagement, most of the economic support that was received by the Obote II Government was wasted on the internal wars and conflicts. During the Obote II period, roads and streets in the country were in disrepair and full of potholes. There were chronic shortages of clean water, electricity, medicine and trained personnel in all Uganda's institutions including the educational system, which had become corrupt with falling standards (Museveni, 1997). It is this state of affairs that was inherited by the NRM when it came into power in 1986.

As part of the democratization agenda, the NRM introduced a *'Ten Point Programme'* as a basis for social, economic and political reconstruction of the country. The programme would also become a vehicle to deliver the NRM's promises to the people; a fundamental change that was intended to set it apart from the past rapacious governments that had ruled Uganda. Commenting about the fundamental change, Njuba, a one-time Minister for Constitutional Affairs, observed that the NRM/A revolution in Uganda was aimed at carrying all the people or at least a great majority through purposive and positive mobilization programmes. The main thrust of the ideology of NRM/A was aimed at doing well for Uganda which was true nationalism (Museveni, 2009). Njuba later on fell out with President Museveni, who he accused of abandoning the ideals of democracy, and joined the opposition FDC.

In line with the democracy, security and unity objectives outlined in the *'Ten Point Programme'*, the NRM expanded the Resistance Councils (RCs) to the entire country. RCs had previously been established in the areas under the NRA/M guerrilla control based on the principle that decision-making power, authority and policy making responsibilities should also be located at the local levels and that citizens should be able to reach and influence representatives and hold them accountable. The overarching question after almost 30 years in power *'is has the NRM administration under President Museveni delivered the fundamental change?'*

During the last two decades that the NRM has been in power, Uganda has managed to maintain an impressive annual economic growth rate of 6.4 percent, largely because of improvement in the policy environment; restoration of peace and stability in most parts of the country; and rehabilitation of infrastructure and increased capacity utilization (Shaw et al., 2008:214). The picture though is still different in northern Uganda where the LRA rebellion which ended in 2006 almost made it impossible for the government to rehabilitate the infrastructure and implement any meaningful development programme (PRDP, 2007). Another factor for economic growth has been due to increased inflow of capital and technology from the private sector involving both foreign and local investors, economic liberalization of the 1990s and donor aid assistance.

Donors pronounced that Uganda was indeed, *'a pioneer of macroeconomic stabilization and structural adjustment in sub-Saharan Africa'*, while even the most strident of critics acknowledged that the Movement's political system deserved to be credited for improving and sustaining peace and security in most parts of the country, allowing a fairly free press and encouraging citizen's participation through a democratically elected government (Moncrieffe, 2004). The dividends of policy reforms that have largely been financed by international donors through foreign aid is evidenced mainly by the expansion in construction, manufacturing (the case of textiles which tapped into the AGOA (African Growth and Opportunity Act), sugar and Ultra Heat Treated (UHT) milk; telecommunications, water, education and poverty reduction. At a broader level, fiscal discipline has ensured macro-economic stability while liberalization, deregulation and privatization have created a relatively 'new nation' (Shaw, 1973). There has also been a marked increase in access to safe water from 49 percent in 1998 to 57 percent in 2000. The number of women in parliament rose from 18.6 percent in 1996 to 26 percent by 2002 thus bringing more women into positions of decision making. Perhaps the most striking development under the NRM government is in the area of education. Since 1997 when government introduced Universal Primary Education (UPE), primary school enrolment increased from 920,000 pupils to 7.2 million in 2002 (Uganda Bureau of Statistics, 2002).

At Makerere University, the country's prestigious university, the total student enrolment has since 1986 increased from the mere 5,000 to over than 25,000 which is more than 450 percent increase in 15 years (Kakuru-Muhwezi, 2003; Muyinda-Mande, 2012). What is even most interesting is that the female enrolment at Makerere University has more than doubled as a result of affirmative action in favour of women introduced in 1989. The NRM can also be credited for the enactment of the 1995 Constitution which was hailed by most observers as a very progressive constitution, re-enfranchising the people by holding regular and periodic elections, and decentralization. The constitution devolved power to the lower levels to increase popular participation of citizens especially those formerly marginalized such as women, persons with disabilities, workers and youths, and political accountability provided for under Article 178 of the Ugandan Constitution.

Over a period of almost two decades, the implementation of decentralization in Uganda has aroused people's interest in democratic ideals of freedom, human rights, civic responsibility and accountable governance. Given that Uganda is a country that was nearly a collapsed state in 1986 when the NRM took power, decentralization provided a lifeline for recovery as it quickly mobilized the citizens and encouraged them to participate in the national development processes. Decentralization promotes broad participation of the majority of citizens in national development and decision-making and became a conflict management mechanism in a country where power and authority had previously been concentrated in the hands of a handful of individuals at the centre. Since majority of citizens participate in socioeconomic and political processes, the violent competition for fewer political positions at the centre reduced, breaking the conflict trap of a vicious cycle of violent conflicts that had characterized Uganda's post-independence politics (Opiyo, Bainomugisha and Ntambirweki, 2016).

While Uganda has registered significant developmental dividends under decentralization, some of the outcomes of the decentralization policy have been mixed and sometimes disappointing in the context of service delivery. The section that follows below analyses the challenges of decentralization.

Challenges of Decentralization in Uganda: A Case for Policy Intervention

While decentralization has been around for more than two decades, one cannot confidently say that it has consolidated local democracy beyond the point of reversal. An analysis of the progress of decentralization reveals serious policy gaps that, if not addressed, could easily result into reversals. Research evidence on decentralization in Uganda suggests that while service delivery has improved with decentralization, efficiency and effectiveness is far from what it should be. Researchers agree that the sticking points are a lack of transparency and insufficient resources at the local government level (Manyak and Katono, 2010). For instance, with decentralization, local government officials must have the resources they need to oversee effective service delivery. However, fiscal decentralization is still a feasible strategy for bringing about improved service delivery in local governments (Nangoli et al., 2015). It has also been observed that attempts to bring about better quality services in most times fail because most contractors hired to provide services on behalf of the government are compromised through corruption and other tendencies such as nepotism, favoritism and abnormal bureaucracies (Nangoli et al, 2015). District-specific research also identifies issues related to transparency as hindering the effectiveness of service delivery (Cankwo, Obandaand Pule, 2015; Obicci, 2015). A study of procurement processes in Nebbi District of Uganda found that significant, effective management of tactical the procurement cycle time can improve service delivery in the District (Cankwo, Obandaand Pule,

2015). Similarly, the same observations were made about public service delivery in Agago District.

In the education sector, the Government under decentralization opened wider the gates of primary school enrolmentin in 1997 which resulted into more than double enrolment of primary school children from 3.1 million to 8.4 million in 2013 (The Guardian, 2015). While the primary school enrolment soared and continues to produce impressive figures, primary school education has continued to experience the highest rates of school dropouts with less than 54 percent of pupils completing primary seven on average. The situation is worse for the girl child where only 30 percent of them complete primary level education. Another matter of concern is that the quality of primary school education has not been improving but declining. Study after study reveals that some of the graduates of the Universal Primary Education cannot read or write and yet they are encouraged to proceed to secondary education level. Unless government deliberately invests in improving the quality of UPE, the country will soon reap negative consequences of poorly skilled and half-baked citizens.

Furthermore, Government has invested significant resources in the construction of Primary Health Care (PHC) infrastructure upcountry to bring health care closer to the people. While PHC infrastructure has largely been expanded across the country, the quality of health care remains wanting in most parts of the country, especially in hard-to-reach areas (Republic of Uganda, Financial Year 2014/2015). Health care suffers the problem of staff absenteeism and understaffing, frequent drug stock-outs, underpaid staff and rudeness of health workers, which threatens patients and drives them to opt for traditional healers.

Another challenge that constrains local governments' ability to deliver on their mandate is poor financing and dependence on the central government for their operations. It should be noted that over 98% of local government financing comes from the central government as conditional grants. The level of budget financing for local governments in comparison with the center has been declining over time. For example, the share of the national budget accruing to local governments reduced from 17 percent in FY 2013/14, to 9 percent in FY 2017/18 (Ministry of Finance Planning and Economic Development (MFPED), Approved Estimates of Revenue and Expenditure FY 2013/14 and FY 2017/18). This is rather paradoxical in a sense that while majority of the population live in the Local Governments (over 80 percent population), a parity 12 percent (and progressively less) of the national budget is being spent on Local Governments. Poor financing, coupled with conditional grants which limit local planning in terms of priority areas for investment, limits Local Governments from delivering on their mandate to the citizens under their jurisdiction.

More so, local governments face the challenge of the creation of new districts some of which are unviable and incapable of delivering quality services due to revenue loss, rampant conflicts between the new and mother districts over resource sharing, demarcation of new borders and inter-ethnic conflicts since the demands directed at serving tribal aspirations. While some of the districts that are divided were very big and required sub-division to increase efficiency and bring services closer to the people, others are created following ethnic sentiments and maneuvers by local political elites to carve out areas for political capital. While decentralization transfers power, authority and resources from the centre, it also transfers grand corruption to local governments. Central to poor service delivery has been serious resource leakages and elite capture of resources meant for delivering services to the communities. It is common practice for local councilors to award themselves tenders through proxies to construct feeder roads and supply other materials to local governments (communities and some local leaders at the Multi-District, Leadership Forum in Arua, and 2015 September). Poor feeder roads in most local governments are a result of this problem.

The roads sector in local governments has remained the most troubled. In spite of the increased financing by Government to the roads sector, most roads in local governments remain a nightmare to the citizens. Most of them are impassable to the extent that farmers fail to access markets to sell their produce. Local governments continue to get fewer funds for the same task compared with Uganda National Roads Authority (UNRA) which defeats the logic of planning. While local governments have consistently raised the issue of underfunding, their appeals have not been responded to by the responsible ministries at the center. The sector has also been bedeviled by large-scale corruption which makes it difficult to deliver quality roads to citizens. The most vivid embarrassing scandal is the construction of Katosi road in Mukono District, where UNRA was duped into paying UGX 24 billion in advance to a dubious firm leading to the stalling of the project (Bainomugisha et al, 2014) As the Government prioritizes infrastructure development including the roads sector, serious steps must be put in place to deal with corruption in the roads sector if local governments are to make progress in service delivery.

ACODE's recent work that examined the governance of public expenditures in the health, education, agriculture and roads sectors adds another layer to our understanding of how decentralization continues to unfold in Uganda. The results of studies suggest that while the systems of decentralized governance have; for the most part been put in place, the functionality of these structures is still work in progress. Lack of coordination between the various stakeholders and government bodies, for example, was found to be especially problematic in the delivery of agricultural services.

Decentralization of service delivery was designed to bring government closer to the people. Indeed, much progress has been made to establish the structures and practices of people-centered service delivery. In spite of this progress, there is widespread recognition that the delivery of efficient public services and political accountability remains a challenge. Moving from rhetoric to practice will involve continuing to invest sufficient resources to enhance the capacity of local government leaders to do the job they have been mandated to perform as well as enhance the capacity of citizens to hold them accountable.

Put on a balancing scale, Uganda has made tremendous strides in social, economic and political development under decentralization framework. The local governance system and its local council (LC) structure are expected to bear important functions and responsibilities in order to consolidate and scale up the gains of decentralization. This includes: empowering local governments to engage in localized planning and programme implementation; local economic development to increase local revenue generation; holding the centre to account based on policies and laws; empowering the citizens to participate fully in the democratic processes and; to demand better public services and political accountability of the elected leaders, while performing their civic duties and obligations. This book interrogates all facets of the promises and practices of decentralization in the context of Uganda. The book volume is organized into ten chapters.

Chapters 2 and 3 take on the two fundamental parts of the assumption that decentralization empowers local governments and that it leads to improved service delivery. In Chapter 2, Ssemakula and Bogere discuss the financing mechanism of local governments and how it enhances or inhibits their ability to deliver on their mandate as provided for in the decentralization policy and the Local Government Act. Drawing on an analysis of thirty districts in Uganda, the authors argue that that the reduction in the contribution of locally-generated revenue for local governments has led to less accountability to citizens, because leaders are more receptive to the demands of the central government and not their local constituencies. Chapter 3 examines the level of citizens' perception and appreciation of service delivery and their level of civic awareness about their roles and duties and obligations. The chapter also seeks to amplify the voices of the voiceless citizens at the community level and to explore the state of decentralized service delivery. Mbabazi, Cunningham and Campillo use the data collected from over 100 community dialogues to discuss citizens' perceptions and their lived experience with decentralised service delivery in the health, education, water, roads, and agriculture sectors. In this chapter the authors argue that bringing service delivery closer to the people creates a governance system that is more responsive to citizens' needs and priorities.

Chapter 4 discusses ACODE's strategic intervention on social accountability strategies designed to unlock the structural and capacity limitations, policy and legal challenges that constrain local governments from delivering better public services to citizens that were raised in Chapters 2 and 3 by strengthening the supply and demand sides of accountable governance. All of the strategies described are linked in one way or another with the Local Government Council Scorecard Initiative (LGCSCI), the focus of Chapter 4. As Tamale and Cunningham describe, LGCSCI uses an action research methodology to enhance the capacity of local governments to deliver on their mandate.

At the core of decentralization was refranchising the formerly marginalized sections of society including the women, youths, persons with disability and the elderly and bringing them into decision-making processes. Chapter 5 focuses on refranchising the formerly marginalized sections of society and connects it to accountability. Asimo and Tamale draw on the findings of an in-depth case study of Gulu district in northern Uganda and posit that because women councillors are elected specifically to represent women as an interest group, they are more responsive and accountable to their constituents in spite of the various challenges including having to service a larger constituency than their male counterparts.

In Chapter 6, Rwengabo and Byarugaba discuss the critical role that communities play in holding their local governments accountable for protecting their rights to land in the face of large scale development. Drawing on the experiences of communities in oil-rich Hoima and Buliisa districts, the authors examine the complex issues surrounding communal land rights, land speculation, and land grabbing. They present an array of approaches that communities use to respond to threats to their land rights and analyses them in terms of their effectiveness in defending communal lands.

Chapters 7 and 8 focus on two social accountability strategies that strengthen communities' capacity to demand for effective and efficient service delivery while at the same time mandating government response. Both were developed and fine-tuned in the context of ACODE's Local Government Councils Scorecard Initiative, but they could each also be used on their own in other contexts. In Chapter 7, Cunningham and Bainomugisha describe the Civic Engagement Action Plan (CEAP) methodology that has proven to catalyse what Fox calls a virtuous circle of mutual empowerment. Taking a how-to approach, they explain how the CEAP process works, and incorporate several short case studies that illustrate the impacts of the process on citizens, local government officials, civil society organizations, and service delivery outcomes. Chapter 8 delves into the set of social accountability tools that fall under the "civic technology" umbrella. Chapter 8 delves into a set of civic engagement tools that encompass "civic technology". Illustrated with several examples around the world, Atukunda and Muhwezi review a broad array of such tools, discussing their strengths and shortcomings, particularly in the context of their ability to amplify citizens' voice in governance. They then describe ACODE innovations - a subject of this chapter - specifically the Local Government SMS platform and the Citizen Monitor Mobile App developed to link communities to their local political leaders thereby strengthening both the demand and supply sides of political accountability.

References

Bainomugisha, A., Muyomba-Tamale, L., Muhwezi, W. W., Cunningham, K., Ssemakula, E. G., Bogere, G. and Rhoads, R. (2014) Local

Government Councils Score-Card Assessment Report 2013/14: A combination of Gains, reversals and Reforms.A combination of Gains, reversals and Reforms. ACODE Policy Research Series.

Buijtenhuijs, R. and Thiriot, C. (1995) Démocratisation in Sub-Saharan Africa 1992-1995. An overview of the literature., Leiden, African Studies Centre Bordeaux. Centre D'Etude d'Afrique.

Cankwo, P., Obanda, P, W. and Pule, S. S. (2015) '"Tactical Procurement Management And Service Delivery In Local Governments Of Uganda: A Case Of Nebbi District Local Government."', European Journal of Logistics Puchasing and Supply Chain Management, p. 3 (1):12-28.

Crook, R. and Manor, J. (1998) Democracy and Descentralisation in South Asia and West Africa. Cambridge: Cambridge University Press.

Danny, B., Hambleton, R. and Hoggett, P. (1994) The Politics of Decentralisation: Revitalizing Local Democracy. London: Mac Millan Press Ltd.

Eric Kashambuzi Eric. (2013). Economic Performance under Obote Governments. Available on website at: http://kashambuzi.com/econ omic-performance-under-obote-governments/

Kakuru-Muhwezi, D. (2003) Gender sensitive educational policy and practice: a Uganda case study. Background paper* prepared for the Education for All Global Monitoring Report 2003/4 Gender and Education for All: The Leap to Equality ;2003 Available from:

Kanyeihamba, G. W. (2002) Constitutional and Political History of Uganda: From 1894 to the present. Kampala : Centenary Publishing House, 2002

Lambright, G. M. S. (2011) Decentralization in Uganda: Explaining Successes and Failures in Local Governance. London: First Forum Press.

Lubanga, S. and Villadsen, F. (1996) 'Democratic Decentralisation in Uganda', in A New Approach to Local Governance. Uganda: Fountain Publishers.

Manyak, T. and Katono, I. (2010) 'Decentralization and conflict in Uganda':, Governance adrift. African Studies Quarterly, p. 11(4), 1-24.

Moncrieffe, J. (2004) Uganda's Political Economy: A Synthesis of Major Thought. Available at: http://www.gsdrc.org/docs/open/DOC44.p df.

Mugyenyi, J. B. (2001) 'IMF "Conditionality and Structural Adjustment Under the National Resistance Movement"', in Hansen, H.B. & Twaddle, M. (ed.) Changing Uganda. Kampala: Fountain Publishers.

Daily Monitor, September, 15, 2009 I am not Responsible for Buganda Crisis- Museveni

Museveni, Y. K. (1997) 'Sowing the Mastered Seed', in The Struggle for Freedom and Democracy in Uganda,. Oxford: Macmillan Publishers Ltd.

Muyinda-Mande, W. (2012) 'Uganda Vice Chancellors' Forum.', UVCF BULLETIN, Volume 1.

Nangoli, S., Ngoma, M., Kimbugwe, H. and Mayoka, K. M. (2015) '"Towards Enhancing Service Delivery in Uganda? s Local Government Units: Is Fiscal Decentralization Still a Feasible Strategy?"', International Journal of Economics & Management Sciences, no. 2015.

Obicci, P. A. (2015) '"Impact of Political Transparency on Public Service in Uganda."', International Journal of Advances in Management and Economics no., p. 4 (1):35-46.

Opiyo, N., Bainomugisha, A. and Ntambirweki, B. (2016) 'Breaking the Conflict Trap in Uganda', in Proposals for Constitutional and Legal Reforms. Kampala: ACODE Policy Research Series 2013., p. No. 58.

Oxhorn, T. and Selee (2004) 'for a cross-national perspective.'

Regan, A. J. (1995) 'A Comparative Framework for Analyzing Uganda's Decentralization PolicyUganda:', in Langseth, P., Katorobo, J., Brett, E., and Munene, J. (eds) Landmarks in Rebuilding a Nation. Kampala: Uganda Fountain Publishers, pp. 90–132.

Republic of Uganda. Annual Health Sector Performance. Financial Year 2014/2015 Kampala: Ministry of Health; [26 January 2016]. Available from: HYPERLINK "http://www.health.go.ug/download /file/fid/553" www.health.go.ug/download/file/fid/553."

Saito, R. (2000) Decentralization in Uganda: Ryukoku University, Japan. Available on website at, Challenges for the 21st Century. Japan: Ryukoku University.

Shaw, E. (1973) Financial Deepening in Economic Development. New York: Oxford University Press.

Steiner, S. (2006) Decentralization in Uganda: Exploring the Constraints for Poverty Reduction, GIGA Working Papers. German: German Institute of Global and Area Studies.

The Guardian (2015) 'Uganda's success in universal primary education falling apart', The Guardian.

The World Bank (2017) 'Uganda's Economic Overview'.

Uganda Bureau of Statistics (2002) 'Statistical Abstract (June 2002).', Uganda Bureau of Statistics.

CHAPTER TWO

Implementation of Fiscal Decentralisation in Developing Countries; Illustrations from Uganda

Eugene Gerald Ssemakula and George Bogere

Introduction

This chapter discusses the implications of local government financing to their ability to deliver services. It is argued in this paper that the changing nature of fiscal decentralisation constrains the ability of local governments to adequately respond to the demands of the citizens, an issue that has implications for accountability and quality of services. Decentralization has been heralded as the necessary and indispensable component to pluralist democracy. It has been argued that it extends democracy and allows it to attain its objectives by enabling citizens to take charge of their affairs by participating in the management of their own affairs (Buijtenhuijs and Thiriot, 1995). The described forms of decentralisation are: decongestion, delegation, devolution, and privatisation (Rondinelli, Nellis and Cheema, 1984). While decongestion transfers responsibilities to central government field offices, delegation involves semi-private organisations outside the official bureaucracy. On the other hand, devolution entails autonomous local government entities with authority while privatisation cedes government responsibility to private entities. Devolution offers significant opportunities to improve government accountability (Rondinelli, Nellis and Cheema, 1984). Decentralisation creates the possibility of exerting stronger pressures on government performance both from below (the demand side) and from above (the supply side) (Yilmaz, Beris and Serrano-Berthet, 2008). The underlying principle remains that regardless of the nature of decentralisation, at least three key dimensions namely; administrative, political and fiscal decentralisation exist (Gubser, 2011). The focus of this chapter is on fiscal decentralisation and how it has been implemented in Uganda. It draws on the experiences in the implementation of fiscal decentralisation and the implication it has on service delivery and accountability.

The World Bank defines Fiscal decentralisation as

The public finance dimension of intergovernmental relations. It specifically addresses the reform of the system of expenditure functions and revenue source transfers from the central to sub-national governments. It is a key element of any decentralization programme. Without appropriate fiscal empowerment, the autonomy of sub-national governments cannot be substantiated and, in this way, the full potential of decentralization cannot be realized" (Feruglio, Martinez-vazquez and Timofeev, 2008).

On the other hand, Paul and Robert refer to the concept of fiscal decentralization as the devolution by the central government to Local Governments (states, regions, municipalities) of specific functions with the administrative authority and fiscal revenue to perform those functions (Francis and James, 2003). Finally, this fiscal decentralisation has been described as the division of public expenditure and revenue between levels of government, and the discretion given to regional and local government to determine their budgets by levying taxes and fees and allocating resources (Davey, 2000). It covers two interrelated issues; the division of spending responsibilities and revenue sources between levels of government (national, regional and local) and the amount of discretion given to regional and local governments to determine their expenditures and revenues (both in aggregate and detail (Davey, 2000).

In essence, fiscal decentralisation deals with the discretion around which local governments receive and appropriate resources. It has a two-way function, on one hand, Local governments internally, collect and appropriate taxes in the form of local revenue while on the other hand, implement the expenditure functions of the grants received from the central government. Seen from the two lenses, fiscal decentralisation therefore deals more with compliance to the set financial policies and standards.

In Uganda, decentralization was introduced in 1992 and was premised on the notion that Local Governments are better placed to respond to the needs of the local communities. It was believed that under decentralization, citizens are able to hold their leaders accountable, thereby improving equity in the distribution of resources and reduction of wastage through corruption and ineffective allocation of resources.

Thus, the ultimate aim of Uganda's decentralization programme was to improve service delivery through transfer of real power (devolution) and reduction of the workload of the central government; ensuring the participation of citizens and democratic control ; achieving good governance as a prerequisite for an efficient public service; bringing political and administrative control over services to the point of delivery ; freeing local managers from central constraints; and improving the capacity of local government councils to plan, finance, and manage service delivery (MOLG, 2014).

Division of Tasks and Responsibilities between Central and Sub-National Governments

The 1995 Constitution of the Republic of Uganda (Republic of Uganda 1995) and the Local Governments Act (1997) (Government of Uganda, 1997) define the functions of the Central and Local Governments. They also provide for the devolution of functions to lower levels following an agreement between the two levels of government. The devolution of the functions is supposed to be accompanied by the transfer of resources for the execution of tasks in form of grants to Local Governments. Lower Local Governments can request progressively higher levels of government (up to central government) to take charge of the functions in instances where the higher level of government retains funds pertaining to the tasks. The functions of the central government mainly pertain to critical and indivisible functions such as defence, security, law and order, national policy formulation, setting national standards, coordination, monitoring, supervision and guidance. The Local Governments on the other hand, are responsible for the direct provision of social services, agricultural extension services and local government planning. Under this configuration, Local Governments are solely responsible for the provision of about 70 percent of the services and share the responsibility of provision of about 15 percent of the services as in Table 2.1.

Table 2.1: Allocation of Tasks and Responsibilities between Central and Local Governments

Service	Allocation of responsibility	Service	Allocation of responsibility
National and Sector Policies	CG	**Community Amenities**	
Local government policies	LG	Water services	SHD
Administration and appointment of technical staff for LGs	LG	Removal and disposal of waste and refuse	LG
Judiciary	CG	Street lighting	LG
Defence	CG	Public vehicle parking	LG
Security, law and order	SHD	**Recreational and cultural affairs**	
Education		Sports and recreation facilities	LG
Nursery	LG	Cemeteries	LG
Primary	LG	Public halls libraries and art galleries	LG
Secondary	SHD	Public parks gardens and recreation grounds	LG
Tertiary and technical education	SHD	**Economic Services**	
Health		Roads (trunk roads)	CG
Referral hospitals	CG	Roads (feeder and community access roads)	LG
District hospitals	LG	Trade and produce buying licensing	LG
Health centres, dispensaries and clinics	LG	Land administration	LG
Primary health care and health education	LG	Agriculture and veterinary extension	LG
Control/management of epidemics and disasters	SHD	Forest and wetlands	LG
Social security and welfare		*GC-Central Government*	
		LG-Local Government	
		SHD- Shared	

Source: EPRC study 1999 on Fiscal Decentralization and Local Government Finance in Relation to Infrastructure and Service Provision in Uganda (EPRC, 2000).

Financing Service Delivery under Decentralization

Fiscal decentralization is one of the ways of enhancing political, institutional and economic development. In Uganda, the devolution of functions and responsibilities to sub-national governments under decentralization was accompanied by devolution of funds to these levels. One of the key features of fiscal decentralization in Uganda is the power conferred on sub-national governments to raise revenues through taxes, fees and levies as well as spend the generated revenues and grants from central government. Local governments are charged with the duty of collecting and appropriating financial resources with the major sources being central government transfers, locally raised revenue and donor funds. The analysis in this paper will mainly focus on intergovernmental transfers and local revenue. The data used herein is based on financial reports over a 4 financial year period covering FY 2015/16-FY2018/19. The rationale is twofold. First, it coincides with the major 5 year term period election circle in Uganda and secondly the first 3 years of the second National Development

Inter-governmental Transfers

Inter-governmental Revenue Sharing: Basis and Considerations

Revenue sharing between central and Local Governments is mainly by a grant system ideally because in most cases, the state does not allow local authorities sufficient tax powers to finance expenditure at that level (EPRC, 2000). Secondly, grants allow the government to bring sub-national authorities into the general macroeconomic management of the economy and also influence expenditure priorities at sub-national levels. In Uganda's case, the onset of decentralisation witnessed vast discretionally powers vested upon the Local governments with regard to the utilisation of finances both locally generated and central government transfers. Challenges, however, arose regarding resource utilisation largely as a result of the limited capacity of the nascent local governments (Jean *et al.*, 2010). This occasioned a response from the central government that commissioned a Fiscal Decentralisation Strategy Paper in 2002 (MoFPED, 2002). Subsequently, the Fiscal Decentralisation Strategy (FDS) became the blueprint for financing local governments. The strategy limited the discretionally abilities that had been originally made available to local governments through devolution. The FDS also imposed conditions on how funds should be allocated across expenditure categories, with three important funding sources within the intergovernmental transfer system: Conditional Grants, Unconditional Grants and Equalization Grants (Jean, Tiphany and Katherine, 2010). The Local Government Finance Commission (LGFC) is mandated to advise the President on all matters concerning the distribution of revenue between Government and LGs and the allocation to each Local

Government (Clause 4 of Article 194 of the Constitution (1995) ('The Constitution of the Republic of Uganda', 1995). The LGFC is expected to establish a balance between the financial needs and the sub-national tasks within the available resources.

Two systems of transfer are utilised; the Recurrent Transfer System (RTS) and the Development Transfer System (DTS). All conditional and unconditional funds for recurrent expenditures are transferred through the RTS, which is based on the annual Recurrent Transfer Budget. On the other hand, the DTS targets non-recurrent expenditures and provides discretionary development and conditional grants for specific sectoral investments. According to the LGFC (2010), grants from central government contribute up to 97 percent of district revenues. Thirty-four out of 41 Central Government transfers to Local Governments are recurrent (19 PAF, 6 Non-PAF & 9 Wage grants) while 7 are development grants. The transfers from the Central Government and donor contributions supplement local revenue collections. The grants can be categorized under three groups including conditional grant, unconditional grant, and equalization grant.

The total resource 'envelope' is determined in the Medium Term Expenditure Framework (MTEF) while the sector priorities are set within Sector Working Groups (SWGs) comprising of donors. It is important to have a clear assignment of tasks and responsibilities among the different levels of Government because the law is not clear about the expenditure obligations of the different levels of government. The allocation of responsibilities between central government and Local Governments should take into consideration economies of scale and the need to reduce duplication. This is the argument for recentralization of procurement of drugs and instructional materials.

Other centralized expenditure priorities include defence, security, power generation, national roads rehabilitation, and construction. Other considerations for allocation of responsibilities include the outcome of the assessment by MDAs responsible for the grants such as the annual assessment of the performance of Local Governments by the ministry of local government. Well performing LGs awarded 20 percent bonus to their allocation, static LGs receive no bonus and poorly performing LGs are deducted 20 percent of the allocation. A National Negotiation Team comprising of representatives of both central and local government is responsible for agreeing to critical areas of funding.

Intergovernmental transfers as a proportion of the national budget

Over the four year period of interest for this analysis (2015-2018), the Uganda national budget increased by 70% from Uganda shillings (UGX) 18,311Bn (511m $) for FY 2015/16 to UGX 31,258 Bn (873m $) for FY 2018/19. This increment was accompanied by an increase of 33% in financing to local governments from UGX 2,361Bn (66m $) to UGX 3,151Bn (88m $). On the contrary, the share of the budget allocated to local governments has continued to decline to close to the 10% mark over the same period as shown in Figure 5.

Figure 5: Trend of Annual Budget and share to Local Governments (FY 2015/16 to 2018/19) UGX Billions

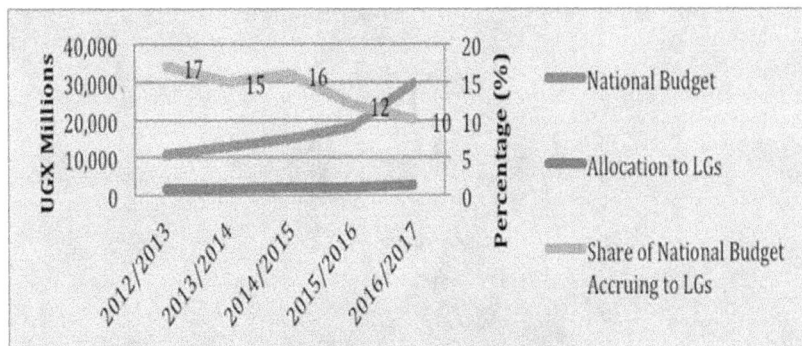

Source: Approved Estimates of Revenue and Expenditure FY 2010/12 to 2017/18

This trend continues to be a point of contention between local and central governments. The local governments argue that the funds allocated are insufficient for delivery of services devolved to them under decentralization. The central government, on the other hand, insists that the growth in the budget has largely been due to national projects in relation to infrastructure and energy development, which are not divisible across local governments.

Transfers and Allocations by sector

Uganda's intergovernmental transfer system imposes conditions on the allocation of funds across sectors. Conditional grants, as a function of national priorities, allocate funds by sector, and these funds are further split across sector budget lines that di

fferentiate between wage expenses and operation costs (GoU 2002). Over a five year period (FY2012/13 to FY2016/17), the allocations to the district local governments were dominated by funding to the education sector with an average annual allocation of 56%, followed public sector management at 21% and health at 14%, as shown in Figure 1.

Figure 1: Average annual allocation of central government transfers to districts FY2012/13 to 2016/17

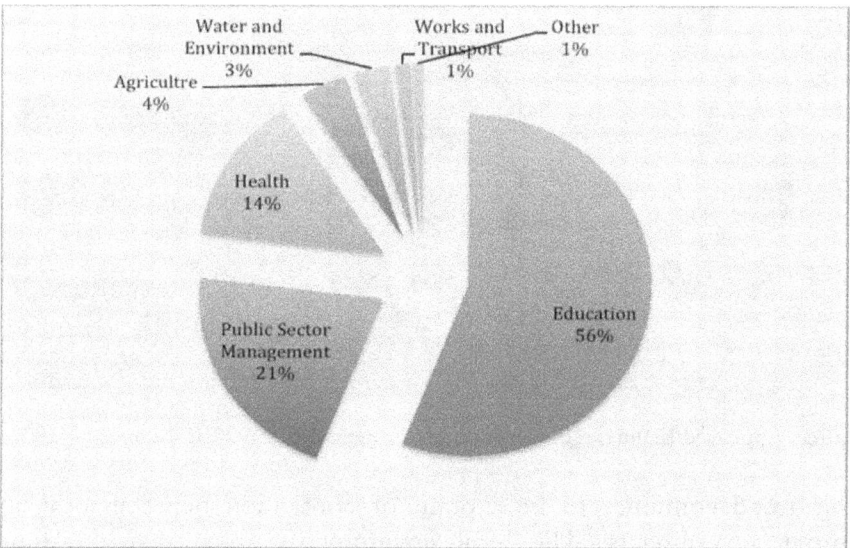

Source: MFPED Approved Estimates of Revenue and Expenditure (FY 2012/13 to 2016/17)

Comparison between Intergovernmental Transfers and other Sources of Local Government Financing As earlier noted, the key sources for local government financing include local revenue, intergovernmental transfers, and donor funding. The analysis of the financing data indicates that Local governments heavily depend on transfers from the central government for their financing as indicated in figure 2.

Figure 2: Composition of financing of selected Local Governments for FY 2011/12 to 2014/15

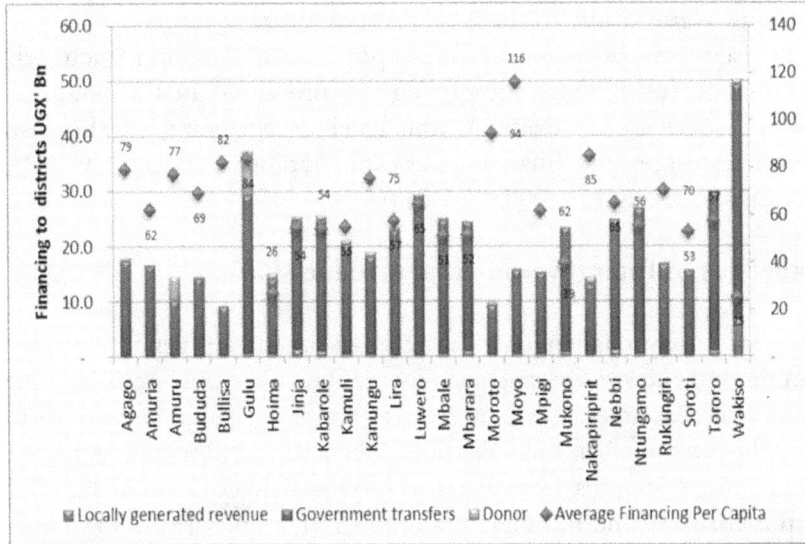

Source: Author's compilation using preliminary census figures 2014 (UBOS) and Annual District Performance Reports 2011/12 to 2014/15

On average central government, transfers account for 92% local government budgets for FY 2011/12 to 2014/15. Donor and local revenue accounted for 5% and 3% respectively. The variation in intergovernmental transfers takes into account the population size, which explains why sparsely populated districts such as Moroto, and Buliisa receive only a portion of what is transferred to Wakiso and Gulu. The performance of districts with regard to donations and local revenue differs individually depending on the individual circumstances obtaining in that particular district. As earlier observed, the criteria for inclusion of the districts in this analysis takes into account the level of urbanisation and degree of marginalisation in the district. The outliers in figure 2 (Gulu and Amuru districts) with significant contributions from donor agencies and Wakiso District with a higher local revenue contribution (12%) can be explained by their uniqueness. Gulu and Amuru districts form part of the greater Northern part of Uganda, where for over 2 decades a civil conflict masterminded by the Lord's' Resistance Army

(LRA) raged. This obtaining situation attracted large volumes of development assistance to these districts. On the other hand, Wakiso District, located next to the country's capital is an urban local government with a high concentration of business enterprises that contribute significantly to the local revenue through taxes.

In real terms, however, when the population demand is factored into the equation, even these meagre figures presented in the picture pale. Over the period, for example, the level of financing of the districts covered translates into financing per capita ranging between UGX 25,000 (7 USD) and UGX 116, 000 (32 USD).

Challenges of Intergovernmental revenue sharing

There are many challenges to inter-governmental revenue sharing; the sprouting of new LGs and administrative structures resulting in the splitting of resources – which reduces funds available for the districts. First, the creation of new districts increases administrative costs and reduces the resources available for service delivery. There has been a sharp increase in the number of administrative units from 56 in 2006 to Districts to 112 by 2016 (Bainomugisha *et al.*, 2017). Secondly, the low level of revenue generation by Local Governments which increases their dependence on transfers from the central government greatly reduces their autonomy. Thirdly, the legal provision, for instance, Section 80(3) of the Local Governments Act - under which Local Governments are entitled to a share of revenue collected on behalf of the central government - is not adhered to. Whereas LGs perform this task within their mandate as a branch of Government, the Law does not clearly define a sharing modality, especially between the central and local government. Fourthly, delays in receipt of funds by local governments- mainly arising from lack of funds at the national level and failure by local governments to comply with reporting timelines - imply delays in implementation of activities are rampant. Data from budget monitoring exercises under ACODE's Centre for Budget and Economic Governance show that local governments and service delivery units continue to be dogged by delays in receipt of funds. This is in spite of reforms aimed at improving predictability and timeliness of funds. The monitoring exercise was carried out between June and July 2015 and focused on funds for quarter 4 for FY 2014/15. The findings show that the average time taken for an institution to receive its quarterly release was five weeks. Funds for district Conditional School Facilitation Grants (SFG) to districts and Conditional Grant for secondary salaries reached the respective institution accounts within three weeks from the start of the quarter (April 1, 2015). District unconditional grant (non-wage) and salaries for primary took up to eight weeks to reach the district and schools respectively. Similarly, the Local Government Management Service Delivery (LGMSD) grant on average took up to five weeks for District local governments and seven weeks for sub-counties. Table 4 shows the details of the time it takes for funds to reach specific institutions.

Table 4: Timeliness of Receipt of Funds by Service Delivery Units

Allocation	Number of units	Minimum time lag (No. of weeks) to receive funds	Maximum time lag (No. of weeks) to receive funds	Average
District LGMSD	24	3	8	5
Sub-county LGMSD	58	1	13	7
District unconditional grant non-wage	21	3	9	5
Sub-county unconditional grant non-wage	45	2	12	8
District production and marketing	13	3	5	4
Sub-county production and marketing	5	4	9	7
District primary education	8	3	5	4
School primary education	84	4	11	6
District SFG	11	3	4	3
School SFG (primary)	7	2	11	6
District primary salaries	7	3	11	7
School primary salaries	23	1	11	8
School secondary salaries	17	1	12	7
District Universal Secondary Education	4	3	4	4

School Universal Secondary Education	39	0	10	5
District PHC development	12	3	8	4
Health Centre PHC development	86	0	12	7
District Road rehabilitation grant	14	3	4	4

Source: ACODE Budget Monitoring Exercise Data Q4 FY 2014/15

Local revenue generation by Local Governments

Local revenue is important for local governments not only because it accords greater discretion to local governments but it also supplements central government transfers and donor contributions. The local government Act provides for a number of taxes to be collected by local governments. These include a) Local Service Tax (LST); to be collected from incomes and wealth of People in gainful employment, professionals, artisans and Businessmen/Women. b) Local Government Hotel Tax (LGHT); to be collected from occupants utilising the services of hotels, lodges, and guesthouses; c) Property rates and land based charges like premium, building plan approval fees, land fees, etc.; d) Ground rent; e) Business licenses; f) User fees (include market dues, parking fees), user charges and permits; g) Royalties from electricity generation, mineral mining and exploration and protected areas; h) Other departmental revenues (include forest revenues; veterinary fees, registration of births; marriages and deaths; fines; etc.) always lumped as Other sources of revenue. Table 2 provides local revenue performance by source category.

Table 4 Trend of Local Revenue Performance (Shs' billions)

Source	2010/11	2011/12	2012/13	2013/14	Average
LST	6,542,312	7,115,367	10,786,472	10,113,773,746	2,534,554,474
LGHT	928,320	1,163,667	1,065,025	1,278,958,104	320,528,779
Property tax	31,557,087	29,289,945	33,648,810	38,678,504,789	9,693,250,158
User fees	21,975,206	20,931,123	29,004,195	34,058,325,346	8,532,558,968

Licences	6,564,179	15,559,527	8,807,180	11,036,713,569	2,766,911,114
Others	43,478,222	43,481,781	56,041,713	57,837,328,767	14,495,082,62 1
Total	111,045,32 7	117,541,41 0	148,483,95 7	153,003,604,32 1	38,345,168,75 4

Source: (Local Government Finance Commission, 2015)

In comparison with the central government transfers, local revenue sources contribute less than 10 percent of the total local government annual budget.

Challenges in the Administration of Local Revenue

Generally, locally raised revenues are meagre, thereby affecting the ability of Local Governments to fund key expenditure needs. Some of the main challenges that impede improvement in collection of local revenues include the following. First, there are ineffective laws and enforcement mechanisms for local revenue collection. The current law for example - property rates and local service tax - which provide for many exemptions that do not effectively support the collection of local revenues. Secondly, political interventions undermine local and other revenue sources and adversely affect compliance. A key example is the abolition of the graduated tax in 2005 partly due to political calculations given its unpopularity but also due to the cost of collection. This led to a sharp decline in local government revenue since total collections from graduated tax amounted to UGX 70 bn. Thirdly, there is weak political supervision of the process, mainly arising from the insufficient capacity of Local Governments to effectively facilitate elected leaders to mobilise the local revenue. Lastly, some of the meaningful revenue sources (veterinary and fishery fees) are collected by central ministries and not shared with Local Governments.

Opportunities for Revenue Generation

Local Governments have opportunities to generate more revenue for service delivery. In order to achieve improvement in local revenue performance, the Local Governments should strengthen the data management systems for local revenue collection and conduct sensitization programs for technical, elected leaders and taxpayers on their roles and obligations in local revenue generation and mobilization. Other options should include the following:

- Reviews of local government financing and local government set up in Uganda will provide an opportunity to examine proposals to remove tax exemptions from the Local Government (Rating) Act 2005 on owner-occupied residential buildings and Local Government Act (Cap 243) on most eligible LST taxpayers, and a possible revert to Graduated tax.
- The Ministry of Trade Tourism and Cooperatives issued statutory instrument No.54 that empowers Local Governments to levy trading licenses on telecommunication masts and professionals among others. This would broaden the tax base for Local Governments.
- The modality for the full collection of Cess on produce by Local Governments is being reviewed by LGFC for use by Local Governments.
- The guide for streamlining the collection of royalty fees for local government was developed and disseminated to beneficiary Local Governments.
- Policies for local revenue mobilization and generation are being proposed by a review of Local Governments financing.

Implications of Current Funding Modalities for Accountability and Service Delivery

Implications for Service Delivery

The concept of decentralization aims at bringing services closer to the people, and to improve service delivery and people's welfare. However, in Uganda, evidence on whether decentralization has improved service delivery is still inconclusive and presents mixed scenarios. Decentralization is not necessarily a guarantee for better service delivery. It is underpinned by three aspects of effective service delivery namely; adequacy of services, quality of services, accessibility, and affordability. Shortcomings of service delivery under decentralization are attributed to several factors.

The level and nature of financing for local governments depicted in this chapter have implications for the level of service delivery. This can be analysed from four perspectives, that is; adequacy of funding, discretionary funding, monitoring service delivery and timeliness of transfers. First, it should be noted that the amount of funding which in some instances was as low as UGX 25,000 (less than USD 10) per capita per financial year is inadequate for service delivery at the Local Government level. The funding available to the local governments is not in tandem with the devolved services and responsibilities. Therefore, the poor services at the local government level are a direct result of the poor funding. Secondly, the funding arrangement limits the discretion over funds by the local governments. Local government funding is dominated by conditional central government transfers, which makes addressing local issues difficult. This has a direct impact on citizens' confidence in the local government and decentralization. While local revenue is associated with greater discretion and flexibility, districts persistently perform poorly on its collection. Thirdly, local governments play a major role in monitoring service delivery. The level of financing greatly influences the ability to monitor service delivery. This is usually in form of funding for political monitoring. The data shows great variation in allocation for Standing Committees and Political Oversight over the 26 districts assessed. The data also shows that districts with higher local revenue have been in a better position to monitor service delivery. Lastly, the timeliness of funding has an impact on the quality of service delivery. The data provided indicate the delay in transmission of funds for service delivery. This is a major concern for implementing activities by local governments.

Lack of commensurate revenue for service delivery by Local Governments: Underfunding sub-national Local Governments constrains the discretion of Local Governments over budget resources. Apart from the mismatch between service delivery responsibilities and resource allocation [less than 20 percent], Local Governments are heavily dependent on central government transfers for revenue [over 95 percent]. This does not support the objective of putting people in charge of their own affairs. It limits people's discretion over budget resources because over 85 percent of the grants are conditional. The low levels of internal revenue generation - which accounts for less than 5 percent of the district budgets – are partly because of the low capacity of revenue generation by Local Governments. The introduction of local service tax and local hotel tax has not yielded much to bolster local revenues. Direct donor funding to Local Governments through project support remains minimal.

Shortage of qualified and experienced staff: The delivery of quality service is anchored on an essential element of any institution - a professionally trained human resource. But most of the positions in the Local Governments are rarely filled and some functions are never performed. Since the freeze on recruitment of civil service at district level was imposed by the central government, the situation has worsened, particularly in hard-to-reach districts. A review of staffing levels in a sample of 66 entities comprising of districts, town councils, and regional referral hospitals revealed that out of the approved structure of 28,454 only 17,871 (63 percent) positions were filled – showing a shortage of 10,583 staff (37percent) understaffing. Other factors responsible for shortage of qualified staff at district level include; lack of training opportunities to develop professional and technical expertise and lack of career progression of staff recruited at district level, low and often delayed pay, shortage of equipment and materials - that makes the positions unattractive to suitors - and ineffectiveness of the District Service Commissions - which are slow in handling recruitment - even when clearance to recruit has been granted by the central government.

Corruption: Like in all other spheres of public life in Uganda, corruption is also rampant at the district level. Corruption is rampant most spheres of public life in Uganda. It takes many forms, including influence peddling by those in positions of authority, undue influence by politicians, abuse of office, bribery, fraud, embezzlement, misappropriation, and misallocation of - limited - resources. The level of corruption under decentralization, particularly the collusion by politicians and technocrats at the districts in awarding contracts and tenders in what is commonly referred to as *"scratch my back, I'll scratch yours"* arrangements, is alarming. This makes supervision very difficult as those supposed to carry out this function are compromised.

Unresolved conflicts over resources: Conflicts stifle development because they consume time, money and energy meant for service delivery. Conflicts cause stress at the workplace, reduces productivity, initiative, and innovation. There are instances when district councils fail to approve district budgets due to conflicts. The most common conflicts at district level are; technical versus political leadership, Resident District Commissioner (RDC) versus District Local Government leadership.

Low demand for accountability by citizens

Demand for accountability of local governments by citizens remains very low and is highlighted by limited citizens' participation in planning and monitoring at the district level. There is a generally negative attitude over civic matters. This is attributed to; widespread lack of knowledge among the citizens of their roles and responsibilities, unavailability of relevant information especially at district level, loss of trust and confidence in government by citizens and absence of effective mechanisms for holding leaders accountable.

Gubser (2011) noted that graduated tax had the effect of strengthening accountability relations between the citizens and their leaders vesting locals in the projects carried out in their name. He contends that the abolition of the tax significantly weakened the accountability relationships between citizens and their local governments. It is not by coincidence therefore that the period before the abolition of graduated tax (1997-2005) witnessed the most vibrant implementation of decentralisation in Uganda with strong local government structures.

The high dependency on the central transfers further distorts accountability relationships in two major ways. First, the dependency on central government transfers means that the principle of counter checks between the local governments and the central government is diminished given that the former are in a very weak position to exert their influence on the latter. Local governments demanding accountability from the central government is tantamount to the proverbial *biting the hand that feeds you* scenario. Secondly, the conditional nature of the grant system implies that local priority setting, a key mandate of local governments is ceded in lieu of the national priorities. In Uganda's local government planning process, the existence of and priority is given to the nomenclature of National Priority Programme Areas (NPPAs) is a key manifestation of this reality. Lastly, the time and resources of the local government officials are spent dealing with reporting requirements as opposed to implementing service delivery. Until recently (beginning of FY 2016/17) local governments had a total of 46 conditional grants, each with reporting requirements (MoFPED, 2002).

Conclusion

The connection between funding, accountability and service delivery cannot be understated. While decentralisation aims to provide citizen control over the quality of services provided, the key aspect of local government funding cannot be overlooked. The current funding arrangements in the Ugandan version of decentralisation present a number of challenges for both service delivery and accountability. Financing the delivery of quality service under decentralization can be enhanced if governance issues are streamlined; actors in the delivery chain, their roles, and relationships to institution enforcement, monitoring and incentives and sanctions for actors are adhered to.

Decentralisation is a political decision. Financing local government requires political commitment. However, there is concern that the commitment to decentralization by the government is waning. This notion is prompted by recentralization of a number of functions that had been devolved to sub-national governments including recruitment of staff and remuneration, procurement, as is the case with the procurement of drugs. This situation is contrary to the thrust of the decentralization policy in Uganda that sought to free the centre of certain functions while at the same time empowering citizens to take charge of affairs. The sub-national governments have over the years become increasingly subjected to central government direction with little discretion. It is widely accepted that the centre of the problems of service delivery under decentralization in Uganda is the political economy of decentralization. Political considerations tend to override the objectives of decentralization. The result is the creation of over 1,350 sub-national governments (112 districts, 22 municipalities, 1,147 sub-counties, and 69 municipal divisions) majority of which are not viable and hardly raise three percent of their annual budgets. Furthermore, the meger funds mainly cover salaries of workers leaving little for the provision of materials and actual service provision.

To address these challenges, efforts have to be made to review the entire fiscal decentralization system, including the allocation of taxes between the central government and local governments with the view of bolstering local revenue generation. Safeguards to proper utilisation of local revenue also need to be instituted, lest it is abused. Six specific measures that can be undertaken include: First, there is need to revise revenue allocation modalities between Central and Local Governments to adequately balance revenue allocation and devolved responsibilities. However, some sectors, especially those that are indivisible and, or are highly sensitive and technical such as defence and security – as well as specific functions such as procurement of drugs and supplies for which economies of scale accrue from centralization - ought to remain under the central government.

Secondly, transparency and accountability need to be strengthened at all levels. Information sharing among actors is a prerequisite for efficient and effective service delivery in a decentralization framework. The lack of information, particularly, about central government driven projects and initiatives results in flaunting of regulations, loss of revenues to Local Governments and duplication. Non-state actors, especially civil society organisations can play a pivotal role in fostering this.

Thirdly, there is need to re-introduce a direct tax to bring back the civic consciousness of the citizens. It is estimated that an imposition of a UGX 20,000 direct tax on every able-bodied Ugandan by local government would rise to over UGX 150 billion. Graduated Tax - the only form of direct tax – which was abolished, partly due to its high administrative costs, remains unpopular. However, it is argued that direct taxation would encourage the citizenry to be more responsibility and demand accountability. There is still a lot of unproductive labour among the youth, and the introduction of a direct tax would arguably, encourage the more youth to work and provide the much needed revenue for Local Governments and encourage people to work.

Fourthly, greater emphasis should be placed on the collection of information for planning purposes at the district level. District officials concede that poor performance in planning is due to lack of funds. Collection of information for planning by districts ought to be a deliberate process to which both financial and human resources need to be dedicated. But very few districts indeed plan for the collection of relevant information for planning purposes. As a result, projections tend to be overtaken by events. The requirement for Local Governments to possess information about revenue sources within their precinct before collecting the same [information] justifies costs incurred in relation to the collection of information. Local Governments are usually required to plan for revenue enhancement on an annual basis although very few of them do so. This is perhaps why there is persistent failure to meet local revenue targets set by Local Governments themselves.

Lastly, local governments should be adequately empowered to enforce laws. Most of the local government offices are not filled – which puts the capacity of local government to implement their own laws in question. There is absence of parish chiefs who are the enforcers of regulations especially those to do with local revenue generation. The abolition of local administration police further weakened the capacity of Local Governments to enforce laws. Thus, it is important to have parish chiefs recruited in all districts, oriented and supervised to ensure that they enforce laws and regulations. Furthermore, Local Governments need to be freed from political interference - which has greatly negated the ability of technocrats at the district level to enforce laws.

References

Bainomugisha, A., Muyomba-Tamale, L., Muhwezi W., W., Cunningham, K., Ssemakula, E.,G., Bogere, G., Mbabazi, J., Asimo, N., Atukunda, P. (2017), Local Government Councils Scorecard Assessment 2016/17: Civic Engagement: Activating the Potentials of Local Governance in Uganda, Kampala, ACODE Policy Research Series No.83, https://www.acode u.org/Files/Publications/PRS_83. pdf.

Buijtenhuijs, R. and Thiriot, C. (1995) *Démocratisation in Sub-Saharan Africa 1992-1995. An overview of the literature.*, Leiden, *African Studies Centre Bordeaux.* Centre D'Etude d'Afrique.

Davey, K. (2000a) 'Fiscal Decentralization: Basic Policy Guidelines for Practitioners', *Transition Newsletter*, 12, pp. 31 32. doi: 10.1017/CBO9 781107415324.004.

Davey, K. (2000b) 'Fiscal Decentralization', *Basic Policy Guidelines for Practitioners. Transition Newsletter.*

EPRC (2000) *Fiscal Decentralisation and Sub-national Government Finance in Relation to Infrastructure and Service Provision in Uganda: Main report. Collaborative study between The National Association of Local Authorities in Denmark (NALAD) and EPRC. Directed.*

Feruglio, N., Martinez-vazquez, J. and Timofeev, A. (2008) *An Assessment of Fiscal Decentralization in Macedonia.* Macedonia.

Francis, P. and James, R. (2003) 'Balancing Rural Poverty Reduction and

Citizen Participation':, *The Contradictions of Uganda’s Decentralization Program. World Development,* p. 31(2), 325–337.

Government of Uganda (1997) 'Local Government Act (Vol. 243).Uganda'. Kampala: Printing and Publishing Corporation.

Gubser, M. (2011a) 'The View from Le Château : USAID ' s Recent Decentralisation Programming in Uganda', 29(August 2009), pp. 23–46.

Gubser, M. (2011b) 'The view from le château: USAID's recent decentralisation programming in Uganda', *Development Policy Review,* 29(1), pp. 23–46. doi: 10.1111/j.1467-7679.2011.00512.x.

Jean, S., Lee, T., Malarkey, K. and McMahon, J. (2010) *Local Government Fiscal Discretion in Uganda.* Kampala: Mdpafrica.Org.Zw,.

Jean, S., Tiphany, L. and Katherine, M. (2010) 'Local government fiscal discretion in Uganda.', *NYU Advanced Project in Management & Policy.*

Local Government Finance Commission (2015) *Annual report 2014/15, 1,.*

MoFPED (2002) *Fiscal Decentralisation Strategy in Uganda, (March),* . MoFPED.

MOLG (2014) *Decentralization and Local Development Local Development.*

Rondinelli, D. A., Nellis, J. R. and Cheema, G. S. (1984) *Decentralization in developing countries.* World Bank Staff Working.

'The Constitution of the Republic of Uganda' (1995).

Yilmaz, S., Beris, Y. and Serrano-Berthet, R. (2008) *Local Government Discretion and Accountability: A Diagnostic Framework for Local Governance.*

CHAPTER THREE

Decentralised Service Delivery in Uganda: The Importance of Citizen Voice

Jonas Mbabazi, Kiran Cunningham & Paloma Campillo

Introduction

Governments at sub-national levels are increasingly pursuing participatory mechanisms in a bid to improve decentralised governance and service delivery. Since the 1980s, many countries started to devolve central government functions to local jurisdictions in response to both internal and external pressures. Centralized states were being pressured from within to enact policies that would provide for more local and regional autonomy. Externally, decentralization was part of the structural adjustment package that many countries adopted in exchange for aid and loans from the World Bank and IMF. It was largely conceived as a vehicle that would improve governance and public service delivery.

Uganda was an early adopter of an ambitious decentralization reform in terms of the scale and scope of the transfer of power and responsibilities to the local level (Steiner, 2006). The process dates back to 1986, when the National Resistance Movement assumed power and there was a desire to break with previous authoritarian regimes and bring government closer to the people (Oluwasinaayomi and Tunde, 2017). It was envisaged that a decentralized system of governance would contribute to development by empowering the people and institutions at every level of society including public, private and civic institutions; improving access to basic services; increasing people's participation in decision-making; assisting in developing people's capacities; and enhancing government's responsiveness, transparency and accountability (Awortwi and Helmsing, 2014).

Improved service delivery was and continues to be at the core of Uganda's decentralization agenda. It was designed to bring political and administrative control of services closer to the actual service delivery point, enable citizens to be more involved in decision-making, reduce the cost of service delivery, and increase accountability, transparency and efficiency in the delivery of public services (Oluwasinaayomi and Tunde, 2017). Indeed, the common mantra and justification for decentralization in Uganda has been "bringing services closer to the people". Decentralization also promised a more local, inclusive democracy as the Local Government Act and the 1995 Constitution ensure that women, youth, and people with disabilities have guaranteed places in the local government system (Ahikire J., 2002).

According to the Local Government Act of 1997, the objectives of decentralization in Uganda were to:

a) transfer real power to districts and thus reduce the load of work on remote and under-resourced central officials;

b) bring political and administrative control over services to a point where they are actually delivered, thereby improving accountability and effectiveness, promoting people's feeling of ownership of programmes and projects executed in their districts;

c) free local managers from central constraints and, as a long-term goal, allow them to develop organisational structures tailored to local circumstances;

d) improve financial accountability and responsibility by establishing a clear link between the payment of taxes and the provision of services they finance;

e) improve the capacities of the councils to plan, finance and manage the delivery of services of their finance and manage the delivery of services of their constituencies; and

f) enhance local economic development in order to increase local incomes.

Those who have studied the impact of decentralization have found that it has, indeed, increased government responsiveness, efficiency and accountability in Uganda (Onzima, 2013), but local governments remain constrained in their decision-making when it comes to allocation of resources. With the abolishment of the graduated tax in 1997, local governments have very few ways to generate own-source revenue (Shah, 2006), and depend on central government transfers for over 90 percent of their finances, on average. This is exacerbated by limited discretion over the funds they receive from the center. By some estimates, local governments only have discretion over 4-5 percent of central government transfers after deducting the wage expenses component of unconditional grants (Bainomugisha et al., 2015). This is consistent with the results of Kazim and Agboda's analysis of decentralization in Africa (2017). They argue that the "political preference" in most African countries, including Uganda, was decentralization without discretionary authority. Most local governments, they found, are bound by "strict constitutional or legal limits on the revenue raising and service provision powers for local authorities, thus, preventing them from operating effectively.

This, of course, creates a contradiction. The local government system is supposed to enable a more inclusive, participatory and responsive system of government, but yet central government retains control over how resources are to be spent. Without the ability to decide how to spend the funds they have, the full realization of the promise of decentralization is impossible, as local governments have very limited power to use the funds they receive from the central government for locally-identified needs and priorities.

While putting a serious damper on the promises of decentralization, the limited discretion they have over service delivery budgets does not totally limit their decision-making power over service delivery. Administratively, districts in Uganda still manage and oversee the way that services are delivered. District-level local governments, known as Local Council Fives (LCVs), are mandated by the Local Governments' Act (1997) (GoU, 1997) to manage and provide services in their areas of jurisdiction. The LCVs have planning, budgeting, legislative, and service delivery powers. They also are mandated with inspecting, monitoring and coordinating service delivery (GoU, 1997). The second schedule of the local government act enumerates the services that LCVs are mandated to provide.

With regard to planning and budgeting, local governments develop annual work plans and budgets that are approved by the local government councils (LCIIIs and LCVs). These work plans and budgets mainly feed into the national priority areas in service delivery such as health, education, water and sanitation, roads, agriculture extension, and environmental protection. The central government, through the Ministry of Finance, Planning and Economic Development (MoFPED), provides indicative planning figures that largely define the confines of the local government budgets. Within the budget cycle, sectors prepare their own budgets that are later combined to form one budget. The relevant committees of council and sector heads scrutinize these budgets before they are tabled in council for further review and approval. This process has a variety of avenues for citizen input and participation. Throughout the budgeting cycle, the local governments are required to conduct budget conferences at the parish level where citizens are asked to provide feedback on their service delivery needs and priorities. Further, in fulfilment of their mandate, the LGVs are empowered to pass ordinances that address specific issues that relate to service delivery challenges raised by their constituents.

Inspection, monitoring and coordination of service delivery are a core function of local governments in Uganda, and are important conduits for interfacing with citizens. The law requires that the technical officers and elected leaders continuously inspect service delivery points and monitor the delivery of services. During these inspection and monitoring exercises, elected and technical local governments officials are supposed to identify and correct service delivery challenges. Where necessary, proposals are sent to relevant committees of council with the goal of generating appropriate recommendations and resolutions of council. The results of inspections and monitoring visits are also included in mandatory quarterly and annual reports, which are shared with MoFPED.

As this discussion of the roles and responsibilities of local governments conveys, decentralization has indeed brought administration and oversight of service delivery closer to the people. The decentralized government was also designed to go a step further and open up spaces for democratic participation and civic dialogue so that the services provided would respond to local needs and capacity (Shah, 2006). The remainder of this chapter examines the degree to which this part of the decentralization promise in Uganda has been fulfilled by exploring what citizens have to say about the state of service delivery in their communities.

Citizen Perspectives on Service Delivery

The voices presented here stem from civic engagement meeting with citizens in over 100 sub-counties in thirty districts in Uganda. These meetings were part of the dissemination of performance results associated with the Local Government Councils Scorecard Initiative (LGCSCI), which is discussed in-depth in Chapter 5 of this book. The meetings, which took place at the sub-county level, involved anywhere between 30 and 90 participants and included a facilitated discussion about service delivery issues in the sub-county. The facilitators, who were researchers with ACODE, compiled detailed field notes from these sessions. The field notes were then coded using the Atlas.ti software programme, and subsequently analyzed for recurring themes that are cross-cutting districts in each service delivery area.

Perceptions of Education

In Uganda, the key policy thrust in the educational sector for both rural and urban areas includes providing equitable access to quality and affordable education to all. The current education policy focuses on expanding the functional capacity of educational structures and reducing on the inequalities of access to education between sexes, geographical areas, and social classes in Uganda. As such Uganda launched the UPE in 1997 and ever since more resources have been allocated to the lower educational public sector through the UPE programme in order to enhance equity of access at that level between boys and girls (ODI, 2006).

The current government efforts in the education sector, especially the Universal Primary Education (UPE) policy are, by and large, premised on the recommendation of the Government White Paper on Education of 1992 (Duclos et al., 2013).

This section, however, focuses on primary/basic education under UPE programme. The Government of Uganda set key objectives of UPE as: (a) making basic education accessible to the learners and relevant to their needs as well as meeting national goals; (b) making education equitable in order to eliminate and disparities and inequalities; (c) establishing, providing and maintaining quality education as the basis for promoting the necessary human resource development; (d) initiating a fundamental positive transformation of society in the social, economic and political fields; and (e) ensuring that education is affordable by the majority of Ugandans by providing initially the minimum necessary facilities and resources, and progressively the optimal facilities to enable every child to enter and remain in school until they complete the primary school education cycle (Duclos et al., 2013).

The policy emphasises equal opportunity for both boys and girls. It is promotes parity in enrolment, retention and performance in primary education. The main achievement of UPE has been a surge in gross enrolment in primary schools, especially for the rural and urban poor. The greatest beneficiary of the UPE has been the girl-child. Enrolment of girls has increased dramatically. Consequently, gender disparities in primary school enrolment have been almost wiped out because there is a steady increase in the number of girls enrolling at school each year. The 1995 Constitution prescribed education as a right, specifying that each child is entitled to a basic education, which is a shared responsibility of the state and the child's parents. Under the Local Government Act of 1997, nursery, primary schools, special schools and technical schools fall under the administration and management of District Councils. Each district has the authority to formulate, approve, and execute its own development plan.

Citizens in Uganda identified on-going issues with the quality of education that reverberate within the sector in other countries, raising significant concerns about how low rates of student success are linked to inadequate educational infrastructure and teacher absenteeism. In the area of infrastructure, citizens reported problems like insufficient classrooms, buildings of poor quality, insufficient latrines and water sources, and a lack of instructional materials, all of which negatively impact students' ability to learn. In addition, issues with teachers arriving late or not showing up at all arose in almost all of the districts.

With regard to educational facilities, citizens commented on the need for more schools, equipment, and staff accommodation. One citizen expounded upon the lack of schools, stating, "We have been requesting for a school in this parish but no response. They are all distant so the children have to walk long distances to reach school." (Discussion conducted on 29 September 2016, in Namalu Sub-county Gulu district) Due to the need for more accessible schools, the education of students across the country is obstructed if not totally compromised. Furthermore, within the schools that do exist, the infrastructure there tends to be insufficient, as one citizen noted: "There is a need for the construction of more classrooms so that the pupils will not have to read under trees." Schools are overcrowded and poorly kept, lacking classrooms, desks, and other materials necessary to meet the needs of students. Accessing schools is only half the battle; once in a school, children are tasked to succeed even though the materials that ought to aid them are either not there or often in an unsatisfactory condition.

Finally, citizens in two districts were rightly concerned about the treatment and potential abuse of female students, as one reports: "Girls do not have a toilet of their own but share with boys. This affects their concentration and they are inconvenienced. Girl pupils could easily be abused due to lack of a private place."(Community Engagement meeting held on 15 August 2016, in Buliisa Town Council, Buliisa District) It is necessary to take vulnerable populations into account when making decisions; girl-students, however, are not given the services and facilities they need in order to fully participate in their education. Thus, the infrastructural inadequacies in the education sector not only inhibit students from receiving an education, but do so disproportionately for girl students.

Infrastructure is not only for students' benefit, but to be used by teachers as well. Given that the distance between home and work is, for many teachers, a challenge, schools are expected to have teachers quarters to discourage absenteeism. Unfortunately, like other areas of infrastructure, the infrastructure for teachers fails to meet expectations. As one citizen explains, "Teachers come from far and there are no staff quarters and this demotivates the teachers, especially during the rainy season."(Community Engagement meeting held on 9 September 2016, in Mukuju Sub-county in Tororo District). Without staff dormitories, teachers have difficulty making the trip to school. Combined with the poor pay that lowers their incentive to work, this causes a lot of teacher absenteeism, creating yet another barrier for students.

Citizens also expressed concern with monitoring service delivery, parent apathy, and the performance of schools, particularly compared to private schools. In regards to poorly performing teachers, one resident explained: "The way government systems work in schools is just amazing - the teacher who doesn't perform well in one school is transferred to the next school to continue failing pupils."(Community Engagement meeting held on 28 August 2016, in Rugando Sub-county in Mbarara District).

There is a need for greater accountability amongst teachers. The current penalty for poorly performing teachers does not resolve any problems, but rather relocates them and does not benefit students. It is apparent that UPE schools generally do not provide students with an acceptable quality of education. One participant lamented: "I am unhappy with the level of UPE schools in the sub-county. Teachers don't teach as well as private schools. The government is not following up on public education."(Community Engagement meeting held on 22 September 2016, in Nyakagyeme Sub-county in Rukungiri District). Here, it is shown that UPE schools, aimed at providing poor children access to education, have instead potentially grown the class rift as the rich are driven to private schools, and the poor are meant to settle for what's available to them, regardless of the difference in quality.

However, the government is not the only key player in the education sector; parents, too, hold a great deal of influence. As one participant explains: "Parents play a leading role in mobilizing children to go back to school. However, children drop out due to poverty. The parents from poor families send their children to town for casual labour work, and others …to collect firewood."(Community Engagement meeting held on 9 September 2016, in Nadunget Sub-county in Moroto District). Parents are ultimately the deciding factor in their children's education, and when the education provided isn't at a level that will likely improve the lives of their children, the practical choice is to send their children to make more money for the family's welfare instead.

While UPE and public schools are largely "free", there is evidence of a trend by which parents and students have to pay increasing fees to compensate for government underfunding. Parents reported that poorer pupils faced exclusion as a result of not being able to pay fees due to the school board committee decisions to charge fees or through the decision of school management to charge fees in response to the delayed release of funds. This was reported to be a significant obstruction to obtaining an education. Examples were reported in several districts. There are accounts of children being sent back home due to failure to pay their fees, which parents explained, they are not capable of paying.

A participant in one district explained: "Parents who cannot afford to pay the money end up having their children at home. UNEB charges UGX. 97,000/= ($ 26.7) for P.7 candidates, the schools charge UGX 2,000/= ($ 0.55) per term for pupils in P.1-P3 and UGX 1,500/= ($0.41) for exams."(Community Engagement meeting held on September 2016, in Manibe Sub-county in Arua District). Due to this practice, many children who were intended to receive free education became unable to do so, contrary to the mission of UPE was entirely cast aside. As another citizen remarked:

> The government started free education to help the underprivileged. Public schools have been privatized, yet most parents cannot afford fees charged by the schools. Many children have dropped out of schools and leaders are watching helplessly.... Government schools are operating as private schools. As established earlier, there is a disconnect between the implementation and intent of UPE schools. Essentially, UPE set a goal that it did not have sufficient resources to meet, and rather than providing poor children empowerment through education, it gave them crumbs and expected them to be satisfied (Community Engagement meeting held on 28 August 2016, in Rugando Sub-county in Mbarara District).

Another issue contributing to citizen inability to access education is geographical accessibility. In Masindi, for example, long distances to schools were reported as a significant impediment for some pupils, this is shown through one resident's testimony: "The whole parish has only one UPE school shared by seven villages which are far distant to the school about 9 km."(Community Engagement meeting held on September 2016, in Budongo Sub-county in Masindi District). As mentioned earlier, there are not enough schools to meet the country's needs. Consequently, schools that are available are meant to be used by a larger radius than is realistic, and children struggle in simply making the journey to their schools.

While accessibility is a challenge in primary education, this challenge is exacerbated as children grow up. UPE does not extend to secondary education; so many families have no means of accessing higher education for their kids. As one participant expressed: "Most of our children do not have access to higher education since we can't afford school fees. When a scholarship comes to this district, only the rich take the opportunity, but poor children stay at home due to the segregation taking place."(Community Engagement meeting held on 20 September 2016, in Kakomongole Sub-county in Nakapiripirit District). Thus, many children's educations are stunted once they leave primary school, and they remain at a disadvantage compared to those students who can afford to advance to the next level. This is assuming the children even make it through the substandard primary schools offered to them. Within the schools, there are high dropout rates, a fact that is best attributed to prioritization. For many families, UPE schools turn out to be more expensive than they can manage, and the education that is provided, is simply not worth the money. As one resident noted: "There was a high dropout rate in the area, as manifested in the ever increasing number of street children. Parents have failed to keep children in school because they are charging fees that many parents cannot afford."(Community Engagement meeting held on 28 August 2016, in Rwanyamahembe Sub-county in Mbarara District). It doesn't make sense to pay great deals of money for an insufficient education that has little to no chance of progressing past primary school, and so many parents decide that it should not be a priority, and focus instead on the subsistence of their family.

Finally, one must keep in mind regional variation in service delivery needs. For example, in the north-eastern districts of Moroto and Nakapiripirit, school security is a concern, with specific requests for schools to be fenced in to deter theft and damages to facilities, and to curtail the movements of students: "Our children freely move in and out of the school because there is no fence and this leads to poor performance."(Community Engagement meeting held on 29 September 2016, in Namalu Sub-county in Nakapiripirit District on September 29, 2016).

The above evidence from communities throughout Uganda confirms that there are both systemic and administrative issues that require intervention of the school head teachers, District Local Government Authorities, and School Management Committees. It is paramount for head teachers to ensure that teachers and pupils arrive at school on time and are in classes. The head teachers need to play their supervisory role to ensure that the learners receive what they ought to receive in class at appropriate intervals. The district authorities need to ensure effective schools' inspection is conducted regularly and remedial actions are taken where necessary to ensure that appropriate conditions for teaching and learning for teachers and pupils respectively obtain across all schools. Regular political oversight and monitoring of education services would be a step in the right direction. The districts should ensure that parents actively participate in the management of schools, support their children to enrol and stay in school and interact with schools administration to ensure that their children are learning. The quality of schooling must be improved if increased access to education is to enhance economic and social development. Careful attention will also have to be paid to promoting good standards of education everywhere.

However, there were isolated cases where citizens reported improvement in school performance largely attributed to competition created by the existence of privately owned schools, and intervention by councils. For example, in Masindi District, Kamengo Sub-county, there are reports of improvement in performance due to competition with the private schools and intervention of local leaders. One resident offers a case of improvement, commenting: "Kinogozi Primary School has improved as a result of councillors' intervention in influencing the transfer of teachers who had overstayed in the school."(Community Engagement meeting held on 18 September 2016 in Kimengo Sub-county in Masindi District). This comment demonstrates the capacity of local players to change and improve their schools, showing that while challenges are there, they can be resolved with adequate commitment and effort. On the other hand, there are cases in which improvement comes from within the school itself, as another citizen noted: "Performance at Kijunjubwa Primary school has slightly improved due to competition with the private school." Thus, action cannot only come from local governments, but the community, parents and students, must recognize the power they have in their schools.

Perceptions of Health Care Services

The Government of Uganda health system consists of the local government health system (including Village Health Teams, Health Centres II, III and IVs). The general hospitals, Regional Referral Hospitals (RRH) and National Referral Hospitals (NRH) are semi-autonomous institutions. The district health system is further divided into Health Sub-Districts (HSDs). Each HSD is supposed to have a referral facility being either a HC IV or a general hospital (GoU, 2010). Local governments manage district health services within their jurisdiction. In line with the decentralisation framework, district health offices have the responsibility of supervising the district health system.

Concerns about facilities, staffing issues, and drug stock-outs dominated citizens' discussions of health service delivery. Staff issues mentioned include reporting to work late, health centres with too few staff to serve the population in need, health centre personnel who are rude, and the lack of staff accommodation. The poor conditions in health centres were also identified as a big problem, with community members describing centres with poor hygiene and a lack of a clean water supply. The need for attention to women's and childbirth services was also expressed, with emphasis on providing maternity wards and services targeted to the needs of women and children.

The most urgent need expressed by citizens focused on building more local clinics to meet basic needs. One citizen argued that a basic discussion of health needs must address the absence of a health centre in the parish:

> You know very well that this parish does not have any health centre; we have been crying for this but see no action. What can we do? (Community Engagement meeting held on 19 August 2016, in Akworo Sub-county in Nebbi District).

Accessibility is the minimum requirement of service delivery, and for the citizens of this parish, that is not met. Residents have no access to essential health services.

Even in sub-counties with centres, more attention needs to be paid to improving the facilities, such as providing adequate beds, basic medical equipment, other supplies (e.g., solar lights and batteries), and expanding space for patients and staff. Citizen concerns in relation to health facilities included:

> There is a need to enlarge patient area to accommodate the incoming patients, especially with the high population growth in our district. Even where facilities are newer, there is lack infrastructure such as beds and equipment" (Community Engagement meeting held on 11 August 2016 in Ndhew Sub-county in Nebbi District).

Following a common trend in service delivery, the infrastructure provided is not enough. Health centres are expected to serve a larger population than they have the resources to, leaving patients unable to benefit from the use of critical medical equipment.

Of all the resources that health centres are lacking, drugs were some of the most common and notable. Drug stock-outs continue to be a major issue that citizens in all districts are facing. Citizens talked about how the unavailability of drugs forced them to go without medicines unless they had the resources to buy them at private clinics where prices could be very high.

> Many times the drugs get finished before the allotted month, hence some sick people must travel to find them or purchase drugs elsewhere . . . When you are admitted to the Nebbi hospital, you will be asked to buy drugs from the clinic or for money for the drugs being given to you for treatment."(Community Engagement meeting held on 9 September 2016, in Erussi Sub-county in Nebbi District).

Consequently, health becomes a commodity, and one's socioeconomic status decides whether or not they can access treatment. Further, the initial drug stock-outs can be attributed back to insufficient health services, as one resident stated: "With a high population for our health centre, there are frequent drug stock-outs." In addition to not providing enough health centres, there are also not enough drugs to meet the needs of the population.

According to citizens, the drugs available need to correspond with those ailments more commonly found in specific districts. In regions with high incidences of malaria, respiratory problems, and worms:

> Service is good but the staff are few in numbers and the medicines for malaria or and other tablets for problems like worms, in general, are difficult to get at the health centre."(Community Engagement meeting held on 25 July 2016, in Mende Sub-county in Wakiso District).

Here, a disconnect between service providers and recipients is illustrated. The health sector is not responsive to the needs of patients, and so the quality of health services suffers.

In addition to insufficient infrastructure, drugs, and equipment, patients are also met with poorly performing or scant medical staff. Health centres tend to be understaffed and have high rates of staff absenteeism, which undermines the treatment provided to patients. As one resident explained:

> health workers are sometimes present. However, health worker absenteeism is worse towards the weekend, especially on Thursday and Friday. It disorganizes patients when they go for health care only to

find that health workers are off duty." (Community Engagement meeting held on 12 August 2016, in Pabbo Sub-county in Amuru District).

Once a citizen has managed to access a health centre, there is no guarantee that they will receive treatment. Moreover, even when staff is present, there are still cases where they are not enough to care for all the patients they receive, as another citizen reports:

> There is inadequate staffing at Nebbi hospital, and the few there are overwhelmed. Quite often there are very long lines of people seeking treatment at OPD."(Community Engagement meeting held in Erussi Sub-county in Nebbi District).

Understaffing is detrimental to both patients and health workers as it creates a strenuous and stressful environment for workers who in turn cannot provide high-quality service to their patients due to exhaustion.

Perceptions of Access to Safe Water and Sanitation

Rural water supply provision covers communities or villages (at the level of Local Council 1 (LC1)) with a scattered population in settlements up to 1,500 people and Rural Growth Centres (RGCs) with populations between 1,500 and 5,000. The main technology options used for water supply improvements in rural areas include protected springs (18%), shallow wells (23%), deep boreholes (44%), and piped water schemes (11%) tanks (GoU, 2016).

Access to safe drinking water continues to be a contentious issue among citizens across the districts. The lack of adequate and safe water sources, poor distribution of safe water sources, non-functioning water sources, irregular water supply for piped water, and health impacts due to poor water quality were the most significant and widespread water challenges that citizens identified.

According to citizens', access and maintenance go hand in hand. An elderly man observed that:

> We have few safe water sources in our vicinity. Boreholes are not well maintained and water management committees are not fully functional

(Community Engagement meeting held on 23 September 2016, Nakapiripirit Town Council in Nakapiripirit District).

Certainly, many regions are hard to reach even as they experience an acute shortage of water. But often the problem is time and expense. Families will spend hours travelling to water sources and waiting in line. One female participant said that the whole parish is served by a two-inch pipe and its pressure was low.

Thus, citizens were quick to applaud efforts by local government officials who supported initiatives that brought access to water to communities. In Rukungiri district, for example, one elder stated that the government has provided water-harvesting tanks to households with iron sheets, and at least 36 tanks have been constructed in the community. In Apac District, the leadership has endeavoured to increase access to safe water; in FY 2013/14, the district drilled 37 boreholes, dug 18 shallow wells, constructed 21 protected springs, and rehabilitated 30 boreholes in an attempt to increase access to safe water (Akena, Obed and Opai, 2015). In other cases, implementing piped water projects can reduce pressure on nearby boreholes and save time. However, some projects of this nature are expensive for citizens. In Jinja District, for example, families are challenged in paying water bills. One citizen explained that her area is served by NWSC but the water is very expensive and many people cannot afford it.

While citizens were aware that there are barriers to universal access to water and sanitation, such as budgeting, maintenance and paying for services, they were less understanding regarding gaps in leadership. Citizens expect that elected officials will do their jobs in advocating on behalf of communities, visit parishes and monitor the services. Non-response is not an option:

> We have never seen these leaders appear in this village, sometimes we wonder why they were elected. See this village - do you see any borehole here? Now, what is the need of these councillors? We keep on voting for these leaders but whenever we need them, they are nowhere to be seen. We drink water with worms from these boreholes (points at borehole) and soon we will die of diseases.

This brings to light the connection between the health and water/sanitation sectors. A nurse from Moroto said that many cases of typhoid had been recorded due to lack of clean and safe water adding that shallow wells and rivers are contaminated, making consumers vulnerable to water-related diseases.

On a positive note, citizens have taken action, raising issues with councillors. Often councillors respond, which reinforces the local governance process. But if they do not citizens will seek solutions outside of local governance. In one story from Moroto, a female participant complained that when a water issue was raised to local councillors – when their borehole broke – they acted as a community to lodge a complaint, writing letters. After a period of inaction, they contacted an NGO, which responded and helped them repair the borehole.

Perceptions of Road Quality

The road network is the backbone of the transport system in the country. Maintaining the road network in a condition that allows for effective, efficient, and sustainable movement of goods and passengers ensures the preservation of past road investments, and conserves the ecology and environment for future generations is critical for the sector. According to the annual sector performance report for the road sector (2015/16), district roads total around 35,566 km and are a mandated responsibility of District Local Governments. Urban roads, which currently total approximately 12,000km, are all those roads within the boundaries of Urban Councils (excluding links maintained by Uganda National Roads Authority) that are a mandated responsibility of Urban Local Governments. Community access roads, the current length of which is estimated at 78,000 km are a responsibility of Local Council III (sub-county) Governments (GoU, 2016).

Citizens' perceptions suggest that the quality of roads has improved, though regular maintenance can be improved: reducing potholes, dust, and poor drainage during rainy seasons, delays, inadequate funding, shoddy construction works impacted maintenance and road quality, and deterioration caused by frequent heavy trucks (e.g., sugar cane trucks in Kamuli). The problematic and even dangerous road issues raised included roads that were washed away by rains, roads that were too narrow, poorly constructed culverts and bridges, and pot-holes – all of which made roads prone to accidents. Citizens complained about the loss of life due to accidents. While local political leaders were often depicted as contributing to solving the problems of building and maintaining roads, citizens viewed the UNRA and Central Government as more at fault, delaying maintenance, payments, and completion of projects, as well as obstructing private sector initiatives to repair roads (Chingos, 2012).

Poor roads and weak transportation systems undermine the delivery of services in many ways. A functioning transportation network is key to accessing education and health. One of the youth from Moroto District remarked that he appreciated efforts by area councillors: "Last month the road from town to Natumukasikou was graded and it is good. This has improved the road network to nearby sub-counties and one can access Kidepo health unit very easily and an ambulance can pick patients who are referred to Moroto at any time without difficulty in accessing the health unit."(Community Engagement meeting held on 4 September 2016, in Tapac Sub-County in Moroto District). While the efforts of the local government are viewed as favourable in many places, citizens can easily recognize situations when councillors are not fulfilling promises or following through on their mandate to deliver services.

> Councillors promised to improve on the roads, but what have they done now? Nothing. Do you see our roads? Today it's fair weather, but otherwise, you would all be stuck here . . . We really don't have leaders, and that's why our roads or bridges are so poor (Community Engagement meeting held on 4 September 2016, in Tapac Sub-County in Moroto District).

In terms of access to education, a man from Moroto District observed that poor quality roads,

> makes it difficult to access school for both pupils and teachers who are commuting daily, especially with the lack of teacher's accommodation and a boarding room for upper primary pupils to help them stay in school and concentrate on their studies. (Community Engagement meeting held on 3 September 2016, in Katikekile Sub-County in Moroto District).

Additionally, quality roads have an economic benefit, bolstering commercial activities such as the marketing of agricultural products. One citizen illustrated the use and benefit of well-maintained roads:

CAIIP (Community Agriculture Infrastructure Improvement Program) roads are routinely maintained through support from Wakiso district. This has enabled us to sustainably transport our agricultural produce from farms to the markets to earn a living. (Community Engagement meeting held on 27 July 2016, in Sissa Sub-County in Wakiso District).

For farmers, transportation is an essential part of sustaining their businesses. Thus, they depend on the regular and effective maintenance of roads to keep their businesses afloat. However, the aforementioned case is not a universal experience, as one resident reported: "We are facing a poor road network problem. During rainy seasons, most of the roads in Ssisa Sub-county, Wakiso District are impassable, rendering impossible the transportation of goods and services to retail outlets."(Community Engagement meeting held on 27 July 2016, in Sissa Sub-County in Wakiso District). When roads are not well kept, business suffers. As noted by one citizen: "We appreciate our leaders' initiative of keeping our roads routinely and periodically maintained. This is not enough, we need tarmacking of our roads to facilitate quick delivery of goods and services, thus reducing the cost of doing business." While regular maintenance does occur, it is still not enough and fails to meet the needs of many citizens.

Citizens often talked about services being neglected unless it is clearly beneficial to political leaders. As one citizen stated: "The problem is that most roads in our sub-county are usually worked on only during elections."(Community Engagement meeting held on 5 September 2016, in Kambuga Sub-County in Kanungu District). Thus, elected officials do not see service delivery as a necessity for the population, but rather as a prop for their own personal and political gain. Moreover, the maintenance provided tends to be sub-par, as one citizen expressed:

> Most contractors don't put murram on these roads. I think the problem is the people who recommend these contractors that end up doing shoddy work."(Community Engagement meeting held on 21 September 2016, in Adekokwok Sub-County in Lira District).

The maintenance provided is inadequate, and yet citizens are expected to be satisfied that it was provided.

An issue frequently voiced by citizens is having access to information about the progress and monitoring of road projects, as well as when hand-overs take place by contractors to the district/community: "It is very difficult for the citizens to monitor the construction of roads for they are ignorant of the terms of service the constructors agreed upon with either the district or sub-county." There is a lack of transparency in the service delivery of roads, thus rendering citizens unable to hold service providers accountable. This ambiguity stems from a lack of interaction between citizens and their elected leaders. In Jinja District, for example, citizens reported challenges in communicating with councillors: "The only avenues for communication with our councillors are through burial ceremonies and village functions like the 'Nigina.' Councillors rarely convene meetings, don't have formal offices, and fear meeting citizens because of the many demands we make."(Community Engagement Meeting held on 12 August 2016, in Kisasi Parish in Jinja District). The lack of communication between local leaders and citizens is highly detrimental and hinders citizen participation, leaders' accountability, transparency in service delivery, and leaders' capacity to be responsive to their constituency.

Perceptions of Agricultural Services

The Government of Uganda (GoU) acknowledges that agriculture has, for a long time, been a core sector of the economy providing the basis for growth in other sectors and significantly contributing to GDP and employment. The sector continues to employ the majority of the workforce with 72% of the workforce and 87% of the working poor being primarily engaged in agricultural activities. Under Operation Wealth Creation (OWC), it is the objective of GoU that national policies, interventions and programmes aim at transforming agriculture from subsistence to commercial agriculture with a target of raising household incomes to a minimum UGX20 million per household per year (GoU, 2016). Agriculture serves as the mainstay of food security as most products are consumed locally and agriculture is practised on a subsistence level (GoU, 2016).

In the previous discussion, citizens observed the connection between roads and agriculture. Citizen voices also reflect and urgency and willingness to work with extension services and local politicians to participate in government programmes. All the same, major concerns expressed by citizens are the timely availability of improved seeds, new implements and tools, advisory services and training, and opening postharvest markets – all of which can help mitigate the fluctuations and vulnerability often associated with farming and animal husbandry in Uganda. In regions where livestock is an important economic resource, such as in Nakapiripirit District, citizens discussed issues of need such as access to cattle vaccines and the problem of livestock theft and raids.

One area of service delivery worth elaborating on is how the government communicates and coordinates with local communities. In some places, citizens reported that the beneficiaries of the distribution of inputs were only those who were informed about the meetings. Even when farmers do receive assistance, citizens lament the lack of follow-through. For example, in Jinja District, three female participants reported that they were told to construct houses for cows and chickens, but the animals were never delivered. In another case, one farmer said that his family wasted money while preparing land for growing crops but the seed delivery was delayed to the point that he could not use them.

Often citizens are left working through the uncertainty of the recent changes in agricultural services with anger and conflict since they depend so directly on the success of agriculture. In one incident, emotions ran high as described in the following engagement that occurred in Luwero District:

> Citizens grew excited and said that agricultural services have moved from worse to worst. The discussion focused on cassava cuttings that were distributed yet they were picked from the very same community. Beans bought to the community were dyed deceiving farmers that they were treated. One man got annoyed and grabbed the microphone in defence of the people responsible for providing agricultural services in the community. However, the people at the meeting began to shout him down, that he should stop. Later, a peasant farmer added that his entire village was mobilized to come for maize and beans seeds but to his surprise, they were given only a small amount to be distributed among the 500 people. Finally, a self-employed citizen with a tough face and a loud voice commented that what annoys him most is the patronage, where the same people always benefit.

Citizens expressed the opinion that local politicians need to play a bigger role as an interface between the extension agents and the farmers. Often times, the agents appear in the village unannounced and even the LC1 chairperson has no knowledge of the activities. If local agricultural services are to be efficient and successful, citizens claim, service delivery must be coordinated within the local governance structure.

Conclusion

In sum, citizens throughout the districts expressed a need for improved services in each of these five sectors. Issues with staffing and infrastructure recur in all areas. Many of the citizen voices reflect the challenges to engaged and meaningful participation in implementing and improving service delivery. However, many of these challenges can be overcome if citizens have access to information and the capacity to engage their leaders effectively. According to Ringold, Holla, Koziol and Srinivasan:

> Citizens and users of services can affect social services by influencing the decisions of policymakers—through voice—and by influencing the behaviour of service providers—through client power. To exert this influence, they need access to information about services and the capacity and opportunities to use the information and transform it into action. Increasing transparency and providing access to information require efforts to improve the availability of information, as well as investments in the quality, relevance, and timeliness of information. Expanding opportunities for using information also involves building the capacity of users to understand and leverage information for action and opening channels to use it (Ringold et al., 2012).

The emphasis here is on both citizen action and politicians embracing and enabling social accountability mechanisms utilized by citizens. These mechanisms include information campaigns to tell citizens about their rights and the standards of service delivery they should expect. Councillors can create the incentives and processes to ensuring that service providers adapt their behaviour and performance in response to citizens' demands.

A better understanding of citizen concerns and priorities enables local government policy to increase the efficiency and effectiveness with which resources are translated into citizens' welfare outcomes. The citizen feedback on the quality of public services may be used to increase accountability by helping to strengthen the ties through which information and sanctions flow between providers, clients, and the local government units that fund and supervise providers. Further, citizens' feedback can enable the formulation of more effective public service policies, as the conditions that ordinary people encounter become better understood. This can be instrumental in re-allocation of resources more successfully. It is critical that local government units appreciate the outcomes of service delivery in their jurisdictions so as to be in a position to conduct rigorous and deliberate measurement of the impact of the services they provide. Attention to citizens' voices and concerns can feed into policy-relevant research to answer a range of questions about the way providers and clients interact and about the way facilities function (Amin, Das and Goldstein, 2008).

Improving the role of local governance in effective service delivery is enhanced by engaging citizens and amplifying their voices. When citizens are given a voice, new pathways emerge for local governance to partner with communities (Richardson et al., 2014). Citizens can offer valuable perspectives on service outcomes. Citizens help councillors by clarifying "demand" through the tools of "voice" – actions that can lead to effective service delivery and greater accountability. The primary challenge for local governance in Uganda today is to recognise that citizen experiences about the quality and nature of delivery of public services can be a very powerful tool that should be embraced by local governments. This, however, will require attendant changes to systems, processes, behaviours, and attitudes within the system and among the leaders so as to accommodate the insights and the new solutions from this interaction. (Richardson et al., 2014)

When we listen to the voices of citizens in this chapter, they have much to say not just about the quality of services provided, but also about how systems are supposed to work. They have heard the promise of decentralisation and understand that they are supposed to be part of the system of local governance by providing input on service delivery needs and prioritization. They also, however, lose hope and stop participating when they feel like their voices aren't listened to, responded to, or even taken seriously. This should be of utmost concern to decision-makers and policy makers at both the local and central government levels because without citizen participation, the promise of decentralisation – and even of democracy itself – cannot be realized.

Just like Goetz & Gaventa (2001) noted, across the different sectors of public service, the potential of citizen's voice and public responsiveness, depends on the features of service design and delivery;

the complexity of the technology involved; and the remoteness, geographical location, social and demographic characteristics of the users. This chapter, therefore, suggests that citizen voice can be enhanced when it goes beyond mere consultation to real influence. Citizens must enjoy more rights through more meaningful participation. This would include formal recognition of citizen groups, right to information about government decision making processes and expenditure patterns and an effective re-dress handling mechanism for poor quality service delivery.

References

Ahikire J. (2002) 'Decentralisation in Uganda Today':, in Institutions and Possible Outcomes in the Context of Human Rights. International Council on Human Rights Policy., p. 2.

Akena, P., Obed, R. and Opai, A. (2015) Local Government Councils' Performance and Public Service Delivery in Uganda: Apac District Council Score-Card Report 2013/14. Kampala.

Amin, S., Das, J. and Goldstein, M. (2008) Governance Leadership for Value-based Care. Are you Effectively Managing Your Career? Washington DC: Worrld Bank.

Awortwi, N. and Helmsing, A. B. (2014) 'In the name of bringing services closer to the people? Explaining the creation of new local government districts in Uganda.', International Reviwe of Administrative Sciences, p. 80(4), 766-788.

Bainomugisha, A., Tamale, L. M., Muhwezi, W. W., Cunningham, K., Ssemakula, E. G. and Bogere, G. (2015) The Local Government Councils Scorecard Assessment 2014/2015: Unlocking Potentials and Amplifying Voices,. Kampala.

Chingos, M. H. (2012) 'Citizen Perceptions of Government Service Quality:Evidence from Public Schools.', Quarterly Journal of Political Science, pp. 411–445.

Duclos, J. Y., Kiconco, A., Levine, S., Enyimu, J., Rodriguez, A. W. and Musisi, A. (2013) Poverty and Social Impact Analysis Universal Primary Education in Uganda: Equity in opportunities and human capital investment., Partnership for Economic Policy (PEP). Nairobi.

Goetz, A.M. & J. Gaventa (2001) Bringing citizen voice and client focus into service delivery. Working paper series, 138. Brighton: IDS.

GoU (1997) Local Governments Act 1997. Kampala: Uganda.

GoU (2010) Second National Health Policy. Kampala: Government of Uganda.

GoU (2016a) Agriculture Sector Strategic Plan 2015/16-2019-20: Final Draft. Kampala.

GoU (2016b) Ministry of Works and Transport Annual Sector Perfomance Report 2015/16. Kampala.

GoU (2016c) Water and Environment Sector Performance Report. Kampala.

ODI (2006) Universal Primary Education: Uganda. Kampala: ODI.

Oluwasinaayomi, K. F. and Tunde, A. (2017) "Decentralisation and local government reforms in Africa: challenges, opportunities and the way forward."', Eastern Africa Social Science Research Review, p. 33(Number 1), 89-113.

Onzima, B. (2013) 'Public Accountability: Explaining Variation Across Local Governments in Uganda in Partial Fulfilment for the Award of the Master of Philosophy in Public Administration'.

Richardson, L., Purdam, K., Cotterill, S., Rees, J., Spuires, G. and Askew, R. (2014) "'Responsible Citizens and Accountable Service Providers? Renegotiating the Contract between Citizen and State."', SAGE Journals, pp. 72–73.

Ringold, D., Holla, A., Koziol, M. and Srinivasan, S. (2012) Citizens and Service Delivery Assessing the Use of Social Accountability Approaches in the Human Development Sectors. Washington DC: The International Bank for Reconstruction and Development / The World Bank.

Shah, A. (2006) Public Sector Governance and Accountability Series: Local Governance in Developing Countries. Washington, D.C: The World Bank.

Steiner, S. (2006) Decentralisation in Uganda:Exploring the Constraints for Poverty Reduction. GIGA German Institute of Global and Area Studies. Hamburg.

CHAPTER FOUR

Strengthening Accountability by Assessing Performance of Local Government Leaders: The Case of the Local Government Councils' Scorecard Initiative in Uganda*

Lillian Muyomba-Tamale and Kiran Cunningham

Introduction

Accountable governments are responsible for what they do and should be able to give satisfactory reasons for their actions. While holding local governments accountable, citizens are fully empowered with knowledge about their leaders' roles, their own rights and obligations, and are fully aware and confident about when and to whom the right questions should be asked. Lee (2011) has argued that accountability is a benchmark of good governance that requires transparency in the relationship between government officials and citizens, a sense of obligation among government officials to be responsive to citizens, and an empowered citizenry capable of punishing their government representatives if they fail to do so (Lee, 2011). Essentially, accountability is more effective when citizens are involved. Social accountability refers to building accountability through citizen. This is referred to as social accountability engagement in which "ordinary citizens and/or civil society organizations participate directly or indirectly in exerting accountability" from public sector officials, often through the monitoring of public sector performance (Malena and Forster, 2004). Social accountability initiatives increase public sector performance by

---

*Portions of this chapter were previously published in the Commonwealth Journal of Local Governance, an open-access journal. See Lillian Muyomba-Tamale and Kiran Cunningham, "Holding local governments accountable for service delivery: The local government councils scorecard initiative in Uganda," Commonwealth Journal of Local Governance, Issue 20 (2017).

bolstering both citizen engagement and the public responsiveness of states. Strategic social accountability initiatives have

> a theory of change that takes into account the relationship between pro-change actions and eventual goals by specifying the multiple links in the causal chain." A tactical approach, by contrast, is limited to a specific link in the causal chain (Fox, 2014).

Effective accountability goes hand in hand with participation. Accountability is effective the degree to which local governments have to explain or justify what they have done or failed to do. The World Bank argues that improved information about local needs and preferences is one of the theoretical advantages of decentralization. However, for this to happen, elected leaders have to feel some sort of pressure to account to citizens. This pressure is related to the periodic elections where citizens may be forced to make decisions based on how best their local priorities were addressed. This makes local elections a powerful form of accountability. Depending on the type of election and commitment to service delivery, the quality of councils elected at district level can also be a meaningful factor to accountability.

For a governance perspective, accountability can be categorised under three broad themes: political accountability, fiscal accountability and administrative accountability. Political accountability is the accountability of the government leaders to the public, other legislative bodies, and accountability agencies of the state with regard to decisions they make. Political accountability is based purely on political responsibility and is generally sanctioned through political means such as being voted out of office, being sanctioned by the appointing authority, and being censored or recalled by constituencies. Fiscal accountability means proper use of and answerability for public funds. Administrative accountability focuses on the conduct of civil servants and how they discharge their public service roles to ensure the effective delivery of public goods and services to the citizens. Administrative and fiscal accountability can be secured through legal sanction and administrative measures.

No matter what form of accountability is talked about, it is important to observe that the concept has two key characteristics: (i) answerability, which is the right to receive a response and the obligation to provide one, and (ii) enforceability, which is the capacity to enforce action and seek redress when accountability fails. These two concepts presuppose that governments accept their obligations to provide adequate, accessible and appropriate basic services, which are of good quality for all citizens. It also means that citizens ought to embrace their obligation to hold their leaders accountable for providing those services.

Scorecards as Tools for Accountability

Scorecards have been used around the world as tools for social accountability and responsiveness from service users both in the private and public sectors. Scorecards have also been instrumental in community engagement and empowerment. The most documented deepening types of scorecards are the Citizens Report Cards (CRC) and the Community Scorecard (CSC).

The World Bank defines a CRC as an assessment of public services by the users (citizens) through client feedback surveys. In practice, a citizen report card goes beyond data collection to being an instrument for exerting public accountability through extensive media coverage and civil society advocacy. Citizen report cards were mainly designed to solicit feedback about the quality of services from the end user of a service. They are also a means through which citizens can rate the quality of services and provide their views about how services can be improved to better suit their needs. According to the World Bank Social Accountability E-Guide, the citizen report card methodology is expected to take into account statistical analyses on transparency in service provision, access, reliability, quality and usage of the service. Citizen report cards have been known to benefit and empower citizens in a number of ways. Most important, citizens are empowered by obtaining information that can be used to hold service providers accountable. Depending on how regular the reports are concluded and shared, service providers use them as a benchmark below which certain standards can't fall. In so doing, citizen satisfaction is upheld and citizen participation in identifying recommendations for change is ensured.

The CRC has some limitations that have been documented by the World Bank. One of them is the fact that CRCs are known to be expensive both financially and in terms of human resource. CRCs often require a sizeable number of human resources. Moreover, the techniques used call for expensive statistical analyses which limits the number of users, particularly at the grassroots.

Community Scorecards (CSCs) have also been used in some countries. In Vietnam, the community scorecard was used as a methodology for the social audit approach with the aim of improved accountability. Implemented by the Ministry of Planning and Investment with support from UNICEF in Vietnam, the social audit approach was modelled to function as a management and accountability mechanism (UNICEF, no date). The methodology was used to assess the processes of government plans and policies through the eyes of the beneficiaries. The community scorecard was guided by a rights based approach that included participation of rights holders on the one hand and the duty bearers on the other. One of the key components of the community scorecard in Vietnam was the interface meetings, which facilitated transparency, knowledge generation and in the final analysis, accountability of the leaders. One of the unique features of the community scorecard in Vietnam was that community members had the liberty to choose their own indicators during any given assessment process. The scorecards were used to measure the level of satisfaction in the health, education and roads sectors (UNICEF, no date).

In both cases, the citizens' scorecards and community scorecards have registered a lot of progress but also have major shortcomings. Both scorecard methodologies focus more on the "voice" and not so much on the "teeth". By design, both types of scorecards are meant to raise red flags by sighting gaps in the service delivery chain, which usually leads to unnecessary conflicts and defensiveness. The stakeholders promoting accountability may unnecessarily be looked at as enemies by those that provide the services. In politically charged environments, they may be looked as as simply being opposed to government programs. On the side of the citizens, a lot of expectations are heightened – that the service delivery problems identified will be resolved within a given time, which is not usually the case. It is against this background that the Local Government Councils Scorecard Initiative (LGCSCI) was started in Uganda, with a view of addressing both the "voice" and "teeth" sides of accountability.

The Local Government Councils Scorecard Initiative (LGCSCI) in Uganda

LGCSCI is a strategic social accountability initiative that enables citizens to demand excellence of their local governments and enables local governments to respond effectively and efficiently to those demands. The scorecard is a home-grown initiative implemented by the Advocates Coalition for Development and Environment (ACODE) working in partnership with the Uganda Local Governments' Association (ULGA). Having worked with local governments for over ten years, ACODE realised that there was a weak accountability relationship between the elected leaders and the citizens. By 2009 when the scorecard initiated, research revealed that improvements in the key service delivery areas of health, education, agriculture and roads were not proportionate to the levels of public investment in the sectors. Rundown health centres and makeshift classrooms existed side by side with emerging state-of-the-art private health centres and schools. Inadequacies in staffing and drug supplies continued to plague health centres, while access to clean and safe drinking water to the majority of the rural poor remained a challenge. The scorecard emerged out of a study whose general conclusion was that fully functional local government councils are the key link in the chain of public service delivery, providing an important source of balance of power between citizens and central government (Tumushabe *et al.*, 2010).

At the time, findings from several studies on the implementation of decentralisation had concluded that local governments were dealing with serious challenges of inadequate financial resources, difficulties with attracting and retaining competent staff, corruption, nepotism and elite capture (Bashaasha et al, 2011). Accountability relationships between the political and technical arms were also not streamlined. For instance, the division of power between district chairpersons and Resident District Commissioners" (RDC) (appointed by the President of Uganda to represent central government's interest and monitor the activities of districts) was ambiguous and often created conflict (Azfar et al, 2006).

The local government scorecard initiative is strategic. Whereas some social accountability initiatives such as the CRC and CSC focus primarily on a single link in the chain – e.g. citizens, civil society organizations, or local governments – LGCSCI focuses on all of these links. The initiative's central premise is that by monitoring the performance of local government councils (LGCs) and providing information about their performance to the electorate, citizens will demand accountability from their local elected officials. This increased demand, which CSOs and local governments will channel upwards to the national level, will ultimately result in a more engaged citizenry, a more responsive government, better performing local government officials, and more effective public service delivery. Activating this accountability chain requires building the capacity of the key stakeholders to demand and supply better governance and service delivery *and* building durable linkages through which the demand and supply can flow. LGCSCI project activities focus on both: enhancing the ability of communities, CSOs, and LGCs to demand improved service delivery, and creating the opportunities for productive engagement between these key actors through which these demands can be effectively made and responded to.

The Local Government Council Scorecard assessment, and the rigorous data collection and dissemination methodology surrounding it, is the centrepiece of the LGCSCI. The scorecards are actually a set of four independent instruments used to assess the performance of the Local Government Council as a corporate body, the District Chairperson, the District Speaker, and individual councillors. Designed in accordance with the roles and responsibilities of LGCs as outlined in Uganda's Local Governments Act, each scorecard comprises 60 to 80 indicators. The indicators are assigned an absolute mark, all of which add up to 100 points. Councillors, chairpersons, speakers and councils are required to provide concrete evidence of their performance for each indicator, and the results are published and disseminated at the community, district, and national levels. (A more detailed discussion of the scorecard methodology is provided below.)

The Scorecard is designed to fit into what some refer to as the *"missing middle"* of social accountability initiatives, turning uninformed citizens into informed citizens, unresponsive government into responsive government, and unaccountable government into accountable government (Odugbemi and Lee, 2011). Its effectiveness as a tool for catalysing accountability and good governance is maximized by the presence of what Fox (2014) refers to as both "voice" and "teeth."

Citizen "voice" is a key component of strategic social accountability initiatives. *Voice* refers to the various ways in which citizens – either as individuals or in organized formations – can express their opinions and concerns, putting pressure on service providers, policy makers and elected leaders to demand better services or to advocate for them (Cornwall and Leach, 2010). Reviews of social accountability initiatives by Lee (2011); Gaventa and McGee (2013); Joshi (2013) and Fox (2014) have shown, however, that results from initiatives that rely solely on citizen voice are generally weak with largely unrealistic demands. Many citizen report card initiatives suffer from this problem. Researchers have found, however, that citizen voices can be strengthened with the involvement of so-called interlocutors or intermediates who facilitate two-way communication between governing bodies and citizens, and bridge cultural and power gaps (Fox, 2014). Within the Scorecard Initiative, both ACODE and local CSO's play this role as they interface with citizens and act as a conduit for citizen voice during the process of scorecard data collection and the dissemination of findings .

Even with amplification of citizen voice by interlocutors, effective social accountability initiatives also need "teeth" – i.e. governmental capacity to respond to voice. This includes the capacity to respond positively to citizen voice through, for example, following recommendations that emerge from citizen engagement processes. It also includes governmental capacity to change practices and structures that inhibit transparency through, for example, investigating grievances and changing incentive structures to discourage wasteful, abusive or corrupt practices (Fox, 2014). The Local Government Council Scorecard Initiative has a variety of teeth. The publication and dissemination of scorecard results to citizens at the community, district and national levels makes visible individual councillors' performance on a broad range of good governance indicators, and provides citizens with very concrete information about their elected officials. It also provides a healthy dose of competition between councils to achieve top performance rankings. Equally significant, is the enhancement of government capacity to respond to citizen voice that is built into the action research methodology underlying LGCSCI. The scorecard was designed to fit into the accountability framework of the local government structure in Uganda.

The Scorecard Methodology

Unlike many citizen report card initiatives, which are similar to consumer satisfaction surveys, the LGCSCI scorecard is grounded in an action research methodology that combines capacity-building with an evidenced-based assessment of political leaders' ability to fulfil their mandate as defined in Uganda's Local Governments Act (Deichmann and Lall, 2007; Joshi, 2013). LGCSCI is not a name and shame undertaking but an intervention geared towards continuous training and equipping of political leaders to be effective in fulfilling their mandate. The initiative is grounded in the project's theory of change. The central premise of this theory of change is that periodic monitoring of the performance of local councils and individual councillors and providing information about their performance to the electorate will trigger citizens' effective demand for political accountability and effectiveness in public service delivery will increase. Citizen demand would then be channelled upwards through the local government council system to the national level (parliament and other line ministries). This would then create an upward demand for political accountability and good governance, resulting in improvement in citizens' quality of life.

The scorecard methodology equips citizens with timely and objective information regarding the performance of their elected leaders. As such, the assessment tools and methods are designed in such a way that the district researchers carry out civic education and on-spot training through the data collection process. One of the unique features about the local government assessment process is that it is evidence based. Unlike many other social accountability initiatives which rely primarily on citizen opinion, the district research team is expected to verify each score before a final mark is awarded.

The first assessment was a pilot phase for FY 2008/09 and was conducted in 10 only districts. The second assessment (FY 2009/10) brought on board 10 more districts. The third assessment for FY 2011/12 was conducted in 26 districts. The third and fourth assessments for FY 2012/13 and FY 2013/14 maintained the 26 districts while the fifth assessment Bainomugisha *et al.* (2014) brought the total of assessed districts to 30.

The Scorecard and the Local Government Structure in Uganda

The policy of decentralisation is operationalized through local governments in Uganda. Central government ministries remain the responsible centres for policy direction while local governments are the implementing bodies of these policies. Local governments are mandated to provide public services such as education, health, road works, water and sanitation and agricultural extension while the line ministries provide the policy guidance in the way these decentralised services are implemented.

The Local Government Act provides for a five-tier local government system comprising of Local Councils I, II, III, IV and V. In this hierarchy LC1, III and V are referred to as Local Governments, which in essence are bodies corporate with powers to generate, collect, plan for and utilise resources in a given locality. On the other hand, LC II and IV are administrative units that carry out functions related to resolution of disputes, monitor the delivery of services and assist in the maintenance of law, order and security. Figure 1 shows the structure of the local governments in Uganda.

Figure 4.1 Local Government Structure in Uganda

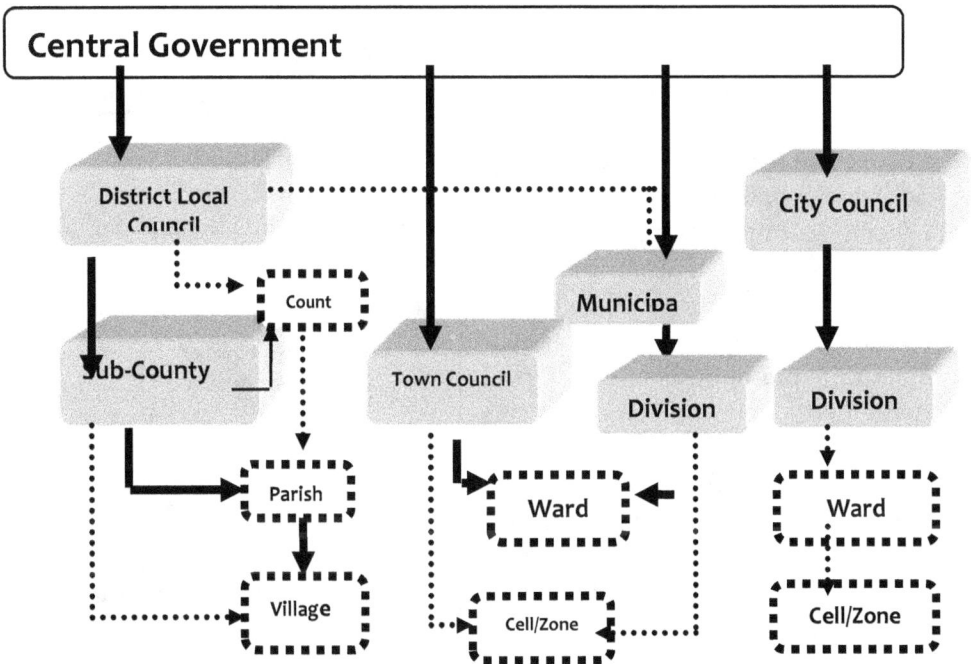

Source; Adapted from Tumushabe *et al.* (2010).

By design, local governments are mandated to undertake service delivery through the technical staff and provide oversight through the political leaders. The political function espouses local governments where decisions are taken at the lowest level possible and provides for citizens engagement in their lower local governments. It involves leadership, participation, inclusion, representation, decision-making, and power relations between central and local governments, and between higher and lower local governments. The service delivery function on the other hand requires local governments to plan and provide services that are directly needed by the citizens through a participatory process. It involves administration, planning, budgeting, financial management, human resources management and development, monitoring and evaluation, supervision and mentoring.

The specific functions of local governments are enshrined in the Local Governments Act (CAP 243) as amended (Government of Uganda, 2015). In general terms, Local government councils perform five interrelated responsibilities: political and representation function; legislative role; financial management and oversight; development planning and implementation and; constituency servicing and monitoring the delivery of public services (G.W. Tumushabe, Mushemeza, *et al.*, 2010).

The local government system therefore presupposes that local government councils are able to perform these responsibilities and through such performance, effective delivery of services and active citizens hip is achieved. These services include education (primary, secondary, trade, special and technical); health (hospitals other than hospitals providing referral and medical training; health centres, dispensaries and aid posts); construction and maintenance of feeder roads; the provision and maintenance of water supplies; agricultural extension service

The tenets of Uganda's decentralization system as enshrined in Article 178 of the Constitution

o   The state shall be guided by the principle of decentralization and devolution of governmental functions and powers to the people at appropriate levels where they can best manage and direct their own affairs.

o   The system shall be such as to ensure that functions, powers and responsibilities are devolved and transferred to local government units in a coordinated manner.

o   Decentralization shall be a principle applying to all levels of local government and in particular from s, land administration and surveying; and community development. Urba n councils are responsible for service delivery in urban areas and they enj oy both financial and planning autonomy.

The district council is mandated to provide oversight over the technical arm. A district council is the highest authority within a district with executive, legislative, planning and administrative powers. In terms of political leadership, district councils are headed by the district chairperson and comprise directly elected councillors and councillors representing special interest groups, including women, people with disabilities and the youth. The district council is a critical player in the social accountability chain because it is the platform where councillors can raise issues affecting their electorates and ensure that resources are allocated for the most pressing service delivery needs.

Local government assessments follow the standard Financial Year (FY) which begins on 1st July and ends on 30th June every year. Essentially, assessments of the concluded FY are undertaken at the beginning of a new financial year and lasts for a period of four months (July to September). The scorecards are designed to assess the work of elected political leaders and representative organs to deliver on their electoral promises, improve public service delivery, ensure accountability and promote good governance. It is important to bear in mind that the Local Government Council comprises councillors elected to represent geographically defined areas. Each council also has members elected to represent special interest groups such as women, youth, the elderly and people with disabilities. Each of the four categories (chairpersons, speakers, councillors, and the council as a whole) has a separate scorecard.

The main building blocks in the LGCSCI scorecard are the principles and core responsibilities of local governments as set out in the Constitution of the Republic of Uganda and the Local Governments Act. These are classified into five categories or broad themes: (i) financial management and oversight; (ii) political functions and representation; (iii) legislation and related functions; (iv) development planning and constituency servicing and (v) monitoring service delivery of the National Priority Program Areas (NPPAs). In the scorecard, these themes are referred to as parameters. The parameters are further broken down into a set of quantitative and qualitative indicators reflecting the statutory responsibilities and functions of the elected leader or institution being assessed.

Assessment Design and Research Methods

The scorecard parameters and indicators represent the detail of political leaders roles outlined in the Local Governments Act. A number of the indicators therein have also been documented as best practices for improved local governance. The tool for conducting the annual assessment of local government councils is what we refer to as the *scorecard.* The scorecard contains a set of qualitative and quantitative measurements as well as the methodological steps for conducting the assessment, alternatively called scorecard administration. The scorecard was developed through an intensive intellectual and empirical process at the inception of the initiative in 2009. The administration of the scorecard is divided into 4 phases, namely: (1) the preparation phase; (2) the fieldwork phase; (3) data collection, management and analysis phase; and (4) outreach and advocacy phase. During the preparation phase, a number of activities including securing buy-in from key stakeholders, customizing the scorecard, selecting the local government councils to be assessed, identification of district research teams and organizing methodology workshops are undertaken. For purposes of quality control and standardization, an Expert Task Group comprising representatives of local governments, academia, civil society and donors was constituted at the onset of LGCSCI to help provide feedback and guidance on implementation as well as assessment.

The action research methodology underpinning LGCSCI combines capacity building with an assessment of elected political leaders' ability to fulfil their mandate as defined in the Local Government Act. The assessment tools and methods are designed in such a way that they lead the research team to carry out capacity building through the data collection process. The main focus of the local government assessments are the elected political leaders (district chairperson, speaker and councillors) at district level. However, a lot of data is gathered from the technical staff, particularly the Chief Administrative Officers (CAOs), clerk to council, heads of department and sub county chief. Procedurally, these are the offices through which most of the final scores are verified through interviews and documentary evidence. Citizens are engaged through civic engagement meetings (CEMs) and the process of drafting and following up Civic Engagement Action Plans (CEAPs).

Data Collection and Verification Processes

Data collection is one of the processes undertaken during the first phase of the assessment – preparation phase. The process of data collection usually begins in June (the last month of the year under review); with assembling the evidence from existing documents that contain recorded evidence of council and councillor performance on most of indicators. With this information in hand, structured interviews are organised with individual councillors, chairpersons and speakers during the month of July. The respondents are at liberty to refer to documents or refer the researcher to documents to corroborate what they are saying. Information from the structured interviews is then augmented and verified through key informant interviews, focus group discussions, and field visits, most of which take place between July and August. Determining the final scores for the scorecards involves the collection and analysis of both qualitative and quantitative data. A brief description of each of these data collection methods follows:

Document Review (First month): This stage marks the beginning of the annual assessment and involves review of both published and grey literature as well as official government reports. Key literature reviewed for LGCSCI annual assessments includes the laws, particularly the Constitution and Local Governments Act, plans which include the district development plan, capacity building plan as well as the budget framework papers, reports which include service delivery and infrastructure reports, public accounts committee and audit reports as well as district and sub county council minutes.

Structured Interviews (Second month): These are carried out as part of administering the scorecard parameters and indicators. As much as possible, the research team is encouraged to schedule appointments in neutral places that will aid the assessment process. Each of the accessible councillors is engaged in a face-to-face interview structured around the scorecard. The process is a vital aspect of collecting verbal evidence that is verified later through written evidence of councillors' performance. Information elicited in the structured interviews is critical to the scoring of the scorecard. As part of the capacity building agenda, the research team is expected to justify in situations where the leader is not awarded a mark. Similarly, leaders are provided with information about how to score better marks and perform better in subsequent assessments.

Field Visits (Second and third months): The purpose of the field visits is to verify the information provided by the district leader. This is done through field visits to specific service delivery units and unstructured interviews with service users at respective service delivery units. Observation of service delivery unit is supplemented with photography to verify assertions of district leaders.

Civic Engagement Action Plans (CEAPs) and Civic Engagement Meetings (CEMs): CEAPs are a final product of the CEMs and are designed to deepen citizen engagement with the Scorecard results and activate citizen demand for better services and introduced in the implementation and assessment of FY 2014/2015. A central part of the CEMs are the CEAPs, which are citizen-generated action plans for using the tools of civic engagement to engage their councillors addressing persistent service delivery issues. The civic engagement tools include petitions, text messages, letters, radio call-ins, participation in meetings called by councillors, inviting councillors to community meetings, and participation in council meetings. These tools act as vehicles for citizen voice. CSOs/Researchers facilitate the CEAP process, thereby deepening their roles as important intermediaries between citizens and elected political leaders. In this role, they both amplify citizen voice and monitor government response to the action plan. The CEMS are moderated by district-based researchers using guiding statements and questions developed from core thematic areas spelt out in the Local Governments Act. Other than data collection, the meetings are platforms for civic education and empowerment about the role of the District Council, Councillors and the District Chairman, as well as the duties of a citizen. At the end of each meeting, a Civic Engagement Action Plan (CEAP) is drafted by citizens. The CEAPs have been very instrumental in improving civic participation as documented in Chapter 8 of this book.

Key Informant Interviews (Second and third months): Key informant interviews are conducted with technical officers in the district, including CAOs, heads of departments, clerks to councils, sub-county chiefs and service delivery unit managers. The major focus of these interviews is on collecting succinct information on the status of service delivery and verifying the actions undertaken by the political actors during the financial year.

The ultimate scores awarded are therefore a result of a multi-faceted data collection process and the triangulation of various types of data. The validity and reliability of the scores is further enhanced by a multi-layered verification process during the final month of the assessment. The process of scorecard generation begins with the district research team responsible for collecting the data for each indicator. These researchers assign the initial scores. The second layer involves the lead researchers in each district who supervise the fieldwork and review the scores assigned by the field researchers. These lead researchers are responsible for drafting the district specific reports through which scorecard results are disseminated. The third layer comprises the LGCSCI core team who are responsible for the final validation of data. This team reviews every scorecard to ensure that the scores awarded are consistent with the evidence provided. After verification, scores are entered using Epi-data and subsequently imported into SPSS where correlations and descriptive summaries are generated for each district. This process usually lasts a period of two months.

The Local Government Scorecard

Table 4.1 is a picture of the first page of a completed scorecard for a district councillor. (The content of the scorecards varies for chairpersons, speakers and councils, but the format is largely the same.) The main headings – LEGISLATIVE ROLE and CONTACT WITH THE ELECTORATE – are the parameters. Column one contains the performance indicators, column two indicates the number of marks associated with each indicator, and researchers use the third column to describe the evidence and justification upon which a score was awarded.

Table 4.1 A Snapshot of a Councilor Scorecard

1. LEGISLATIVE ROLE	(25)	Comments
i) Participation in plenary a) Attend at least four times b) Debate at least 4 times c) Debate issues related to service delivery		a) Attended district council meetings held on 27th August 2013,13th November 2013,21st December 2013,21st March 2014,17th April 2014 & 6th June 2014 b) MIN/DC/82/2014 on education
ii) Participation in committees a) Attend at least four times b) Debate at least 4 times c) Debate issues related to service delivery		a) Attended Education, Health, And Community Based Service Committee meeting held on 25th 06 2014, 12th 05 2014, 10th 02 2014, 12th 12 2013, 03rd 10 2013, 19th 08 2013, 23rd 07 2013. b) Debated in Education, Health and community based service committee meetings as follows: 10/14/2013 on health (Kagoma hospital), 10/14/2013 on staff and work; education, council procedures
iii) Moved a motion for approval as resolution of council a) Moved at least one motion b) Moved at least one motion in relation to NPPA		No motion
iv) Provided special skills/knowledge to the council or committee: a) Written and presented a paper to guide council b) Written and presented a paper to guide committee c) Evidence of having provided explanation/guidance on the special issues during the council proceedings after request to the speaker		a) No paper presented b) did not write but presented an oral one c) was asked to prepare but it was oral
2. CONTACT WITH ELECTORATES	(20)	
i) Meeting with electorates a) Evidence of programme of meetings b) At least four community meetings held c) Giving of official communication on service delivery at least 4 times d) Organizing of the community to demand for accountability		a) Program is the ACODE diary b) Called only one official meeting c) Verbally told the clerk of Bugembe town council what the district was intending to do d) Did not organize the citizens
ii) Office or coordinating center in the constituency a) Existence of an office/ center b) Evidence of the electorates visiting the office c) Evidence of documents and records		a) Office in the carpentry workshop in Bugembe town council b) Possession of a visitors' book c) has a file for the documents

On the Scorecard, we see the indicators, scores and comments related to the councillor's performance in two of the five parameters – legislative role and contact with the electorate. Councillors have four primary responsibilities within the legislative area: participation in plenary sessions, participation in committees, moving motions for approval as resolutions, and providing special skills and knowledge to the council or committee. In dialogue with a task group of key stakeholders, including ULGA, the LGCSCI team developed specific indicators to assess performance in each area. For example, good performance in the area of participation in plenaries (i.e. district council meetings) is measured using three indicators: attending at least four times, debating at least four times, and debating issues related to service delivery. In the example included, this particular councillor attained the minimum threshold of least four meetings (attended 6 meetings in total), debated an issue related to service delivery (in this case, education), but did not debate at least four times in council. Thus, he received marks for the first and third indicators, but not for the second. Since scores are "all or nothing," he received five out of the eight marks possible in this performance area. The scorecard example also illustrates the verification process.   Focusing on the first performance area (Meeting with Electorate) in the Community Engagement parameter, we see that the field researchers initially awarded the councillor marks for the second and third indicators (note circled scores), but a subsequent review of the scorecard by a member of the LGCSCI core team noted that there was insufficient evidence for those marks to be given and crossed them out.

Presentation of Final Scores

Once scores have been finalized, scorecard reports are prepared for each district. These reports contain the scores for chairpersons, speakers, the council as a body, and each individual councillor. A district report is produced for each of the districts to ease reference by ordinary citizens. By design, the district report is much shorter and focuses on the factors that led to the performance of the leaders. The centrepiece of each district report is the table with councillors' scores, ranked in order of highest to lowest overall score. A synthesis report comparing performance of all district leaders in the scorecard districts is also compiled and launched at the national level. The synthesis report is mainly used for national level advocacy with key policy makers in parliament and the relevant ministries. Figure 2 contains part of a table from a district report (Namara-Wamanga *et al.*, 2014).

Table 4.2: Summary of Councillor Performance

Summary performance of Wakiso District Councillors FY2013/14																												
Identifier				Performance				Legislative Role					Contact with Electorate		LLG	Monitoring NPPAs												
Name	Political Party	Commitment	Gender	Terms	2011/12	2012/13	2013/14	% change	Plenary	Committee	Motions	Special skill	Sub total	Meeting electorate	Office	Political	Sub-county meetings	Health	Education	Agriculture	Water	Roads	PWD	ENR	Sub Total
POINTS POSSIBLE									8	8	5	4	25	11	9	20	10	7	7	7	7	7	5	5	45
Norman Ssemwanga Kabagambe	NRM	Kira TC	M	1	69	68	91	3	8	8	6	1	17	11	9	20	10	7	7	7	6	7	5	5	44
Abudu Ndawula Kayondo	DP	Ssisa	M	1	58	83	88	6	8	8	0	0	16	11	9	20	10	7	7	6	7	3	5	5	42
Harriet Nvubuga Kitto	NRM	Namaa TC	M	1	66	85	87	2	8	8	5	0	21	11	9	20	10	7	7	5	6	7	1	5	36
Immaculate Nakimbugwe	NRM	Kakiri SC/TC	F	1	58	76	85	12	8	8	0	0	16	11	9	20	10	7	6	7	6	7	5	1	39
Sarah Nanyonga	NRM	Masulita & Namayumba	F	1	57	76	85	12	8	8	5	0	21	11	9	20	10	7	7	3	6	7	5	1	34
Alice Ssentongo	DP	Nsanga TC	F	1	62	76	80	3	5	8	0	2	15	9	9	18	10	7	6	7	4	3	5	5	37
John Paul Mayende	DP	Katabi	M	1	65	54	76	41	8	8	5	0	21	9	9	18	10	5	7	5	4	1	0	5	27
Khasifa Rashid Sebyara	NRM	Nabweru	M	1	67	77	75	-3	8	8	5	1	22	9	9	18	10	5	5	1	6	7	0	5	26
Norah Naluli	NRM	Mende	F	1	45	69	74	7	5	8	5	0	18	9	9	18	10	7	5	7	0	1	5	5	29
Herbert Wanda	NRM	Kakiri TC	M	1	69	74	73	-1	8	8	5	0	21	9	9	18	10	1	1	7	4	1	5	5	24

Source: (Namara-Wamanga *et al.*, 2014)

The first five columns of the table contain basic information about the councillor (name, political party affiliation, sub-county represented, gender, and number of terms in office). Following that are columns associated with the overall performance of each councillor. While this scorecard report was for FY 2013/14, scores from the previous two financial years are also included so that citizens and others can see trends in their councillors' performance over time. In addition, the report includes a column showing the percentage change in the overall score from the previous year. In the example used in Table 4.2, citizens from Kakiri Town Council are able to see that their female councillor, Immaculate Nakimbugwe, performed very well as she tied with another female councillor for 4th position overall. Her performance has been steadily improving from 58 in FY 2011/12 to 76 in FY 2012/13 and then to 85 points during the year under review. Her current score represents a 14% increase from the previous year. This kind of presentation makes it easy for citizens to track the performance of their councillors over a period of time, an important aspect of being able to hold their councillors accountable before any election.

The scorecard report also includes scores for councillors' performance on each parameter. Recall from the discussion of Figure 1 that there are multiple indicators for every parameter; the score on the report is the sum of the scores for each indicator. For example, the scores for monitoring each of the National Priority Program Areas (NPPAs) comprises the sum of the councillor's score on three indicators: a) conducting visits to service delivery sites, b) preparing quarterly monitoring reports on site visits, and c) taking follow-up action on issues raised in the reports.

The reports also include an accompanying narrative that highlights particular achievements and challenges and provides additional information connected to factors affecting performance. Below is an excerpt from the Wakiso District Report, associated with the scorecard in Table 4.2, that highlights and offers an explanation for the higher scores of councillors who sit on the District Executive Committee (DEC). *Membership in certain committees also played a role in the high level of performance of councillors. For instance, councillors that also served as members of the DEC had greater opportunities and facilitation to fulfil their roles more effectively compared to councillors who were not members of the DEC. A councillor that serves as a DEC member is entitled to the full time service of council, presents him/her privileges of an office, emoluments and allowances making execution of his/her roles easier.*

Not only are the parameter-specific scores and accompanying narrative context important for citizen "voice," as people are able to use the data to hold their local elected officials accountable in specific performance areas, this level of detail is also helpful to those being scored as it highlights jobs well done and provides specific targets for improvement. Moreover, they give the LGCSCI team a sense of where more "teeth" are needed as well. For example, referring again to NPPA performance areas in Figure 2, monitoring of the service delivery sectors continues to be a challenge for practically all but the very top scoring councillors. When the team dug deeper into this, they realized that there are significant budgetary and transportation constraints that impinge on councillors' ability to meet their responsibilities in this area. Armed with this information, the project team, ULGA, and the councillor's themselves have begun to demand that more resources be provided to them from the central government, especially for monitoring service delivery. This is an excellent example of how the scorecard, and the

LGCSCI project more broadly, triggers upward demand for accountability, not just from the citizens to the local governments, but from the local governments to central government as well.

Impact and Lessons Learned

When the scorecard was initiated in 2009, there was initial resistance by political leaders who feared that the assessment would be used by their political opponents to defeat them. This attitude has since changed because politicians have come to appreciate the usefulness of the scorecard in making them effective and efficient in their work. The partnership with the Uganda Local Government Association (ULGA) in 2010 was strategic as it provided legitimacy for our work within the local governments. After eight years of the initiative, local leaders are aware that even if they do not achieve the status of top performer, being able to document improvement in performance is appreciated by voters. The capacity building work that accompanies the scorecard process is multifaceted and has evolved over the course of the initiative. From the beginning, each round of assessment begins with an "inception meeting," organised to prepare the leaders for the next round of assessment. During these meetings councillors are reminded about what they are not doing right and how they can do things better. Because the scorecard itself is set up in accordance with the official roles and responsibilities of local government leaders and standard best practices, councillors, understanding of their own roles is deepened through this process.

Deeper Civic Participation and Engagement

The CEAPs methodology has been instrumental in deepening citizen voice and accountability in service delivery at the national and local government levels. The CEAP methodology provides another opportunity for non-partisan and constructive dialogue across the demand-supply lines where service-users can voice their service-delivery challenges, preferences and priorities, and engage with their elected officials using the tools of civic engagement. The CEAP methodology was first piloted in 2015 in the five districts of Gulu, Amuru, Nwoya, Lira and Agago in the sub-counties of Awach, Pabbo, Anaka and Lira-Palwo respectively. Citizens were supported to come up with strategies of mobilizing themselves to engage their district leaders and local government on issues of service delivery in their communities. Communities developed action plans for writing letters, petitions, sending SMS, holding community meetings, and attending council meetings, among others. Currently, CEAPs are being implemented in all 33 scorecard districts in Uganda, with many positive results of social accountability.

Improved Legislative Performance

By design, the scorecard methodology mainly focuses on the district council which comprises the district chairperson and elected councillors. Over the years, remarkable improvement has been registered in the legislative role of councils around the country. Having realised that most councils' performance was often hampered by a poor culture of political accountability and dysfunctional statutory bodies, the LGCSCI therefore focused on addressing the challenges by providing tailor-made training of both political and technical leaders in areas with capacity gaps. As a result of these interventions, almost all local governments covered by the initiative have, for example, been able to improve the quality of debate in council meetings. Before the intervention, most council debates were dominated by personal issues such as councillor allowances, as well as petty conflicts between the speakers and chairpersons which bogged down council business.

To date, it has become a common practice in LGCSCI districts for district councillors to hold civil servants to account in the delivery of much-needed public services. Additionally, whereas it used to be common practice to find council debate being dominated by a handful of councillors, lately, all councillors have to ensure that they debate so that their contribution is captured by the Clerk to Council in the minutes of council. Thus, councils have become much more deliberative than previously. Results from the most recent scorecard assessment for example, reveal that councillors' performance improved. For instance, the number of councillors scoring 80 and above increased from 6 to 29 to 40 to 52 in Financial Years (FY) 2011/12, 2012/13, and 14/15 respectively. The highest total scores for councillors have also been increasing from 85 to 89 to 91 to 99 points.

Improved Accountability and Oversight over the Technical Arm

As a social accountability tool, the local government scorecard has been hailed for improved oversight of the political leaders over the technical staff. One of the core functions of councils is providing oversight over the technical staff of the district. As analysts have argued, functioning local council oversight rely on the assumption that local elected councillors have more incentives to respond to the needs and preferences of local citizens and that they are more downwardly accountable than local bureaucrats (Bainomugisha *et al.*, 2015). At the beginning of the initiative in 2009, most councils lacked requisite capacity to perform the oversight function due to limited knowledge of the Council Rules of Procedure, councillor roles, limited education as well as frequent conflicts between the technical staff and councillors. After years of capacity building through trainings, peer-to-peer exchange learning visits; the oversight function across most districts has greatly improved. Findings from the 2014/15 scorecard report reveal that the district chairpersons who scored 3 to 4 points in oversight were 16 in FY2012/13 compared to 19 in 2013/14 and 20 in 2014/15.

Improved Monitoring of Government Programmes

Monitoring government programs is critical in ensuring accountability. Yet, one of the major failures that had characterized most local governments that inspired the design of LGCSCI was poor monitoring of service delivery by the elected leaders. Consequently, the scorecard was designed to draw the attention of councillors to focus a lot of their effort on monitoring service delivery. As a matter of fact, a significant proportion of the scorecard points (45) are devoted to monitoring service delivery. As a capacity building endeavour, local leaders were provided with a monitoring checklist with minimum service delivery indicators for each sector. In spite of councillors' recurrent complaints regarding the lack of adequate facilitation to carry out monitoring of service delivery, there has been a marked improvement in monitoring, with most of them submitting written reports of their field visits to the chairpersons and chief administrative officers. The monitoring reports usually mirror the status of services at the service delivery units and local communities. This feedback is very instrumental in providing leads and basis for follow-up and addressing service delivery deficiencies reported about (Bainomugisha *et al.*, 2015).

Improved Contact with the Electorate/Citizens

After eight years of implementing the local government scorecard, leaders' contact with their electorate has greatly improved (Bainomugisha *et al.*, 2015). One of the critical responsibilities of elected local leaders around the world is representation of the issues or development challenges facing their electorate in either parliament or councils. Evidence from the first two local government assessments revealed that this was a poorly performed function by district councillors who always cited poor pay, and an electorate that demands transport refund and allowance for attending meetings convened by their leaders. There were many cases where councillors simply migrated to urban centres upon being elected and abandoned their constituencies. This situation is different. Through civic engagement meetings (CEMs) and the CEAPs with citizens and their leaders, citizens have been educated not to demand money but rather demand service delivery, thereby delivering civic education and strengthening the social contract between the leaders and the citizens.

Conclusion

The performance of local government councils, as indicated by their scores over the years, has steadily increased and councillors themselves express increasing confidence in their ability to do their work. Indeed, the aftermath of the 2016 general elections in Uganda pointed to the fact that the scorecard impacted on voters' choices and decision making. During the campaigns that culminated into the 2016 general elections, a number of district leaders including chairpersons, speakers and councillors with relatively good performance used their scorecard performance to campaign and were re-elected (Bainomugisha *et al.*, 2015). Overall, only 17 percent of incumbent councillors were returned in the 111 districts in Uganda. However, statistics from the 30 districts where the scorecard was implemented present a more pleasant picture with 42 percent of incumbents being re-elected to various positions in the district council. In districts such as Moroto, Lira and Nakapiripirit, the return rate was as high as 75 percent, 74 percent and 64 percent respectively. A number of councillors also made it to parliament having campaigned using their previous scorecard performance. This is attributed to the capacity building interventions that have been consistently implemented under the initiative. As a social accountability tool, the scorecard methodology has influenced political processes that in turn have a bearing on economic and social welfare of the lives of citizens.

The local government scorecard has evolved since 2009, and a number of positive lessons have been learned and applied to ensure adaptability with the changing political times. As a strategic social accountability initiative designed to build both the "voice" and "teeth" necessary for responsive governance, the scorecard initiative focuses on building the capacity of citizens to demand for effective service delivery and the capacity of local governments to meet that demand by providing services effectively and efficiently. While LGCSCI does much to strengthen the "voice" – or demand side of social accountability, its centrepiece is focused on the "teeth" – or supply side. In contexts such as Uganda, where decentralization is a fairly recent phenomenon and local governments have only recently been established as the governing bodies responsible for ensuring effective and efficient delivery of services, focusing on the teeth side of social accountability cannot be underestimated. Indeed, the LGCSCI experience suggests it may be an essential place to begin.

References

Azfar, O., Livingston, J. and Meagher, P. (2006) 'Decentralization in Uganda', *Decentralization and Local Governance in Developing Countries: A Comparative Perspective*, p. 223–257.

Bainomugisha, A., Muyomba-Tamale, L., Muhwezi, W. W., Cunningham, K., Ssemakula, E. G., Bogere, G. and .....Mbabazi, J. (2015) 'The Local Government Councils Scorecard Assessment 2014/2015', *Unlocking Potentials and Amplifying Voices*, Vol. 70.

Bainomugisha, A., Muyomba-Tamale, L., Muhwezi, W. W., Cunningham, K., Ssemakula, E. G., Bogere, G. and ACODE (2014) 'Local Government Councils Scorecard Report 2013/14', in *A Combination of Gains, Reversals and Reforms. ACODE Policy Research Series*. Kampala:

ACODE., p. No. 64.

Bashaasha, B., Mangheni, M. N. and Nkonya, E. (2011) *Decentralization and rural service delivery in Uganda.* Kampala: International Food Policy Research Institute (IFPRI).

Cornwall, A. and Leach, M. (2010) *Putting the Politics Back into 'Public Engagement': Participation, Mobilization and Citizenship in the Shaping of Health Services.* Brighton: IDS.

Deichmann, U. and Lall, S. V. (2007) *Citizen feedback and delivery of urban services.* World Development.

Fox, J. (2014) *Social Accountability: What does the evidence really say?, Global Partnership for Social Accountability.* Washington, DC.

Gaventa, J. and McGee, R. (2013) 'The impact of transparency and accountability initiatives', *Development Policy Review*, p. 31(s1), s3–s28.

Government of Uganda (2015) *Government of Uganda: Act 16 Local Governments (Amendment) Act 2015, CVIII.* Kampala: Government of Uganda.

Joshi, A. (2013) 'Do they work? Assessing the impact of transparency and accountability initiatives in service delivery', *Development Policy Review*, p. 31(s1), s29–s48.

Lee, T. (2011) *The (Im) Possibility of Mobilizing Public Opinion.* Inertia to Public Action.

Malena, C. and Forster, R. (2004) *Social Accountability An introduction to the concept and emerging practice.*

Namara-Wamanga, S., Ssali, M. K., Ainembambazi, R. and ACODE (2014) *Wakiso District Council Scorecard Report FY 2013/14: ACODE Public Service Delivery and Accountability Report Series.* Kampala.

Odugbemi, S. and Lee, T. (2011) *Accountability through public opinion: from inertia to public action.* World Bank.

Tumushabe, G. W., Mushemeza, E., Muyomba-Tamale, L. and Ssemakula, E. G. (2010) *Monitoring and Assessing the Performance of Local Government Councils in Uganda: Background, Methodology and ScoreCard.* Kampala:

Tumushabe, G. W., Muyomba-Tamale, L., Ssemakula, E. and Lukwago, D. (2010) *Uganda local government councils scorecard report 2008/09: A comparative analysis of findings and recommendations for action. ACODE Policy Research Series.* Kampala.

UNICEF (no date) *Community scorecard manual, A social audit tool to monitor the progress of viet nam's socio-économic development plan.* Vietnam

CHAPTER FIVE

Women as Agents of Accountability at Local Government Level

Naomi Asimo & Lillian Muyomba-Tamale

Introduction

Progressively, the number of women in political leadership has continued to increase around the world. With policies such as affirmative action, the numbers are much higher at local government level where there are more opportunities for representation within the decentralized frameworks. Studies have shown that women at the local government level are more likely to present themselves as candidates to contest for positions at the national level, especially parliament, having acquired sufficient experience in their previous political careers. Despite the growing numbers, gender inequality persists across the world. With a few exceptions, women continue to work more yet earn less and have less direct access to productive resources than men. Moreover, much of the value of women's work remains *invisible* due to the association of *"work"* with income, leading to a lack of recognition of their practical and strategic needs especially, as those differ from work by men. This imbalance presents a disconnect between the three closely interlinked principles of empowerment – agency, resources, and achievements (Kabeer, 2010). In the face of this persistent gender inequality and an increasingly sophisticated understanding of the differing roles, responsibilities, and needs of women and men, many countries, especially in the global south, have focused on increasing women's representation in government. This has been adopted as a strategy for ensuring that the specific interests of women are taken into account when policies and programmes are developed and implemented.

For many countries, Uganda inclusive, this move has been primarily in response to the changing discourse on good governance. For donor-dependent governments, particularly in the less developed countries, the practice has also been inspired by mounting pressure largely from development partners (F. Saito, 1998; Binda, 2004). It has most recently been driven by the mandate to realize the targets under Millennium Development Goal (MDG) 3 and later goal 5 of the post-2015 Sustainable Development Goals (SDGs) as adopted by the United Nations. Both goals are intended to attain gender equality and empowerment of women and girls (Sam, 2016). They set out to realize gender equitable societies by promoting women's social, economic and political participation. MDG 3 stressed the elimination of gender disparity in education at all levels and empowerment of women particular as regards access to health information and control of resources. This goal was set to be realized by 2015. Goal 5 of the post 2015 SDGs builds on MDG 3 with a target period of 2030. Through target number five of this goal, all the UN member states commit to *"ensure women's full and effective participation and equal opportunities for leadership at all levels of decision making in political, economic and public life"* by 2030. These two goals have further driven political restructuring in several political institutions.

Within the political restructuring, the desire to address persistent gender inequality culminated into other interventions that have progressively drawn focus to increased incorporation of women in the previously male-dominated political spheres. Affirmative Action for women in politics is one such intervention. Constituency demarcation and gender quotas, particularly electoral gender quotas under affirmative action, have been widely adopted to reverse the phenomenon around women being one of the historically underrepresented social groups. Affirmative action can generally be defined as

> programmes which take some kind of initiative either voluntarily or under the compulsion of the law, to increase, maintain, or rearrange the number or status of certain group members usually defined by race or gender, within a larger group (Bachi, 1996).

Bachi maintains that affirmative action is a form of preferential treatment in favour of discriminated or minority groups. Whereas different states have embraced the concept in different forms and at different levels including under education, employment, constitution of boards and so on, in this chapter, the term "affirmative action" is used in reference to such intervention mandated by law in electoral offices.

Over the last three decades, women's participation in elective offices, especially resulting from affirmative action, has become one of the most popular ways of shaping democratic political institutions worldwide (Tamale, 2004). Underlying the realization of gender inclusive governance and administration is the evolution in national and international legal structures and policies (conventions and constitutional provisions); as well as the evolution and dedication of activists, both individual and institutions (Tamale, 2004). Several countries are increasingly introducing gender quotas to address the issue of under representation by women in leadership positions (Pande and Ford, 2011) and to make governments more responsive to their specific needs. Electoral quotas for many states have been targeted to national parliaments and lower levels of government either through constitutional amendment or by electoral law reforms. Uganda was an early adopter of gender quotas in 1989, and today, meets the threshold of 30 percent of legislative seats reserved for women at both the central and local government levels.

Ahikire, (2013) maintains that quotas for women should not be seen as a favour but rather as a means for society to correct what was wrong from the very beginning. She further argues that quotas for women should be seen as a compensation for the structural and societal barriers, both direct and hidden, that women meet in the electoral processes (Ahikire, 2013). While most research and studies have revealed a significant increase in the number of women taking on electoral offices, the vast majority of these findings focus on numerical representation of women in parliament and higher political offices. There has been limited work done to show the impact of their presence in electoral offices on decision-making processes and the delivery of public services. In view of this, Akihire argues that the realization of numbers and percentage representation of women is not sufficient to reflect the impact of their presence in decision making structures.

This chapter discusses the question of women as agents of accountability at local government level. It addresses the role local elected women leaders' play in changing the status quo of services in their constituencies. While reference may be made scantily to a wider perspective of local elected women leaders, the greater focus will be drawn from the Ugandan context with an inclination to findings from a private academic study undertaken by one of the authors of this chapter (Asimo, 2016) and those from a social accountability intervention - the Local Government Councils' Scorecard initiative - discussed in Chapter 4 of this book.

From Governance to Gender - Conscious Governments

On the global scene, the public advocacy for women's rights, including political representation and participation, was formally triggered by the 1848 Women's Rights Convention in Seneca Falls, New York (Wellman J., 1991). This culminated into the *"Declaration of Sentiments and Grievances"* fronting injustices of the then role of women in society including their lack of political access. Over time this campaign spread to other parts of America, to Europe and later to the African continent. Up until the 1970s and early 1980s, the women's movement was more inclined towards gaining women citizenship rights like the right to vote and the right to ownership of property (Duflo, 2004). This was fronted at the international level. It is in the second phase of the women's movement in the late 1980s and early 1990s that the focus shifted to securing women political power through electoral quotas at national level. It is then that the women's movement put substantive pressure for the institutionalization of women political representation through the inclusion of quotas in the constitutions of countries (Duflo, 2004).

On the whole, it is evident that women and men by nature have inherently unique policy priorities (Taylor-Robinson and Heath, 2003) based on their divergent social needs. This diversity needs to find its way into the planning and implementation processes at different levels of government (Duflo, 2004). In view of this Pitkin asserts that "in this complex modern society, representation is a significant avenue for furthering local interests; be they based on group or cause" (Pitkin, 1967). For women therefore, as a minority, Razavil argues that representation is critical "despite the debate as to whether they can be considered a coherent constituency for political processes given their differences of class, race, age, and location" (Razavil, 2000).

This ideally means that women, like men, need to be represented equitably at each level of planning if their needs are to be effectively and efficiently addressed. There have been significant advances made in promoting inclusive participation in education and political spheres particularly during the 21st century. However, gender gaps, though reversed in some communities, continue to exist in others particularly in low-income countries. Women remain substantially under-represented in leadership positions, in politics and business across the globe despite the increased female suffrage (Pande and Ford, 2011) and despite the fact that they constitute a larger population than men (Duflo, 2004).

As such, the need to empower women worldwide increasingly forms a greater part of the global development agenda in recent years. The worldwide recognition of affirmative action is in itself a symbol of commitment to end discrimination against minorities (*women inclusive*) and to make governments more responsive to their specific interests (Kellough, 1992). There has been an array of legal frameworks, considerations and commitments gradually leading to the increased visibility and participation being enjoyed by women today. These have basically provided ground for reconstructing the identity of women in as far as public spaces are concerned. In 1979, the United Nations General Assembly adopted the "Convention on the Elimination of all forms of Discrimination Against Women (CEDAW)" to which many countries, including Uganda conform. This was an instrument adopted with the aim of ensuring women's equal access to, and equal opportunities in, political and public life, including the right to vote and to stand for election (M.M. Hughes and Green, 2006). The same convention aimed at promoting equal access and opportunities in education, health and employment. Nearly two decades later, there was the 1995 Beijing Declaration. In it signatory states, Uganda inclusive, countries re-affirmed their commitment to ensure women's empowerment and their full participation in all spheres of society including participation in decision-making processes and access to power. These are considered fundamental for the achievement of equality, development and peace. They therefore set a platform for women to realize their aspirations and for their abilities and endeavours to be recognized in society. The more recent MDG 3 and Goal 5 of the post-2015 SDGs further deepened the drive towards women's empowerment in many states.

In response to this global drive, domestic governments have incorporated policies and practices in different forms and at different levels in favour of groups that have suffered discrimination and under representation. Unique to women, several countries have taken on to demarcation of electoral areas and political seats in political parties, parliaments and local councils through quotas (Tripp, 2001). In India, for example, the 74th constitutional amendment provides for reservation of 33 percent of seats in local elected bodies within the towns and in the countryside (the *panchayats*) for women (Hust, 2002; Duflo, 2004). Ideally, the numerical provision presents a window of opportunity for increased articulation of and response to issues affecting women constituents. Duflo observes that the rapid rise in number of Women's International Inter-governmental Organizations and the global network among these organizations has created some form of structural consensus and conformity in as far as incorporation of women in public spheres in concerned. In Uganda, the introduction of the gender quotas was a political landmark *"that marked the beginning of the end of the historical exclusion of women from the decision-making process at both the local and national levels"* (Tamale, 2004). As such, the number of women involved in government has been growing over the years.

By increasing the role of women at different levels within governments, gender parity can be guaranteed. There exists a lot of literature about women in government though these focus more at the national level (parliament, ministries, organisations and heads of states). In a study conducted by the Inter-Parliamentary Union in 2013 (Inter-Parliamentary Union, 2013), the number of women in government, particularly parliament stood at 21.8 percent. In the same study, the statistics indicated that more developed countries such as Norway and Sweden had relatively higher numbers when compared to developing countries such as Sri Lanka (Inter-Parliamentary Union, 2013).

In Uganda's parliament, statistics reveal that participation of women has specifically been increasing in terms of numbers since 1986. The 2006 parliamentary elections saw a rise in number of women elected as "district women representatives" in parliament from 75 to 84. In addition, 24 women contested for the direct constituency seats in which 15 of them won. Besides the Ugandan cases, diverse examples from India have also shown that women in local governments have the potential to advance social issues.

In Uganda, the women's movement was sparked off by their heavy involvement in the guerrilla war that brought the National Resistance Movement (NRM) to power in the 1980s (Ahikire, 2004). During this period, women, both rural and middle class, took on roles in the armed struggle, an activity that was hitherto seen as a male preserve. This drive according to Ahikire set the pace for affirmative action in Uganda. Given the sudden discovery made, the women earned their place because of their potentialities. As a country, therefore, Uganda's efforts towards gender equality were formally adopted through a constitutional reform in the mid-90s and structural reforms that followed it. The policy on decentralization was one outstanding structural reform that saw more consideration for women in leadership positions

The implementation of the policy on decentralization and the growing number of districts in Uganda, particularly during the last fifteen years, has had a direct bearing on the increase in women's representation in parliament (U. Kashaka, 2017). The same effect has been registered at local government level as women seem more inclined to contest for political positions on the affirmative action ticket. As such it is arguable that the vast majority of women in Uganda have been politically empowered as a result of the local council system which in itself has been an essential pillar of decentralization as a structural reform (Umaru Kashaka, 2017). Women have been able to compete with their male counterparts for seats traditionally believed to be for male candidates. Yet, the reality of a Uganda that is struggling to shed the trappings of a traditionally patriarchal society has been reflected in the extent to which women exercise their political power both inside and outside the confines of their political offices. As such, women in government face a number of challenges that are mainly attributed to patriarchy. Even after so many interventions globally, most societies are still dominated by men with an assumption that women's spaces are the private and not public spaces. Historically, a number of factors work against the advancement of women in government. These include: gender inequality within families, cultural attitudes and inequitable division of labour within the household. Once elected, women leaders usually undergo a lot more scrutiny compared to their male counterparts. For instance, it matters who a female politician is married to, whether she has children, what she wears and how she says what she says. The media has been at the forefront of making analyses about how feminine or masculine leaders, particularly the former, appear in public. Male political leaders rarely have to deal with this.

Intrinsically, women in government, at national level, tend to hold the less valued posts once elected as cabinet ministers. With a few exceptions, women usually deputise male ministers and thus take the second best position in management. Uganda is no exception to this despite strides achieved towards increased women participation in leadership. Gender analysts have argued that it is not sufficient simply to hire women leaders in government, it also matters which positions these women hold. In many cases, women in government do not necessarily hold executive decision-making authority but are rather relegated to the softer ministries such as health and education that are considered more motherly. Ministries that are regarded as more technical and demanding such as defence, finance and the military are mostly considered to be more masculine and therefore account for very few women leaders globally.

Beyond the national level, state governments embraced policy restructuring as an avenue through which the objective of the policy on affirmative action would infiltrate their local governance systems. For Uganda, the policy of decentralisation that introduced the local governance system was one such reform. At its forefront was the need to deconstruct the centre-controlled power to lower levels of governance in a bid to bring planning and decision making closer to the people (Fumihiko Saito, 1998; Kiyaga-Nsubuga and Olum, 2009). The local government system, therefore, necessitated the creation of clear political structures at lower levels to draw an array of local leaders (elected and appointed). These local leaders would apparently be better placed to undertake more effective planning (fiscal or otherwise) and supervision of services delivered at this level given their assumed proximity to the local communities. This system would therefore aid in addressing the different service delivery needs for the different social groups.

In essence, participation of women in Uganda's local government politics has been growing since 1995. This growth is associated with the policy on affirmative action, which is guaranteed in the Constitution (Tamale, 2004) and the Local Government Act. Uganda took a bold step in 1995 to protect and enforce the rights of groups of people who had been marginalized in previous government systems by including a clause on affirmative action in the then new Constitution (1995). Article 32.1 of this Constitution (Republic of Uganda, 1995) provides that

> … the State shall take affirmative action in favour of groups marginalized on the basis of gender, age, disability or any other reasons created by history, tradition or custom, for the purpose of redressing imbalances which exist against them.

Objective XV, one of the 8 social and economic objectives set out in this Constitution, particularly mandates the state to recognize the significant role that women play in society. Article 33 of the same constitution clearly outlines the specific rights of women, as one of the marginalized groups noted above (Republic of Uganda, 1995; Fumihiko Saito, 1998). Such legal provisions have created an unchallengeable basis for women's empowerment through their inclusion in political and administrative processes both at national and local level.

The institutionalization of the 1997 Local Governments Act (as amended) starting with the 1998 local government elections saw the official implementation of quotas both in the demarcation of electoral areas and constitution of decision-making political organs at these lower levels (*see Annex 1 for local government structure*). Women's inclusion in public policy-making structures at lower tiers of government was concretized during this process. Section 108 of the 1997 Local Government Act (as amended) provides that

> the population quota for demarcation of electoral areas for women representatives shall be determined by the requirement of women constituting one-third of any local council being considered.

This provision is further augmented under sections 10 (e) and 23 (1e), (2e), (3e), (4e) and (5e). For lower local governments in particular, Section 47 (2i) provides for women councils at parish and village level whose chairpersons are mandated to serve as secretaries for women as well as public health coordinators at these levels. In addition, Section 47 (3) provides for women constituting at least one-third of the executive committee members at the village and parish levels (Republic of Uganda, 1997).

We, however, find that even with this provision, women representation still encounters debilitating factors. While Uganda's 1995 Constitution clearly defines women's political rights, Section 8 sub-section 1 of her 1997 Local Government Act articulates the duties of a local elected leader. Both male and female leaders are elected to represent pre-defined political constituencies. The leaders are mandated to: maintain close contact with the electoral area, consult the people on issues to be discussed in the council where necessary; present views, opinions and proposals to the council; attend sessions of the local council and meetings of committees or subcommittees of which he or she is a member; appoint at least a day in a given period for meeting the people in his or her electoral area; report to the electorate the general decisions of council and the actions it has taken to solve problems raised by the residents in the electoral area; bring to bear on any discussion in the council the benefit of his or her skill, profession, experience or specialized knowledge; and take part in communal and development activities in his or her electoral area and district as a whole. The challenge is that these roles, which apply to both male and female elected leaders are not cognisant of gender-related barriers and the constitutional variance in constituency size in addition to other crosscutting financial and non-financial impediments.

Women as Drivers of Responsive Local Governments: A Case of Gulu District in Uganda

Gulu District is one of the districts in the Acholi sub-region in the Northern region of Uganda. It is considered the regional capital of the north and a gateway through to South Sudan. Gulu District was at the centre of the Lord's Resistance Army (LRA) war which ravaged the entire Northern (Van Acker F., 2004), North Eastern and parts of the Teso sub-regions and left close to 2 million Ugandans displaced for over two decades. By December 2006, relative peace and calm had returned to the region and displaced persons began to return from the Internally Displaced Persons (IDP) camps.

This background paints a picture of a district that has had so much to deal with in terms of social, economic and political recovery. After schools had been destroyed during the war, almost all the children of school going age missed out on close to 15 years of education. Residents were unable to receive modern health care and access to safe drinking water was far from a reality. With support from the central government and international development agencies, Gulu, as well as other affected districts, are being helped to recover the lost decades. These institutions are providing additional support to boost local economic activities, create employment, and rebuild new infrastructure in schools, health centres, roads and farm inputs. Through the Peace, Recovery and Development Plan (PRDP) and the Northern Uganda Social Action Fund (NUSAF), districts affected by the LRA war have been able to access additional equalization grants with a view of fast-tracking economic and social progress in the region. By December 2008, a survey conducted by the Office of the Prime Minister (OPM) in Uganda revealed that Gulu District emerged as a model district with the highest number of enrolment for primary school children, increasing numbers of health care access and improved connectivity between and among sub-counties due to the improved road network. In the same study by the OPM, 82.3 percent of the communities in Gulu were satisfied with the quality of services from NUSAF while 43 percent of those were highly satisfied.

In 2010, Gulu District was identified and included in the second cohort of the Local Government Councils Scorecard Initiative (LGCSCI). The scorecard initiative is discussed in detail in chapter 4 of this book. The choice of Gulu was based on the quality of leadership that had been credited for successes in the recovery programs implemented by the government of Uganda. Gulu was identified to provide a comparison between districts emerging from war and districts from other regions within the country that had enjoyed peace. During her first scorecard assessment in financial year 2009/2010, Gulu District Council emerged the best out of 20 district councils assessed with 78 out of 100 points. The then district chairperson, Hon. Nobert Mao was ranked second best chairperson among the 20 district chairpersons (Tumushabe, Muyomba and Ssemakula, 2011).

The general and local government elections of February 2011 ushered in a new five-year political term (2011-2016). In Gulu district, a new council was elected with a total of 31 councillors, 13 of whom were women. Out of the 13 women, only one was directly elected as the 12 were elected through the affirmative action ticket. During the first assessment in this 5-year political period, covering FY 2011/12, Gulu District Council once again emerged the best council with 82 out of 100 points. Correspondingly, Chairman Martin Ojara Mapenduzi, the then district chairperson, also emerged winner among all the 20 chairpersons that were assessed during that financial (Tumushabe *et al.*, 2013). Since then, the performance of the district council and chairperson continued with excellence in either the first or second positions. The most recent scorecard assessment for FY 2016/17 still paints Gulu District as a model district with both the district council and the district chairperson rated as the best performing among the 35 district councils and district chairpersons assessed (Bainomugisha *et al.*, 2017). This level of excellence is attributed to a number of factors including the active involvement and participation of women leaders in the district.

Evidence from the annual local government scorecard assessments points to the fact that female leaders indeed affected policy, the delivery of services, as well as attitude and behavioural changes among their electorate. In comparison, the outcomes of women's mobilization in the local communities have been widely registered across Uganda as is the case in countries like India (Duflo, 2004) where similar studies have been done. The Gulu case is an outcome of an academic study (Asimo, 2016) that was conducted among the women councillors elected to represent citizens for a 5-financial year period from 2011 to 2016.

Gulu's unique political history that is punctuated with the deep scars from the LRA war presented both male and female leaders with a lot more work to do in terms of influencing policy. Women leaders rose to the occasion and adopted specific strategies to respond to the community challenges especially those related to health, education and enhancing the economic welfare of their electorate. By 2012, a women's caucus had been formed with support from women's rights NGOs such as Gulu Women's Economic Development and Globalisation (GWED-G), a local women's organizations; Association of Women Lawyers in Uganda (FIDA-U), a national women's rights organizations; and the Forum for Women in Development (FOWODE), a women's organization based in the capital. The Women's Caucus was a pressure group through which women councillors at the district level were able to first of all overcome the challenges arising from competition amongst themselves. Conflict among the district women leaders had been registered strongly and evidently undermined the performance of women leaders. This pressure group was also employed as a platform to front women-specific issues. Through it the women leaders would mobilize quorum, drawing both male and female leaders from the higher and lower local governments, to push for action in response to specific service delivery needs, particularly those affecting the women in the district. The strength of this forum was evident in the ability of these leaders to strategically engage their communities through dialogues, as well as in their monitoring. As the former deputy speaker, and female councillor representing youth explained during an interview conducted on 23rd of February 2017,

> We had a woman caucus as female councilors through which we conducted community dialogues and carried out monitoring of the various sectors in the district.

Through the caucus, the women were able to influence and in some cases spearhead the drafting of several local policies including: the District Cholera Outbreak Response Plan (passed by the district council in 2014); the District Gender-Based Violence ordinance (passed on 24th December 2015); the Education Ordinance for Gulu district; the District Hygiene and Sanitation Ordinance and the most recent Gulu district Alcohol Ordinance (passed by the District Council in January 2016). The involvement of the women leaders in these processes was by far a direct response to societal needs. While they lobbied their district council and the central government (through their district leadership and local NGOs), they, on the other hand, conducted massive community awareness campaigns to sensitize citizens on the actions that were being undertaken and went ahead to solicit their participation in tackling the problems.

As part of their mobilisation strategy and with support from local development partners and the district council, female councillors convened community dialogues on November 2012, participated in radio talk shows, conducted door-to-door campaigns, mobilized women savings groups, and lobbied support from local NGOs to enhance their technical capacity and provide financial support to some of their activities. Speaking on the effectiveness of dialogues as a strategy adopted by women councillors, the district chairperson remarked:

The female councillors in Gulu have performed so well under their caucus. A number of people are now well informed. The community is more knowledgeable and I think that came as a result of those constant dialogues and engagement.

He further adds that "I remember the women used these dialogues to talk about land conflicts, early marriage and early pregnancy, and gender-based violence".

The study also revealed that women councillors had significantly influenced education services in the district. In February 2012, leaders in Gulu district championed campaigns to promote education for both boys and girls. The campaign, which was supported by the United Nations Children's Fund (UNICEF), was launched in Awach sub-county and aimed at increasing enrolment which had dropped as a result of the effects of the LRA war and slow return from the Internally Displaced Camps (IDPs). The female councillors specifically supported the component of the campaign dubbed *"the stay in school campaign"* whose focus was on encouraging the girl child to stay in school. Such interventions and the councillor's effort were fostered by local NGOs like Child Voice whose work and support are centred on the girl child, derailed by early motherhood. By December 2015, the enrolment rate had risen from 65,075 children in 2011 to 121,544 in 2015 (Ministry of Education Science Technology and Sports, 2015). At a higher level, up to 14 underprivileged girls (one from each of the selected sub-counties in Gulu District) benefited from a University bursary scheme (all costs paid for the 3-year academic period) as a result of the campaign by women councillors. This bursary, which was supported by the district, was intended to benefit both girls and boys as the then district chairperson explained that:

> this bursary was meant to benefit both boys and girls. The council allocated one hundred million shilling in FY 2012/13. But the women lobbied so hard that it ended up paying for only girls.

The female councillors took on other approaches to motivate girls in particular to attain the much needed formal education amidst the post-war effects. One female councillor observed that:

As women leaders, we tried to advocate for girl learning which the government accepted and at the district level we have a "girl learning school" and we advocated for those who can afford to open girl learning schools to do so.

It is important to note that this is different from the FAL programme. According to the interview held on 20th of February 2017 with the female councilor representing Bungatira Sub-county, Gulu District, as secretary for the standing committee on education in health, she narrated that One such institution is located in Alliance Girls School and I even sat for my *Senior* there because I wished to inspire other girls and as a result many girls are going back to school.

The women councillors also registered substantive achievements in as far as improvement in the health sector was concerned. Between 2012 and 2013, Gulu district women councillors spearheaded a health campaign against open defecation in the community. The campaign was initiated in Lalogi Sub-county. Through combined efforts under their women caucus, they mobilized their male counterparts and local NGOs to support the processes. They also mobilized local women's groups in this sub-county to petition the district against open defecation. They collectively conducted household inspections and contributed to the drafting of the ordinance on Hygiene and Sanitation which covered open free defecation. Through their relentless efforts, the ordinance was passed by the District Council and ultimately Lalogi Sub-county was declared an open defecation free space by 2016. During an interview with the then Executive Direction of GWED-G, a local women's NGO, she explained that:

> … in relation to health, there were petitions that these women pulled out especially if you look at community health. I remember in Lalogi, after one year the area was rendered open defecation free space because everybody there was going to the bush and there were no hand washing utensils … There was an ordinance which was passed that people must first of all get latrines and also put hand washing facilities outside and that, in addition, they should put in place stands where they dry their utensils. But where the councillors inspired me was by

doing household inspections until that area was declared open defecation free.

While some of the health issues were addressed locally, the women councillors also mounted pressure that drew action from the central government. In the spirit of their caucus the women leaders mobilised women from across the district's sub-counties to participate in processes that culminated into a petition following the prevalence of Hepatitis B that had plagued the sub-region for over three years. The petition was drafted with support from LCV and LCIII female councillors. The female district councillors conducted monitoring visits to Health Centre IIIs at sub-county level. By December 2016, the central government had responded by supplying the vaccine to the District Health Office. Gulu District was one of the 11 districts that received free vaccines for Hepatitis B in 2016. The then Executive Director of GWED-G in clarifying this explained that:

> Gulu is the only district in Northern Uganda which is giving free Hepatitis B vaccine. That came about because our women petitioned the district. We wanted to take them (the district) to court. The district called a special council meeting to look into our petition.... It was not just the women councillors but the women in the community as well working with the council. ...immediately the council selected 11 members including the Chairman LCV who went to the Ministry of Health, and met the minister separately ... the minister got threatened and he promised to include Gulu in the list of the 11 districts that would get the free vaccine . . . Gulu was the first to get it... went and sampled five health facilities just to cross check. When I went to Awach Health Centre, I found 2000 vaccines and 350 people already vaccinated.

On matters of maternal health, the study revealed even greater levels of engagement by the women councillors. The then District Chairperson highlighted a number of efforts by the councillors as he explained that:

> ... female councillors worked so closely with Reproductive Health Uganda, going to health facilities and educating women. Actually, they even organized a dialogue to look at family planning and all that. It was a debate that attracted even the male councillors at the district level.

> But there were several other dialogues at sub-county level, going to the community and talking about reproductive health issues. I also remember women councillors involved in mobilizing women to participate in cervical cancer screening (District Chairperson, Gulu District, 2017, personal communication, 19 February).

In the same year mothers in Gulu district received a significant number of delivery kits *(locally known as "mama kits")* following a petition to the central government. Given their limited technical and financial capacity, this group of women leaders lobbied and were provided technical and financial support by local women's NGO, GWED-G.

Outside the confines of women councillors in general, the female councillor representing persons with disability (PWDs), with support from her male counterpart and fellow women councillors spearheaded a campaign to address accessibility issues for citizens with physical impairment. In response to this, the then district council passed a resolution mandating all public offices in the district to construct ramps at the entrance of the district administrative building to enable PWDs access the public services they provide. This decision further mandated the inclusion of a component on disability-friendly services (ramps in particular) in every physical development contract awarded by the district. In response to the peaceful demonstration by the PWDs spearheaded by their female representative, the district chairperson was allocated an alternation office on the ground floor of the district's administrative block to enable easy accessibility for the PWDs.

The study also found that women councillors had fronted unique economic enhancement interventions to improvement of household incomes and financial management among the rural women. The study revealed that by 2016, a number of women's savings groups, popularly known as *"Bol I Cup"* in the local dialect, had been constituted across Gulu District as a result of attempts by the women councillors to improve the economic status of rural women. The councillors started a similar savings arrangement among themselves way back in 2012 before rolling it out to the communities. This programme in the community was supported by the National Union of Disabled Persons in Uganda (NUDIPU). One female councillor, also a member of the then District Executive Committee explained:

> ...we saw a lot of cases of domestic violence against women and we encouraged the women in the communities to constitute groups and form SACCOs to save money and to help the members of those groups. This saving initiative was implemented by NUDIPU and it was a very vital program which I participated in (Chairperson for Standing Committee of Council on Production and Natural resources, 2017, 20 February).

The saving schemes were intended to enable women whose household obligations have doubled over time to particularly ensure they can afford services that require some little financial resources such as education for their children and the necessary household basics.

Discussion: Improving the Performance of Women in Local Accountability

We earlier recognized the positive influence of the international and local policy in ensuring incorporation of women in political positions (especially through gender quotas) and recognition of their endeavours. In Uganda, the reservation of seats through affirmative action has propelled the confidence of women representatives in local councils. When asked how he thought women had benefited from the policy on affirmative action, the then District Chairperson of Gulu, on 20 February 2017 confirmed the benefit of this policy for women in his district noting that the policy had raised women's confidence in local governance. He explained that:

> I think the most prominent benefit that I would talk about is the representation aspect because making sure women are given a special kind of representation to make sure their voices are heard and I think their level of participation has very much created an impact. I think that is really the most important benefit.

This agrees with findings from the scorecard assessments which present a pleasant picture of improved performance among the women leaders at local government level in districts like Gulu where the intervention on affirmative action is being implemented. During the first two assessments, the performance of female councillors was largely below average across the scorecard districts. However, after a series of capacity building initiatives, female councillors have greatly improved their performance in terms of the quality of debate during council and committees. Equipped with more knowledge about what elected leaders should be doing, women have been at the forefront of monitoring service delivery, particularly in the health and education sectors. In turn, this has contributed to the improved quality of debates as the women debate from an informed point of view, focusing on real issues that affect women, boys and girls from their constituencies.

Findings from the academic study re-affirm those from the most recent scorecard assessment which reveal that despite the structural barriers such as larger constituencies, more women were rated among the top 10 performers in each of the 35 districts assessed. At the national level, the scorecard has been instrumental in helping women to advance into national politics, particularly, parliamentary politics. An analysis of the gender performance over the last five years reveals that women who perform better usually inspire fellow women leaders. The case of Gulu based on the independent academic study in reference in this chapter attributes such achievement to a combination of other enabling factors.

The effective response to service delivery needs identified by councillors was a joint effort by different actors including the political and technical offices as well as the local NGOs and media. The local NGOs offered both technical and financial support for the processes and activities involved. For women, in particular, these institutions conducted regular capacity building trainings including translation of critical legal and working documents into the local dialect to enable the female councillors engage with the communities and the development processes more meaningfully. The women's caucus which created opportunity for the women councillors to register significant policy outcomes was supported by GWED-G, a local women's organization. These local NGOs also provided financial support during the community dialogues and other community activities as one female councillor who served as the Secretary to the standing committee of council on Education and Health explained:

> … GWED-G offers us support by providing us with transport to access hard to reach areas as well as facilitation for the meetings,

facilitation for some participants who come from very far, and refreshments. This is something the local leader cannot do as a councillor because they do not have the funds. But with the help of such partners, we can reach out to communities and deal with women's issues.

The deliberated support from the offices of the district chairperson and speaker of the district council was manifested through remarks by the respondents. It is a unique approach by the district chairperson to empower women by appointing them into the district executive committee through offices of secretaries to the committees of council and rendering them continuous support. Along with these offices, these women were appointed to represent the district council on boards of government-supported and private institutions like schools and hospitals. This was not only to facilitate information flow between council and these institutions but also to specifically ensure that issues relating to gender especially for the females were adequately planned for and followed through. To this, the Chief Administrative Officer explained that:

> In Gulu, Chairman Mapenduzi has been consistent with his choice of leaders. The secretary for health and education has always been a woman. That is deliberate. And she sits on the Boards of a number of schools as well as on the Board of Lacor Hospital. She is a powerful woman, an extremely influential person. She's not very highly educated but she is a force to reckon with. And the objective is that she can influence the planning for girls and women (Deputy Chief Administrator Officer, Gulu District, 2017, Personal communication, February).

The female councillors that took on such offices individually acknowledged that while in these offices, they were inspired by the chairperson's support to the extent that a number of them were inspired to take on short courses to enhance their performance.

The media participated actively during council and committee activities and in joint response to service delivery issues. In fact, some of the local radio stations offered free airtime for talk shows to women leaders to sensitize and empower citizens on an array of service delivery issues.

In spite of such achievements, both studies - ACODE's scorecard assessments; and the independent academic study find that women leaders at local government level continue to face a number of challenges while executing their duties.

At the forefront, the local policies have not supported women fully in their uniqueness - with consideration to their gender limitations. Uganda's constitutional provisions establish election of councillors, both male and female alike, through adult suffrage (Local Government Act section 117 (1-2). This provides room for women to be elected on two fronts: as directly elected whereby they contest against their male counterparts for the unreserved 70 percent seats; or under the affirmative action ticket whereby they contest against fellow women for the 30 percent reserved seats. By this provision, councillors are elected by both male and female constituents which in its self is a challenge. Yet Uganda's rural society remains largely patriarchal despite national attempts to shift towards gender-balanced systems and structures. The then Gulu District Chairperson noted that "... it is a fact that our culture, our political environment, and the way that society has developed sometimes gives a lopsided position for women".

Secondly, both studies show that a significant percentage of female councillors at district level often represent two or more sub-counties while their male counterparts are responsible for just one sub-county. This is made worse by the fact that despite the big coverage, both male and female councillors receive the same remuneration for their work and are expected to deliver in equal measure. As a result, these women have found it challenging to particularly undertake effective monitoring of government services in their second or third electoral areas. The double or multiple representations also implies that women councillors are more likely to miss out when it comes to participation at sub-county meetings. The possibility of conflicting schedules for meetings at sub-county and district levels is higher for women than it is for men.

The academic study finds that women in Gulu district still face cultural barriers which undermine their professional aspirations. This finding resonates with that in the scorecard assessments and as such is reflective of the situation across many other rural communities in Uganda. In most of rural Uganda, the question of gender equity has not yet taken root. Women are still considered the weaker sex whose place is in the kitchen and the backyard. Nursing mothers and female councillors on maternity leave do not receive any special support from the local government. They are expected to perform just like any other male councillor as one of the Gulu District female councillors recollected:

> Personally I happened to conceive and even deliver during my time in council and it was not very easy. But good enough as a councillor for disability, government has a policy to support us through an assistant so that helped me. But of course you cannot move to many places with the child. It constrained me a lot especially because I was a single mother. If possible I would advise that women elected into council should first concentrate on council work and deliver later because council work is very hectic (Woman councillor, representing persons with disabilities, Gulu District Council, 2017, personal communication, 10 May).

The academic study also finds that the performance of individual women councillors is greatly defined by the changing domestic responsibility. The Secretary to the standing committee of council on Education and Health, who was re-elected into office, explained that:

> Women have taken on almost all of the domestic responsibilities. You find a woman is the one to: cater for feeding at home; making sure the children are dressed; school fees are paid; see that when a child is sick, medical attention is given. Women are overloaded with the responsibility of carrying all the domestic duties which is beyond their traditional expectations (Female councillor representing Bungatira sub-county, Gulu District, 2017, personal communication, 20 February).

The study further finds that men in rural areas are increasingly engaging in polygamous relationships and are indulging more in non-productive activities excessive alcoholism. This draws their attention and resources away from their natural function of providing for their families, a gap women are forced to bridge. As such, women have to play the role of breadwinners and ensure the welfare of their children including matters of education and health. They have to spend a substantive amount of their time in farmlands and other small-scale businesses in order to sustain their households. It remains a challenge for them to balance these roles with their mandated political responsibilities.

Clearly, women at these lower levels are still openly limited by their spouses or not rendered the necessary support by the electorate most of who still prefer male leaders. This attitude from their spouses and society holds them back from contesting against their male counterparts for directly elected positions despite their interest and capability. We therefore find that women at these lower levels remain more comfortable contesting under the shield of affirmative action. The question on whether it would be more politically productive to have women elected by a defined female constituency remains unanswered.

The pressure from the material demands by the citizens cannot be downplayed. A majority of the rural communities in Uganda, experience high poverty levels. Their relationship with the elected leaders is therefore not largely driven by service delivery needs as ideally expected. For many, this relationship is grounded essentially on individual material needs. This, however, may have been a solvable puzzle had it not been for the political trend whereby elected leaders make untenable and misleading promises even when they are aware of the limits of their power. With this hindsight, citizens across the board continue to make material demands and because the elected leaders need to sustain themselves in these offices they are either forced to make all attempts to meet these demands including losing their personal property or at the worst absconding from their responsibilities. Research under the scorecard initiative has shown that a good percentage of elected leaders are not well established financially yet they invest a lot in material demands from the electorate.

The assessments reveal that women, in particular, are victims of this technical gap since they present lower education levels than their male counterparts. The assessment finds a causal relationship between the low levels of education and their overall performance in their roles. Findings from the scorecard assessment indicate that the legislative function is not effectively performed by majority of women councillors and this has been associated with the lower levels of education. The female councillor representing youth who also doubled as the deputy speaker to the district council explained that the councillors' limited understanding and interpretation of information undermined their participation particularly in legislation. She explained that

> ... most of the councillors did not utilize their power to influence the budgeting process because of lack of education to a certain level and a poor reading culture in our society. You would find that most leaders do not read the budgets presented to them.

Although a number of councillors, like in Gulu have been seen to take on programmes to upgrade their academic levels, this has only yielded fruit in a few councils particularly those where there is deliberate effort by the senior leaders to create room for them to do so. It was found that women leaders had lower academic qualifications compared to their male counterparts. They also have limited financial resources, bigger constituency size - with some representing up to three constituencies, and other domestic responsibilities that society seems to sweep under the carpet. The low academic levels have evidently taken a toll on some women especially with regard to their legislative function.

In light of the challenges encountered by women in local leadership, as found by the study in reference and scorecard assessments alike, the scorecard reports which establish the same gaps make recommendations to improve the capacity of elected leaders at local government level. Local leaders operate under the presumption that they know what to do and how to do it, yet majority interface with this leadership function without prior experience in political offices. Local leaders are elected from citizens with a spectrum of career and professional backgrounds. This means that there is need for intense and continuous support especially from the central government for them to deliver reasonably.

Relatedly, conclusions drawn from the past scorecard reports speak to the need to improve financing to local governments as a means to enhanced implementation of the decentralisation policy. Gender-based budgeting is sighted as one of the strategies that should be adopted to ensure that both men and women actively participate in the budget formulation and budgeting processes. The reports also speak to the need to deepen civic engagement that allows special interest groups such as women, youth, PWDs and the elderly to determine priorities that enhance their well-being.

Conclusion

There is no doubt that women are indeed instrumental agents of accountability at local government level. This chapter has revealed that all that women in leadership need is support and recognition of their unique roles and responsibilities both at the household and at the political levels. The participation by women in politics is still a relatively young phenomenon in many developing countries, Uganda inclusive. Whereas it is generally acknowledged that women have indeed registered substantive political and social outcomes over time with regard to policy and delivery of services, the levels of this achievement evidently vary from country to country. This is mostly so because of the diverse cultural, social structural and internal country political characteristics that impacts the level of response to the global demand for women empowerment and inclusion in public -particularly political spheres (Melanie M. Hughes and Green, 2006).

The Gulu case study presents an interesting phenomenon where women can become effective agents of accountability if they get support from their leaders, especially the male folk. We can comfortably argue that on the whole, women in politics have sufficient potential to bring about desired policy and service delivery change with conducive and supportive environment. By this, we acknowledge that these leaders, particularly the women persistently grapple with the effects of lower education levels, limited resources, material-minded electorate and challenges from a patriarchal mindset. Women in the rural communities are increasingly taking on the role of heading the households although the degree may arguably be dependent on the social and political history of a local government. The cases used in this chapter clearly show that patriarchy has undermined women's confidence to contest for directly elected positions while at the same time burdening the women with more domestic roles that overwhelm their capacity to balance their family and public roles.

Governments around the world should remain engaged in the advancement of support to women in government, both at national and local levels. The success stories sighted from Gulu have come at a cost with so many sacrifices. It is the case of individual women who have overcome the structural barriers with great recognition and to the benefit of their societies. It is also the case of a supportive leadership of men ready to give a hand to women by first of all acknowledging them as partners in development. The ground is not yet levelled for both men and women but the path is clear. Laws should be reviewed to ensure equal representation where inequality exists, women in leadership should be supported with more resources and time to enhance their academic qualifications and society should be sensitized to support women leaders.

References

Van Acker F. (2004) 'Uganda and the Lord's Resistance Army:', *The new order no one ordered. African Affairs,* p. 103(412), 335–357.

Ahikire, J. (2004) 'Towards Women's effective Participation in Electoral Processes: A review of the Ugandan experience', *Feminist Africa,* 3(80), pp. 1–14. doi: 10.1039/c3cc45319g.

Ahikire, J. (2013) 'Affirmative Action for Women in Uganda Today: Navigating through the Muddy Waters and pushing on', *The Daily Monitor,* March.

Asimo, N. (2016) *Women in Governance and Quality of Rural Women's Health: A Case of Gulu District Local Government.*

Bachi, C. L. (1996) 'The Politics of Affirmative Action: "Women"', in *Equality and Category Politics.* London: Sage Publications Limited.

Bainomugisha, A., Muyomba-Tamale, L., Ssemakula, E. G., Bogere, G., Mbabazi, J., Asimo, N. and Atukunda, P. (2017) 'Local Government Councils Scorecard Assessment 2016-17':, in *Civic Engagement: Activating the Potentials of Local Governance in Uganda.* Kampala.

Binda, F. (2004) *The Implementation of Quotas: European Experiences Quota Report Series.*

Duflo, E. (2004a) 'Women as Policy Makers':, in *Evidence from a Randomized Policy Experiment in India.* The Econometric Society Stable.

Duflo, E. (2004b) 'Women as Policy Makers: Evidence from a Randomized Policy Experiment in India Author (s): Raghabendra Chattopadhyay and Esther Duflo Published by: The Econometric Society Stable URL: http://www.jstor.org/stable/3598894', *Econometrica,* 72(5), pp. 1409–1443. doi: 10.1111/j.1468-0262.2004.00539.x.

Hughes, M. M. and Green, J. L. (2006) 'The I nternational W omen's M ovement a nd Women's P olitical R epresentation, 1 893–2003', 71, pp. 898–920.

Hughes, M. M. and Green, J. L. (2006) 'The I nternational W omen's M ovement a nd Women's P olitical Representation, 1 893–2003,' p. 71, 898–920.

Hust, E. (2002) *Heidelberg Papers in South Asian and Comparative Politics Political Representation and Empowerment : Women in the Institutions of Local Government in Orissa after the 73 rd Amendment to the Indian Constitution by Political Representation and Empowerment W.*

Inter-Parliamentary Union (2013) 'Women in Parliament in 2013: The Year in Review'.

Kabeer, N. (2010) 'Gender equality and women's empowerment:', *A critical analysis of the third millennium development goal 1. Gender & Development,* p. 13(1), 13–24.

Kashaka, U. (2017) 'Why Female Representation in Politics is not Increasing.', *The New Vision*, March, p. 34–35.

Kashaka, U. (2017) 'Why Female Representation in Politics is not Increasing', *The New Vision*, March, pp. 34–35.

Kellough, J. E. (1992) 'Affirmative Action in Government Employment.', *The Annals of the American Academy of Political and Social Science,* p. 523(1), 117–130.

Kiyaga-Nsubuga, J. and Olum, Y. (2009) 'Local Governance and Local Democracy in Uganda', *Commonwealth Journal of Local Governance*, (2), pp. 26–43.

Ministry of Education Science Technology and Sports (2015) 'Education Statistical Abstract.' Kampala.

Pande, R. and Ford, D. (2011) 'Gender Quotas and Female Leadership : Development Report on Gender, 1–42.', *A Review Background Paper for the World Development Report on Gender. Background Paper for the World.*

Pitkin, H. F. (1967) *The Concept of Representation.* California:

Razavil, S. (2000) 'Women in Contemporary Democratization.', *International Journal of Politics, Culture, and Society,* p. 15(1), 201–224.

Republic of Uganda (1995) *Constitution of the Republic of Uganda.* Uganda.

Republic of Uganda (1997) *The local Governments Act.* Uganda.

Saito, F. (1998) 'DECENTRALIZATION IN UGANDA - Saito.pdf. In Decentralization and Democratization in Sub-Saharan Africa.'

Saito, F. (1998) 'DECENTRALIZATION IN UGANDA - Saito.pdf', in

Decentralization and Democratization in Sub-Saharan Africa.

Sam, K. L. (2016) 'Women's leadership in local government in the Caribbean.', *Commonwealth Journal of Local Governance*, p. (18), 68.

Tamale, S. (2004a) 'Introducing Quotas: Discourse and Legal Reform in Uganda. The Implementation of Quotas: African Experiences.' Johannesburg.

Tamale, S. (2004b) *Introducing Quotas: Discourse and Legal Reform in Uganda. The Implementation of Quotas: African Experiences.* Johannesburg.

Taylor-Robinson, M. M. and Heath, R. M. (2003) 'Do Women Legislators Have different policy priorities than their male colleagues? A critical case test. Women and Politics', p. 24.

Tripp, A. M. (2001) 'The New Political Activism in Africa.', *Journal of Democracy*, p. 12(3), 141–155.

Tumushabe, G., Muyomba-Tamale, L., Ssemakula, E. G. and Muhumuza, T. (2013) *Uganda Local Government Councils Scorecard 2012/13: The big service delivery divide.* Kampala.

Tumushabe, G., Muyomba, L. T. and Ssemakula, E. (2011) 'Uganda Local Government Councils Score-card Report 2009/2010':, in *Political Accountability, Representation and the State of Service Delivery.* Kampala.

Wellman J. (1991) 'The Seneca Falls Women's Rights Convention:', *A Study of Social Networks. Journal of Women's History*, p. 3, 9–37.

CHAPTER SIX

Civic Engagement and Community Land Rights in Uganda's Albertine Graben

Sabastiano Rwengabo & Gerald Byarugaba

Introduction

Land is central to human progress. Peasant and non-peasant societies, agrarian and non-agrarian economies alike, depend on land for food production, natural resources for industrial production, and service sectors like tourism and hospitality. This central role of the terrestrial resource is at the root of abuses and violations of land rights against landowning communities, especially those inhabiting resource-rich regions of the global south. Implicated in these abuses and violations are the powerful, non-peasant actors with sub-national, national, regional, and global links and networks (Miranda, 2007). These abuses and violations are driven by the desire to access, control, and expropriate land-based natural resources like minerals and oil and gas, for large-scale agriculture, to develop physical infrastructure, or for the sheer creation of geo-social spaces for amusement and social amenities, such as hunting, games and sports grounds, open urban public spaces, socio-cultural functions, and tourism. In these processes, local, regional, and international factors and forces seem to converge to complicate land governance in these societies. As a result, affected communities are torn between accepting 'development' and losing their land-based livelihoods.

Whether or not these large-scale acquisitions driven by global interest in farmlands in the global south provide equitable benefits is a question the answer to which is not to be found in contemporary develop mentalism (Deininger *et al.*, 2011). The deceptiveness of current emphasis on average gross domestic product (GDP), which is measured in terms of quantities of farm and non-farm production arising from lands acquired via dispossession of landowning communities, cannot be overemphasized.

Large-scale land acquisition's may lead to increased GDP without engendering corresponding improvements in the livelihoods of communities whose lands have been acquired and/or expropriated. This disconnect, between land acquisitions and livelihoods, generates local-level political-governance problems that affect broad natural resource governance regimes, practices, and their consequences. Nowhere is land as serious a political-governance question as in petroleum- and mineral-rich but also fertile areas that support agrarian livelihoods and where low-cost land transfers are needed for non-farm economic activities. Land is also highly contentious in underdeveloped societies where large-scale land acquisitions for capitalist development oftentimes undermine local communities' desire to preserve land-based livelihood traditions or reap benefits of investments on their lands (Deininger *et al.*, 2011).

In the bid to develop Uganda's nascent petroleum sector, people's land rights were violated in the country's Albertine Graben. The case of Rwamutonga internally displaced peoples, in Hoima district, is telling. Rwamutonga has been so documented that it is difficult to determine whether the government is solely responsible for the suffering of these peoples or whether petroleum companies are equally responsible (Anyuru *et al.*, 2016)[1]. Similar violations took place during the acquisition of land for palm oil production in the country's Ssese Islands, in a process Carmody and Taylor (2016) call "ecolonization", an unfolding process by which new frontiers are being conquered in the quest for expanded accumulation, to create territory, and to offset the ecological consequences of the on-going expansion and deepening of the capitalist mode of production (2016:100).

Communities in Uganda's Albertine Graben have been victims of this paradoxical relationship between land acquisitions and development discourses (Kizito, 2015). Displacements in Teso and Karamoja (in the country's eastern and north-eastern regions respectively) reveal the local-foreign actor nexus and collusion in these violations (Carmody and

---

[1] In Focus Group Discussion (FGD), held on 10 August 2016, in Nile Parish, Ngwedo Sub-County, Buliisa district).

Taylor, 2016). A balance has not been struck between massive land-based developments and the livelihoods of affected communities, a reality revealed by observers of recent in-country large-scale developments (Anyuru *et al.*, 2016). Socially, these challenges assume gender, generational, and social-class dimensions (Nickel, 2016).

Grasping these challenges helps us to unravel community agency in these complex land-governance experiences. It improves our thinking about, inquiries in, and practical responses toward, land rights protections in agrarian economies. This in-depth understanding reveals safeguards that involve the participation of affected communities, hence bottom-up, not top-down, prescriptions from central power locales. The challenge, then, is to develop and apply a conceptual model for understanding how affected communities can defend and/or promote their land rights—to uncover ways and means of community response to e-colonisation and current land grabs that, Carmody and Taylor believe, result from "ecological scarcity and the opportunities this [scarcity] presents for accumulation and logics of state building" (Carmody and Taylor, 2016).

This chapter formulates a new conception of the relationship between civic engagement (CE) and communal land rights. This framework is tested against cases of community responses to land rights violations in Uganda's Albertine Graben using ethnographical methods of inquiry. The chapter is based on qualitative investigation of community responses to land rights violations and community agency in land governance at the local level within the petroleum-rich Albertine Graben districts of Buliisa and Hoima in western Uganda. Data on CE was gathered through focus group discussions (FGDs), in-depth key informant interviews with community leaders, local government leaders and officials, field visits to and observations of areas of contestation, attendance to workshops and seminars addressing communal land rights, and in-depth literature review. The findings reveal that:

(a) land rights violations tend to take place under conditions of ignorance of land rights, when land governance structures are dysfunctional and/or weak, and when pressure for land acquisition for capitalist accumulation becomes unbearable;

(b) where these violations endanger entire communities, affected communities can develop collective responses to these violations despite the collective action problems that tend to bedevil the pursuit of common goods; and

(c) Contrary to the view that poor masses are unable to articulate and defend their rights against more powerful actors, communities in the Albertine Graben have been able to articulate and defend their rights. They have tried to fend off perceived land grabbers and/or prolong land-acquisition processes, creating difficulties for e-*colonisation*.

The argument that civic agency has the potential to protect communal land rights can be sustained when we consider the various reasons for public investment in guaranteeing property rights to land (Deininger, 2003). Notwithstanding the fusion between powerful capital and the state in the land-acquisition processes now unfolding in the global south (Carmody and Taylor, 2016), collective efforts can strengthen communities to resist the powerful over land rights violations. This assessment is made for the petroleum-rich Albertine Graben, western Uganda.

Why the Albertine Graben when land governance challenges straddle the whole country and global south? The recent past has seen an upsurge in land conflicts and rights violations in the Graben (Uganda Human Rights Commission, 2013; Kizito, 2015; Nickel, 2016). Local land administration structures in the region have not effectively addressed these complex land governance challenges. As a result, persistent land conflicts have been exacerbated largely by developments in the oil and gas sector with their attendant land acquisition processes, which, suffused by speculation, is a necessary step toward developing the petroleum sector (Byakagaba and Twesigye, 2015). These processes are characterized by lack of transparency, violations of human rights of evicted communities, illegitimate and often violent evictions (such as those that took place in Rwamutonga village, Hoima district), contestations over property values, misgivings about delayed compensations and resettlement, and quarrels over perceived and actual fraud, and other concerns. These mishaps thrive on inadequate knowledge, by Project Affected Persons (PAPs), of the available options and redress mechanisms (Anyuru *et al.*, 2016).

Examples are not hard to find. The process of acquiring 29 km² of land for the construction of an Oil Refinery in Buseruka Sub-county,

Hoima district, for example, affected about 1,221 households accommodating an estimated total population of 7,118 people. This number included an estimated 3,514 women; 1,344 children; 181 elderly persons; and 2,079 men (Elizabeth and Paulat, 2014; *The Observer*, 2014). In 2014, more than 250 families were evicted in Rwamutonga village, Hoima district, to pave way for the construction of an oil waste treatment plant (*Oil In Uganda*, 2015) In Buliisa district, conflicts associated with oil exploration erupted, among other areas, in Ngwedo and Buliisa sub-counties, and Buliisa Town Council, leading to violent clashes involving local communities (Tumusiime, 2014). In all these instances, communities were either ignorant of what awaited them or were misinformed for reasons beyond this study.

Civic Engagement and Community Land Rights

There is an inevitable but always ignored connection between civic engagement (CE), on the one hand, and promotion and protection of communal land rights and forms and practices of local-level land governance on the other. A highly engaged community, which exercises its civic rights and agency, is more likely to affect land governance than a disengaged community, whether or not we are talking of agrarian communities or hunter-gatherer or fishing communities inhabiting areas where land is of interest to external actors (state and non-state alike). This relationship can be conceptualized, empirically demonstrated, and implications drawn for land governance at local level. CE and communal land rights fall within the broad theory and practice of land governance, which concerns itself with the management of land and land-based resources with the view to improving people's land-based livelihoods. Rational choice theorists view land governance in terms of decision-making processes related to land, whereby land is taken as a resource about which people make rational decisions to maximize their benefits. Political Scientists, however, consider politics to be central to land governance. They stress power (ability to coerce others to act or behave in desired ways) and interests of the powerful (elites) and structures in land acquisition, ownership, and control. Economic theory stresses public choice/rational choice, where individual behaviour is informed by market-based decisions and self-interest in the available or potentially accessible land. This may lead to self-interest, struggles for land in the political market-place, and influence on regulatory instruments and structures as power is fused with rent-seeking behaviour (World Bank, 2016).

In defining governance, attention is always paid to the role of the state in regulating non-state actors' behaviours in land acquisition, control, ownership, and management processes. This emphasis on authority, control, and legitimacy of government and its relationship with non-governmental actors over land is useful for it analyses actors, their interests, incentives, and the constraints and relationships that evolve in the process (ibid, Slide 7).

This underlines issues of how land is acquired and lost, the structures involved in that, the rights enjoyed on land, and how those rights can exchange hands: all those policies, processes, and institutions by which decisions about land are made and implemented (Mugyenyi, 2016).

Community land rights are both individual and collective rights to access, control, own, utilise, and exchange land for the benefit of the landowning individual or community. The rights may be natural, such as the right to life through food production and settlement, or property rights, including land and land-based property ownership. In Uganda, land rights are protected by the constitution (Republic of Uganda, 1995) just as are property-ownership rights (Ibid, Art. 26). Constitutionally, land cannot be taken away from the owner for development or in the public interest—unless timely and adequate compensation is provided (Mugyenyi, 2016). These constitutional and legal protections were aimed at protecting communities' land rights from violations by both powerful actors and the State (Republic of Uganda, 1998, 2004, 2013). Land rights are rooted in land tenure systems, that is, ways in which land can be acquired and owned (Otsuka, 2002). Some land tenure systems, such as leasehold, limit the right to access and utilize land for a period specified in the lease agreement. Other systems, such as the changing customary tenure (Cotula, 2007), grant full rights over land: most customary tenure holdings in Uganda, though transferable to freehold and leasehold, are not registered. Where customary lands belong to communities, community efforts are needed to protect land rights. Where several land tenure systems co-exist simultaneously, and the community is threatened with loss of land, civic engagement becomes necessary to safeguard community rights.

In this conception of CE, we stress that community members have civil rights as protected by the constitution and national laws. In no way do we assume that all community members are citizens in the traditional use of the concept; we are aware that communities can best make legitimate demands upon the state to which they owe allegiance. Thus, CE is conceived within the context of the state-citizen relationship. We define CE as the centrality of local communities in governance processes, via participation and inclusion in decision making and actions, with resulting ability of communities to influence governance.

CE presupposes a shift from the individual to the collective, from the person to the community. It entails people's involvement through mobilization, conscientisation, and provision of information for purposes of engendering community, as opposed to individual, action on issues of common interest. This involvement may lead to reproduction or accentuation of problematic social relations within the community and between communities and other actors (Dempsey, 2010). The term also entails a planned process of working with identified local communities, which may be connected by geographical location, special interest, affiliation or identity, to address issues affecting their collective well-being. CE requires civic agency, which is the capacity of human communities and groups to collectively and cooperatively act on common problems regardless of their differences (Harry and Boyte, 2016).

CE is important in Uganda due to land tenure insecurity which bred manifold violations of community land rights. These violations were exacerbated by land acquisitions amidst post-2006 oil and gas developments in the Albertine Graben (Uganda Human Rights Commission, 2013). This trend also feeds on increasing global pressure for land in Africa, in which foreign companies, states, organizations, and individuals alike, scramble for African land and participate in struggles for large-scale land acquisition for agriculture, industry, and extractives sectors (Carmody and Taylor, 2016).

We assume that: (a) CE improves land governance generally and land rights protections specifically; (b) where communities are collectively endangered, by violations of their land rights, communities can develop collective responses to these violations despite the collective action problems that tend to bedevil the pursuit of common goods. CE is more likely to become beneficial when land is governed according to community norms. This norm-based land governance facilitates community participation in making and implementing decisions on how their land is accessed, controlled, and utilized, thus insuring communities against land rights violations. This people-driven initiative facilitates the development of responsive policies and programs on land: community cooperation smoothens the implementation of such measures. This is not to say that such policies and programs are always more efficient and effective than elite-driven ones but to underline community agency in these undertakings.

Not only does CE build a sense of cooperation and joint purpose by generating social license for developments on land; it develops confidence in government and private sector agencies that genuinely engage, respect, and respond to community concerns. CE also builds an inclusive society reflecting participatory democracy which is co-constitutive of Uganda's local governance. With CE citizens become active development agents, not mere onlookers of government and private-sector investments. In a setting of complex social relations amongst different ethnic groupings and conflicting land use forms, CE makes it possible to develop more acceptable and sustainable solutions to the numerous challenges of community-level land governance. For instance, citizens' cooperation is necessary for a more secure oil and gas sector, prevents oil conflicts, and enhances people's responsiveness to petroleum-sector developments (Watts, 2001). Contrarily, the marginalisation of communities leads to community resistances as witnessed in the Niger Delta and Ecuador (Kimerling, 2006; Becker, 2013).

It needs no further emphasis that CE enhances social license for land-based developments that affect indigenous communities, facilitates state-society solutions to land governance challenges facing a given community, encourages cordial relationships between investors and local communities, and fosters community learning that is a *sine qua non* of an active citizenry. Development results from the active participation of the people for whom it is intended. CE is one major channel and method of encouraging such participation. This participation can emerge from within the community, that is, it can be organic in evolution. CE can also be prompted by interactions between communities and foreign actors, state and non-state alike. This implies possible typologies of CE the understanding and empirical demonstration of which enriches our grasp of the contextual and changing realities of CE in the country's Albertine Graben and how land rights issues have been addressed through different forms of CE.

Typologies of Civic Engagement

We categorise the different forms of CE into: (a) autonomous; (b) induced; and (c) state-centric. The dividing line between these typologies may often be blurry. But it is possible to theoretically distinguish them based on their origin. Table 1 illustrates the different typologies of CE.

Table 6.1: Typologies of Civic Engagement

Typology of CE	Nature and Explanation	How it Operates
a) **Autonomous**	This is organic and originates within the community. ▪ Neither engineered from outside nor inspired from without ▪ CE of, for, and by the community itself.	Community self mobilizes to address a common problem. ▪ *Organic* elites/leaders emerge within the community, in response to existing problems affecting community members. ▪ Elites/leaders mobilize the community, then organise it into some structure revolving around the problem. ▪ Community overcomes collective action problem, undertakes to defend land rights.
b) **Induced**	Facilitated/Fuelled by non-state actors from outside the community ▪ Inducement based on problem observed by external actor ▪ External actor has interest (rational, ideological, moral-ethical, political, etc.) in mobilizing community	Non-state actor, the "Inducer", often from outside the community, identifies a problem, mobilizes, conscientizes, and organizes the community for joint response. ▪ External non-state actors involved following reports, research, rumours, claims, etc., on land conflicts. ▪ Inducers (academic, researchers, civil society, elites) mobilize and organise communities. ▪ May build on pre-existing/nascent autonomous processes. ▪ Inducers provide information, resources, capacity to develop documents and other tools

| c) | **State-Centric** | Sate policy-led; in response to community problem

▪ Indicates state response
▪ May be rooted in tactical or strategic interests
▪ Convergence of interest (bureaucratic and political) | Government, having identified a policy problem, encourages, organizes community into an engagement framework
▪ State seeks to develop policy responses to the identified problem.
▪ May or may not involve non-state actors
▪ Policy circles develop frameworks to address the problem
▪ Political and bureaucratic support and resources dedicated to developing CE frameworks |

Source: Developed by the Authors

From Table 6.1, there may be overlaps, complementarity, and convergence between the different typologies of CE. For instance, while a non-governmental organization (NGO) may organize a community against an impending land eviction, the organization will likely build on pre-existing forms of organization or response, however weak or nascent. Pre-existing community organization is a necessary—though not sufficient—condition for inducing the community into action. Otherwise, it would take time, effort, and resources to swing a community, lacking a nucleus organization, into action against a more organised and resourced party.

We distinguish *autonomous* from *induced* and *state-centric* CE. Autonomous CE is neither engineered from outside nor inspired by examples from without. It is CE of, for, and by the community itself. The community mobilizes, organizes, and constitutes itself into a structure for interacting with other stakeholders to address a shared problem. Since mobilization and organization are not spontaneous, and always require minimum leadership, ***organic elites*** and/or leaders emerge from within the community in response to problems affecting their community. These leaders analyse the problem at their levels, articulate it to the people, assess its ramifications (no claim about the accuracy of the assessment), and mobilize the community for action. This *organic leadership* may constitute itself into a structure or remain just coordinated without hierarchy. These elites organize their community into some kind of social structure revolving around the problem. The community, due to the education, articulation, and self-sacrifice of leaders, overcomes collective action problem. At the convenient moment, such a community can respond to threats to their land by demanding explanations, preventing perceived encroachment, and/or demanding certain terms on the matter. Where threats to land persist without a solution, the community undertakes to defend their land rights.

Induced CE involves external "Inducers", usually non-state actors from outside the affected community. Inducers, be they academics, other researchers, political pundits, or civil society elites, can mobilize and organize communities either for philanthropic reasons or for selfish motives disguised as unselfish assistance. Inducement is a function of problems observed by the external actor with interest (rational, ideological, moral-ethical, political, etc.) in mobilizing or helping the community. This may base on reports, research, media campaigns, and observation of land conflicts in the area. The inducer identifies a problem, mobilizes, sensitizes, and organizes the community for joint action. Following inducer intervention, the community is able to grasp the problem, defend its rights, and/or seek external assistance to overcome that problem. These inducers *may build on already-existing but nascent autonomous processes*, or start new processes by identifying and capacitating community-level elites through the provision of information, resources, developing capacity, and other tools of engagement.

State-centric CE entails state-level, policy-tailored, intervention. Always indicative of state response, state-centric CE may be rooted in tactical or strategic political interests of ruling elites or perceptions of the country's development strategists. It combines bureaucratic and political convergence of interest, at least temporarily, in addressing community problems at a given time. After identifying a policy problem, the state develops engagement frameworks, with or without the involvement of non-state actors. The state may develop policy responses, if none already exist, to the identified problem or build upon existing but hitherto related governance frameworks to direct the community into action. Policy and legal responses are developed and articulated to the community. The process need not be articulated in any formal policy and/or legal document. One can think of vigilantes and militias organized during counterinsurgency operations as a form of state-centric CE to address a civil conflict. Uganda undertook a similar CE during the early 1990s in the fight against HIV/AIDS. Emergency responses always take the combination of state-centric, induced, and autonomous CE. Political and bureaucratic support and resources may be dedicated to developing CE frameworks when work is already ongoing. Evidence of these forms of CE exists in Uganda's Albertine Graben.

Land Rights Violations in the Albertine Graben

Land rights violations in the Albertine Graben are part of a broader land governance crisis facing the country, a crisis that is not unlike other land-governance failures facing the developing global south. These challenges consist of land grabs, contentious land tenure systems, speculative land acquisitions, eviction of land-dependent agrarian and pastoralist communities, and encroachment on conservation lands and protected areas. Both state and non-state actors are involved, at different levels, in different locales, and use different methods that suit the contending actor—but all with a similar motive: access to, control over, ownership, and appropriation of land. Natural-resource-rich and fertile regions have suffered these acquisitions, their communities becoming victims of the evolving complex, global, problem of land governance. Mention can be made of countries like Nigeria, Angola, Ecuador (Ikelegbe, 2001; Kimerling, 2006; Becker, 2013) not forgetting Zimbabwe, Kenya, South Africa, where colonial land acquisitions led to dispossession en masse.

In Uganda, these problems are more pronounced in the oil-and-gas-rich Bunyoro-Kitara sub-region (Byakagaba and Twesigye, 2015), but Karamoja (north-eastern Uganda) is equally affected following recent expansions of mining activities. In Buganda (central) region, multiple land tenure systems, the inharmonious relationship between the state and Buganda kingdom over land, antagonisms between landlords and tenants, and fraudulent deals in the land market constitute land governance challenges. In the Rwenzori region, conflicts among traditional authority structures over land; between these structures and communities; between and within communities; and between and within families prevail. There are also conflicts between state agencies responsible for game and forest reserves and other protected areas, and communities neighbouring these areas, over boundary demarcations (KRC, 2012). In northern Uganda, conflicts between communal land ownership and the emerging land market engendered apprehensions about the potential loss of community lands.

These countrywide land-governance problems breed land rights violations in three ways. First, unequal power relations favour the more powerful: when the powerful clash with the powerless, the powerless mostly lose out because of weak institutional protections. Judicial struggles are rarely helpful for delays, corruption, case backlog, and under-facilitation in court-based land adjudication tend to exhaust poor contenders. Second, land governance structures are weak, corrupt, and/or impervious to ideals of respect for communal land rights, hence unable to surmount these challenges. Third, community responses are not coordinated and organized enough to defend community land rights against powerful state and market players. The resulting dispossession of land-dependent communities by government institutions, private companies, and powerful individuals is fuelled in part by limited citizens' awareness about, and defense of, their land rights given the limited tools with which these communities can advance their land rights. Though some of these violations have historical origins, recent developments exacerbated the problem in the Graben.

The discovery of oil and gas deposits in the Albertine Graben, commercial deposits of which were announced in 2006, had two consequences. First, land suddenly appreciated in value. Petroleum-related infrastructure developments intensified pre-existing tensions by encouraging speculators, necessitating land acquisition by oil companies, and causing contentious evictions and resettlements. Second, multinational corporations, local speculators, fraudulent individuals position themselves to earn from compensations for lands needed for petroleum infrastructure developments, hence a new rush for Graben land. Add the global commoditization of land and a national land governance infrastructure that promotes monetization of land in a capitalist world. Due to lack of documented evidence of customary ownership, communities continue to lose land to powerful individuals and groups, who, when confronted, resort to formal justice systems. These systems are inaccessible to, and exhaust, the poor, due to the high cost, delays, and corruption, further inflicting injustice upon affected communities (CRED, TIU, and DGF, 2015).

Local land governance structures in the region, such as District Executive Committees (DECs) and Local Councils (LCs), District Land Boards (DLBs), Area Land Committees (ALCs), and responsible bureaucratic offices are equally unhelpful. They are under-staffed, under-facilitated, corrupt, and in some cases incompetent. There are also fears of how Bunyoro-Kitara Kingdom—the biggest land owner will treat squatters on her land should local governments in the region embark on issuance of Customary Certificates of Ownership (CCOs). The local governments' political and technical leaderships, together with national-level actors like the Ministry of Lands, Housing and Urban Development (MoLHUD), remain custodians of policy-related matters on land. But the magnitude of land conflicts in the region necessitated direct intervention from the President who sought to halt all titling of land, highlighting failures in the institutional structures for managing land.

Violations of land rights in Bunyoro-Kitara sub-region contradict local and international protections. Article 237 of the Constitution recognises customary land as lawful tenure. Section 3 of the Land Act, cap 277, provides for customary land ownership as does the National Land Policy, 2013. The Land Regulations, 2004, outline procedures for registration of customary land. Despite these legal-constitutional provisions and protections, customary land tenure features strongly in communal land rights violations. Ironically, while 70-80% of land in Uganda is held under customary tenure (USAID, 2010), land titles however fraudulently some may have been acquired—tend to supersede customary claims (CRED, TIU, and DGF, 2015). In 2016, President Yoweri Museveni assigned officials to investigate land conflicts in the region (*Oil In Uganda*, 2015) where community associations, including the Bunyoro-Kitara Reparations Agency (BUKITAREPA) and other groupings in Buliisa district, had emerged to counter threats to their land (Ssebuyora, 2013). In other words, land rights violations led to counter-developments aimed at securing communal lands (Byakagaba and Twesigye, 2015), as though in a cyclic spiral, land-rights violations also entail conflicts over illegal and often violent evictions CSCO (2014), contested values attached to land-based property, delayed compensations, fraud and corruption involving land-governance institutions, and inadequate knowledge of the available options and redress mechanisms for Project Affected Persons (PAPs) (Anyuru *et al.*,

2016). CE initiatives respond to these issues. Fears, suspicions, and uncertainties about the future of land ownership for especially poor, land-dependent households, ignited community responses. As a result, communities attempted to reposition themselves to counter intensifying land rights violations.

The question of land rights protection in Uganda circulates governmental, civil society, and community circles as it relates to questions of low-cost access to land concurrent with property rights (Deininger, 2003). Several considerations remain prominent in this issue, such as: the kind of information needed to, at least minimally, protect land owners then suffering under the weight of capitalist land acquisitions; the effectiveness of interventions designed to ensure coexistence between land-based developments and people's land rights and livelihoods; and who stands to lose/gain in the long run. Simultaneously, land conflicts are also prevalent at the family level (related to inheritance by widows and orphans), inter-family/household (over neighbouring pieces of land). Others involve competition between different forms of livelihoods, mainly between pastoralists and cultivators, over the same space or area for these different livelihood activities. In some areas, entire communities were engaged to evolve their own initiatives as community apprehensions against land rights violations extended to religious institutions, [2] ethnolinguistic groups, and state and market actors. Our findings revealed evidence of all three forms of CE being put to use in the defence of land rights in Buliisa and Hoima districts.

Responding to Land Rights Violations: Different Typologies of Civic Engagement

The different forms/typologies of CE previously presented can be shown. In response to land rights violations, the Albertine Graben has witnessed an avalanche of different interventions. Some are informational and educational. Others involve community mobilisation and creation of structures for facilitating engagement and interaction

---

[2] in FGD, held on 11 August 2016, in Kibingo Village, Kyabigambire Sub-county, Hoima District

between communities and other actors. In the process, these innovations have acquired the typological appearance of autonomous, induced, and state-centric CE. To these empirical unfolding, we now turn.

Autonomous Civic engagement (ACE)

There were several examples of autonomous civic engagement (ACE). In Kichoke village, Buliisa Sub-county, Buliisa district, for example, the community learnt, via a notice displayed at the sub-county headquarters, that a rich man processed a Certificate of Title over their communal land. The area LCI chairperson had apparently colluded in this transaction. By-passing the LC structure, members of the community mobilized themselves to defend their land. The group selected its own leadership which was parallel to the existing local governance structure to fill the vacuum created by the apparent collusion of their LCI Chairperson with those who were planning to sell communal land to the rich man. The group wrote a letter to the ALC of Buliisa Sub-county asserting their rights on the said land. The LCI Chairperson refused to stamp their letter. Subsequently, the group petitioned the RDC and was able to stop issuance of a freehold title to the rich man on their land. [3]

Another example of ACE comes from Kiziranfumbi sub-county in Hoima district. There, a common threat from a man (name withheld) who has been attempting to evict the community and 'grab' land in these parishes since 2003, brought together residents from the six parishes of Kigabo, Kisonko, Kijunza, Kyamukonjo, Kakende, and Kalungu. The affected community members mobilized themselves into a group, contracted a lawyer and took legal action against the man. The case has been on-going for more than eight years. The group has managed to avert or at least postpone a possible eviction from their land.

There also emerged a more structured and coherent ACE under the umbrella called Bunyoro-Kitara Reparations Agency (BUKITAREPA). This is an organization of indigenous peoples who belong to nationalities that were under Bunyoro-Kitara Kingdom prior to colonial occupation. BUKITAREPA has, since 2004, become a mobilizing force for collective

---

[3] In FDG conducted on 10 August 2016, in Kichoke village, Bugana Parish, Buliisa Sub-county, Buliisa district.

action toward addressing "historical injustices" in the region, most of which revolve around land (Bigiriwenkya, 2016). Its goal is to bring together all people of the "original Bunyoro-Kitara Kingdom", as one of its officials called it, in order to create a united, self-driven, and coordinated critical mass aimed at achieving a prosperous and egalitarian society in the kingdom. It is unclear whether the group understands what an egalitarian society is, but the group claims they aspire toward what they call socioeconomic egalitarianism—social and economic equality—which hardly existed in the kingdom even prior to colonial subterfuge. One of the stated objectives of BUKITAREPA is *"To recover, preserve and protect the land of Bunyoro Kitara sub-region".* This feeds upon narratives and historical references to British colonial disenfranchisement of native Banyoro communities in matters of land tenure. What fuels this anger is the discontent about the continuous influx of people in the post-colonial era, who have interest in acquiring land in this region.

BUKITAREPA has established itself as a force to reckon with. The state perceives the group's operations as threatening security in the region. A senior security official in Hoima district revealed that the state perceives BUKITAREPA to be a "very dangerous group" that threatens to undermine law and order in Bunyoro region. Though not yet constituting a strong agent of domestic instability, as Kathman and Shannon (2011) prognosticate, the pressure group has demonstrated the zeal to confront government and other stakeholders in the region. In June 2014, BUKITAREPA sued the government of Uganda and three oil companies over petroleum exploration in the Albertine Graben, specifically for carrying out activities that resulted in land and resource dispossession against indigenous people. The suit also alleged underhand methods by government officials who encouraged fraudulent acquisition of oil-rich land in the region, while disregarding the principles of free, prior and informed consent as articulated in Article 26 of the Constitution. The agency accused the government of failing to reach an agreement with communities on what would constitute just and fair compensation for their land.

In a separate case, in 2016, BUKITAREPA sued all District Land Boards from the Bunyoro-Kitara region districts of Kibaale, Hoima, Masindi, Buliisa, Kagadi, Kakumiro and Kiryandongo, for allegedly giving out indigenous peoples' customary land to oil companies and other persons without communities' consent. Both cases have not been decided [as of May 2017], but the group hopes to reap concessions from this legal process. The group has also been involved in frustrating genuine land transactions between the Banyoro and people from other ethnolinguistic groups, especially those not resident in Bunyoro region. Its influence is equally strong in Kibaale district, where some of its members reside. These attempts demonstrate that autonomously organized collective action, when well guided, can go a long way in pursuing common interests through constituted institutional channels compared to action by isolated individuals and small groups. In some areas, autonomous CE occurs concurrently with induced CE.

Induced Civic Engagement (ICE)

ICE is demonstrable by reference to several cases of intervention by NGOs to mobilise citizens to defend their land rights in Buliisa and Hoima districts. In order to overcome lack of documented evidence of ownership of communal land in both districts, Civic Response on Environment and Development (CRED) mobilizes communities to form and register CLAs as a step toward registration of communal lands and ensuring the security of tenure. In Kisiimo and Kakindo cells, Buliisa Town Council, Buliisa district; as well as Kigoya, Kihukwa and Kisansya in Buliisa Sub-county, CLAs have been formed. In Hoima district, CLAs were formed in Buseruka Sub-county, for example in Kiryamboga village. Other organizations, including AFFORD-Africa and USAID-SAFE Programme, have also supported different efforts aimed at securing community land rights.

Interestingly, even private, for-profit organizations, including Post Bank and Swiss Consult, are also engaged in processes that support but also trigger new forms of CE for land rights protection in Hoima district. Through the *Kyaapa Loan* product, Post Bank, Hoima Branch, advances loans to individuals who are interested in processing freehold titles for their unregistered customary land but who may be unable to meet costs involved in surveying and other charges. Under the arrangement, the client who takes up a *Kyaapa Loan* entrusts Post Bank to work with its surveyor and process freehold titles from the MoLHUD in Kampala on behalf of the client(s). The client(s) keep(s) depositing stated amounts of money to the bank to service the loan advanced and associated interest for a period of between one month and a maximum of ten years. The loans started from UGX 2.1 million for a 50"X100" feet plot of land but vary for land above that size. Depending on the land size and the estimated value of the land the money may be higher. Once ready, the land title is kept as security by the bank until the client fully settles his/her loan obligations and the certificate of title is handed to the owner.

Our interactions with a Post Bank official revealed that the product has been working since 2008, with increasing community interest. Between February and August 2016 a total of UGX 150 million (more than US$ 400,000) worth of loans was involved, while a total of 60 land titles are said to have been successfully processed through this arrangement. Apparently, uptake of the *Kyaapa Loan* product has been growing as more and more community members realize the need to protect their land in the face of increasing land conflicts and interest in land in the region. Documented evidence of these revelations was not readily accessed.

State-centric Civic Engagement (SCE)

The state has not sat back and watched land rights violations evolve unabated. It has acted as well. SCE was demonstrated in neighbouring Buhuka parish, Kyangwali sub-county, Hoima district. In this case, the Ministry (MLHUD) responded to tenure insecurity on communal land by encouraging the formation of CLAs as legal entities through which the community could register and own communal land. The MLHUD successfully processed a freehold title for a CLA in the area but had not handed it over to the community. The ministry was also encouraging and registering CLAs in the region, as has been experimented in other regions of the country.

The president's intervention in 2016 to suspend the issuance of land titles in Buliisa district; the establishment of the Land Fund for purposes of compensating absentee landlords in the region and return land back to its current occupants; and the establishment, in 2017, of a (Commission of Inquiry Effectiveness of Law, Policies, and Processes of Land

Acquisition, Land Administration, Land Management and Land Registration in Uganda) (Republic of Uganda, 2017) are some of the state-centric responses to cries from communities about land rights violations. Many civil society groups, including the Civil Society Coalition on Oil and Gas (CSCO), made oral and written submissions to the Commission (CSCO, 2017; UWONET, 2017). The inquiry has traveled countrywide seeking communities' views on how land governance can be improved upon. Already experienced with ACE and ICE, the communities articulately demand government interventions to prevent land rights violations in their respective areas. Conducting the inquiry, and reporting, by the Commission, is one thing. Implementing its recommendations is another and more of a political than technical problem.

State-centric CE is a function of state responsibility and policy exigencies. The MoLHUD, ULC, DLBs, ALCs, are charged, under the constitution and land-related laws, with registration and management of land tenure. Internationally, Uganda is a member of the International Centre for the Settlement of Investment Disputes (ICSID) and the Multilateral Investment Guarantee Agency (MIGA). These domestic and international establishments constitute a reasonably comprehensive regulatory and institutional structure that places substantial responsibility in the hands of the state to manage land on behalf of the citizens (Carmody and Taylor, 2016). The state can hardly sit and watch as local, regional, and international/global interests in Uganda's land create difficulties for communities and for the state's development agenda. Land remains a serious governance question countrywide, in petroleum- and mineral-rich but also fertile areas.

The Sukulu Phosphate Mining Project, signed off by the president on 4th December 2015, in Usukuru sub-county, Tororo District, threatens loss of land to approximately 4,800 households (Muhindo, 2017). It is alleged that there are fraudulently signed lease agreements that give concession to the Chinese company, Guangzhou DongSong Energy Group, to appropriate about 26.5 square Kilometres of land, spanning 14 villages in Osukuru and Rubongi Sub-counties, Tororo district, eastern Uganda. Only 122 out of 4,800 project-affected households have since signed the Surface Rights Lease Agreement (Muhindo, 2017). It is contended that while the community agreed to lease their land for 21 (twenty-one) years, the agreement the communities were made to sign stipulates a period of 99 (ninety-nine) years, indicating potential fraudulent collusion by the agreement drafters and the Chinese company to defraud and take advantage of the mainly illiterate and unrepresented community (Muhindo, 2017).

We have demonstrated that communities in the Albertine Graben are victims of land acquisitions, amidst a specific development discourse, where fraud, displacements, and compensation quarrels have not been unlike experiences in Teso, Karamoja, and displacements involving a British company, New Forests or a multinational company in Bugala Island, Kalangala district, or where villagers in Buliisa District "were beaten by hired thugs and detained by police. . . after contesting the fraudulent sale of community land, including a plot where Tullow Oil's Kasmene-3 well is located" (Carmody and Taylor, 2016). The state, therefore, has been compelled to respond to this crisis with state-centric CE interventions in order to protect its interests, the interests of foreign investors it is hungry for, and strike a balance between massive land acquisitions and community livelihoods in order to assure community buy-in in the extant state-market investment agenda (Anyuru *et al.*, 2016). Has state-centric CE embraced local governments or have LGs been its champions?

State-Centric CE and the Role of Local Governments

Local governments (LGs) structures—Executive Committees, bureaucracies, Councils (elected local-government legislative organs) at districts, municipalities, sub-counties, town councils—are lower levels of state governance and service delivery. In theory, they are directly involved in SCE. As lower-levels of the state's policy and technical authority structures, local government institutions are the first points of contact between affected communities and the state. An engaged, organized, and well-led community may demand and protect its land rights. Where state institutions are weak, especially at local level, an organised and politically awake community can galvanize collective interests and even interfere with government programs and/or complicate governance (Deutsch, 1961; Huntington, 1968). Ironically, local governments have mixed roles in SCE: some of its officials are spoilers, others struggling with the general institutional malaise afflicting land governance in Uganda. Instead of augmenting SCE, LGs seem to do otherwise. Discussing the role of LGs, therefore, requires looking at: (a) the way they are implicated in the problem; (b) how they could be more positive players; and (c) the role of CE in both filling the void when LG is ineffective, but ultimately how CE can enhance the positive role of LG by holding them accountable and catalysing responsive government.

LGs are implicated because of dwindling state legitimacy and trust in government institutions. Communities in the Albertine Graben, like elsewhere in Uganda, fear for their land rights and consider that government institutions have not been very helpful to them. This fear arises from LGs' failure to help citizens to overcome current threats of mushrooming projects that negatively impact on communal land rights. The inevitable cooperation between LGs and the central government on the systematic land demarcation program, which is perceived to threaten Bunyoro-Kitara Kingdom's land interests, is also seen as unhelpful. The failures of sub-county and district LGs to address land governance issues have reduced people's trust in these state structures. Accusations and counter-accusations between the central ministry and LGs create the impression that the state, though attempting to use SCE to solve the problem, is not coherent. There is alleged connivance between LG leaders and land grabbers, which is also consistent with the failure of LG leaders to convince central state authorities to address people's fears.[4]

This perceived failure of local authorities adds to inefficiencies and corruption involving District Land Boards (DLBs), Area Land Committees (ALCs, which are levels of land governance below DLBs), and technical officials. Within LGs, some DLBs blame ALCs for land rights violations. The DLBs claim that ALCs, basing on mere desk surveys, forward applications to DLBs before visiting the locus to ascertain the existence and ownership of lands in question. The DLBs forward these applications to the ministry for the issuance of Certificates of Title, only to learn afterward that the land in question, and the titling process on it, was fraudulent. Officials from MoLHUD also decried this

---

[4] FGD conducted on August 2016, in Buliisa district Nyanseke and Nyairongo villages, Kaseeta Parish, Kabwoya Sub-county, Hoima district.

improper practice during a dialogue in Hoima in October 2016—further implicating LGs in land rights violations. In some areas, communities fear that LG officials are complicit in these violations. The FGD conducted on 11 August 2016, in Kichoke village, and Waiga II P/Sch., Buliisa SC, Buliisa district; and Mubaku Parish, Ngwedo Sub-country, Buliisa district revealed suspicion that LC leaders connive with powerful land speculators to sell communal lands.

The chairperson of one of the LCs in Buliisa district is accused of frustrating people's attempts to jointly protect land rights by refusing to stamp applicants' documents for unclear reasons. This indicates that LGs fail to resolve land conflicts because some of their personnel may be involved in these violations. Some LG leaders sell communal lands claiming to be legitimate owners: for instance, one chairperson of Local Council Three (LCIII) in Buliisa reportedly sold communal land of which he claimed ownership. Attempts to access some of these individuals and verify these claims were futile. These leaders, either out of corrupt intents or inadvertently, cooperate with powerful actors to violate communal land rights. Called "land grabbers" and "land speculators" by respondents, these actors are both from within and outside the region, and names were mentioned of such personalities[5]. The lands ministry has ***cancelled*** some land transactions in the region due to suspected fraud which, in some instances, involved connivance with LG leaders and officials.

On how LGs could be more positive players, the findings reveal that LGs are the first levels and channels of engagement in land rights protections. They are also last channels through which top-down land rights violations take place at community level. Land acquisition necessarily requires approval from DLBs and ALCs. There is limited capacity and institutional weaknesses in local governments that create land governance gaps. These gaps are then filled by community initiatives. LG institutions can appropriate community initiatives to address land governance challenges within their areas of jurisdiction in three ways.

---

[5] (A FGD conducted on 10 and 11 August 2016, in Kabwolwa village, Kigoya Parish, Buliisa sub-country)

First, DLBs and ALCs rely on people-initiated communal land associations (CLAs) to register customary lands and issue Certificates of Customary Ownerships (CCOs), which are issued to owners of customary lands. Some of these CLAs are induced by NGOs like CRED. Others organically evolve from community initiatives. Autonomous CE presents potential to improve land governance, but this requires support, linking groups with each other, training, and guidance to the isolated pockets/cases of community action so that they can collectively achieve positive results. LGs have since realized the importance of these CE initiatives. The benefits of this relationship include: making the documentation of land ownership less costly; and increasing the ability of communities to work with LGs to safeguard their land. Amplifying positive outcomes of the communities' own efforts would inspire and encourage people to join these groupings and overcome collective action problems.

Second, LGs can work with CSOs and communities to ensure the positive evolution of ICE by working with civil society to design and implement CE interventions that are consistent with state policy. Induced CE is needed in Buliisa and Hoima district where community awareness about land rights remains low. Communities have since requested civil society organisations (CSOs) to scale up awareness creation on community land rights protection, and hence increase respect for rights of landowners. But civil society needs to cooperate with the government to uphold these rights. Therefore, local governance institutions are key actors in the process.

Finally, LGs can initiate and/or support state-centric CE because most land-governance challenges stem from dysfunctional land administration institutions and non-implementation of existing frameworks despite government's constitutional, legal, and political mandate to protect citizens' land rights. State-centric CE need not be a top-bottom process; it can as well be bottom-up as demonstrated in Kasese district where the LGs cooperated with communities to register and issue CCOs for customary lands.

On the role of CE in filling the void created by LG ineffectiveness and how CE can ultimately enhance the positive role of LGs, the findings reveal that: first, CE holds LGs accountable by creating pressure to respond to prevailing governance challenges; and second, CE catalyzes responsive government. Autonomous community initiatives would not be necessary where LG institutions and other state structures effectively address land governance challenges at the local level. ACE emerges as a form of self-help. Communities fend for themselves in defence of their land rights, thus forcing LGs to liaise with other state structures to address intra-community conflicts and disputes between communities and state agencies. The planned process of systematic land demarcations is illustrative of this community-driven accountability.

Where LGs violate land rights contrary to their legal-constitutional, administrative, and political mandate to protect land rights, community initiatives cause uproar which forces the lands ministry to blame LGs, arouses civil society interests in the issue, and creates space for dialogues wherein commitments are made and sometimes acted upon. During several of the dialogues that were observed in the region, LGs and the ministry made commitments to take certain actions. In terms of forcing responsiveness, CE incentivizes LGs to liaise with central-state institutions like wildlife and nature conservation agencies to prevent encroachment on protected lands, provide people with alternatives, or relocate them. Strengthening CE, using different strategies of community mobilization and capacitation, makes LGs more responsive. It complements their work on land governance. Strengthened CE exposes the urgency with which remedies to land rights violations are needed.

Conclusion

Contrary to some reasoning that poor communities are incapable of responding to land rights violations by powerful market and state actors, and are thus unable to counter e-colonisation, CE has had mixed outcomes in Uganda's Albertine Graben. For one it has forced LGs to become more responsible and held them accountable. Second, CE has led to the emergence of complex relationships between local governance structures and community initiatives the outcome of which is difficult to predict: in some instances, it has led to conflicts with LGs; in others, it has engendered cooperation with LGs. The outcome of CE is dependent upon the exigencies of the time and the issues at hand. Inasmuch as CE helps to safeguard community land rights, there have also been undesirable consequences. The violent clashes we witnessed on 3rd

December 2014, at Rwengabi village, Kabwoya sub-county, Hoima district (Tumusiime, 2014) plainly remind us that CE, regardless of which form it takes, can unfold dangerously to the negation of peaceable local governance. Promoters of CE ought to put in place mechanisms for controlling the course taken by the community in pursuit of their land rights and minimize unintended consequences. The levels of organisation, nature of leadership, and prior conscientisation, influence the trajectory and effects of CE. While land conflicts between communities and LGs indicate weakness in local governance institutions, violence is always counter-productive and ought to be as much selective as it ought to be justified as the only available choice of engagement.

A gap exists in our understanding of this phenomenon in two respects. We tend to suppose that land dependence is typical of developing, agrarian, societies and thus present industrialized societies as though they operate off-land. This supposition—that rural and/or peasant communities depend on land while urban and non-peasant ones depend less on land, and more on technology and services—is misleading for most techno-scientific products and/or services that we depend on are based on land. Attention to land rights challenges, which now afflict the global south, would reveal the relationship between CE and communal land rights. At what level would CE work when these challenges are rooted in global, regional, and local interests in land and the attendant commercialization of lands (Carmody and Taylor, 2016) in especially resource-rich agrarian societies in the developing world?

This study reveals that effective CE for the promotion and protection of land rights requires prior awareness about the forces that drive land rights violations in given areas, key actors, and gaps in existing redress mechanisms. It demands the difficult but important process of understanding and overcoming political and bureaucratic corruption that promote impunity, hinder implementation of existing and new land-governance frameworks and reforms, and stymie institutional effectiveness at different levels of state governance. The starting point for local governments' intervention in SCE, for instance, is to document actors who promote communal land rights, expose and sanction perpetrators of land rights violations, and forge cooperation between communities and LGs in protecting land rights. But where local authorities are complicit in these violations, there is no resource beyond autonomous and induced CE. This complex link between political and bureaucratic goodwill and capitalist pressure, to undertake development projects in ways that hardly respect community land rights, it useful: it enriches our understanding of citizens' suspicions and mistrust that sometimes engender conflicts between communities and their local leaders who would be responsible for protecting land rights. Amidst these governance failures, CE becomes a useful tool, and viable alternative, for protecting community land rights in agrarian societies.

References

Anyuru, M. A., Rhoads, R., Mugyeni, O., Manoba, J. A. and Balemesa, T. (2016) 'Balancing Development and Community Livelihoods: A Framework for Land Acquisition and Resettlement in Uganda - A Study of Communities Affected by Conservation in Kibaale District, Oil Development in Hoima District, and Hydro Electric Power Development in', *ACODE Policy Research Series*, (75).

Becker, M. (2013) 'The Stormy Relations between Rafael Correa and Social Movements in Ecuador', *Latin American Perspectives*, 40(3), pp. 43–62.

Bigiriwenkya, A. (2016) 'BUKITAREPA sues Attorney General, Oil Companies for Outrageous oil activities. Masindi'': Greater Masindi Media Practitioners Association', *GMEPA News*, 24 June.

Byakagaba, P. and Twesigye, B. (2015) 'Securing Communal Land and Resource Rights in the Albertine Region of Uganda: The Case of Hoima and Buliisa Districts', in. Kampala.

Carmody, P. and Taylor, D. (2016) 'Globalization, Land Grabbing, and the Present-Day Colonial State in Uganda: Ecolonization and Its Impacts', *Journal of Environment & Development*, 25(1), pp. 100–126.

Cotula, L. (2007) *Changes in customary land tenure systems in Africa*. Hertfordshire: Russell Press.

CSCO (2014) '[Civil Society Coalition on Oil and Gas in Uganda] Rwamutonga Eviction and its Implications on Rights and Livelihoods of Peasant Communities in the Oil-rich Region of Uganda.', in. Kampala: CSCO/ACODE.

CSCO (2017) *A Submission by Civil Society Coalition on Oil And Gas (CSCO)* in Uganda, to the Land Inquiry.* Kampala: CSCO/ACODE.

Deininger, K. (2003) *Land Policies for Growth and Poverty Reduction.* Washington DC: The World Bank.

Deininger, K., Byerlee, D., Lindsay, J., Norton, A., Selod, H. and Stickler, M. (2011) *Rising Global Interest in Farmland: Can It Yield Sustainable and Equitable Benefits?* Washington DC: The World Bank.

Dempsey, S. E. (2010) 'Critiquing Civic engagement', *Management Communication Quarterly*, 24(3), pp. 359–390.

Deutsch, K. W. (1961) 'Social Mobilization and Political Development', *The American Political Science Review*, p. 55(3), 493-514.

Development, C. R. for E. and (2015) 'Against Giants', *Oil-influenced land injustices in the Albertine Graben in Uganda.* Kampala: CRED.

Elizabeth Paulat (2014) *Land Eviction Breeds Violence in Oil-Rich Hoima, Voice of America.*

Harry, C. and Boyte, H. C. (2016) 'Building Civic Agency: The Public-Work Approach', *Open Democracy*, (25 Oct 2016).

Huntington, S. P. (1968) *Political Order in Changing Societies.* New Haven & London: Yale University Press.

Ikelegbe, A. (2001) 'Civil society, oil and conflict in the Niger Delta region of Nigeria: Ramifications of Civil Society for a Regional Resource Struggle', *The Journal of Modern African Studies*, 39(3), pp. 437–469.

Kathman, J. and Shannon, M. (2011) 'Oil Extraction and the Potential for Domestic Instability in Uganda', *African Studies Quarterly*, 12(3), pp. 23–45.

Kimerling, J. (2006) 'Indigenous Peoples and the Oil Frontier in Amazonia: The Case of Ecuador, Chevron Texaco, and Aguinda v. Texaco', *International Law and Politics*, pp. 38, 663.

Kizito, N. (2015) *The Political economy of Land grabbing in Oil resource areas: The Uganda Albertine Graben.* Linnaeus University.

KRC (2012) *Kabarole Research and Resource Centre. Stuck in the Mist: Contextual Analysis of the Conflicts in the Rwenzori Region.* Fort Portal.

Miranda, L. A. (2007) *The Hybrid State-Corporate Enterprise and the Violation of Indigenous Land Rights: Theorising Corporate Responsibility and Accountability under International Law.* Lewis & Clark Law Review.

Mugyenyi, O. (2016) 'Land Rights and Obligations of Key Actors in Land Governance: A Presentation during the Multi-Stake Holder

Dialogue on Land Governance', *Land Governance Challenges for Inclusive Development in Buliisa and Hoima Districts*, (17–18, 2016).

Muhindo, J. (2017) *"A Brief on the Two Cases I Cited before the Land Inquiry 2017 - The Plight of Project-Affected Persons under the Sukulu Phosphate Mining Project"*. Kampala: Global Rights Alert.

Nickel, C. (2016) *Following the Oil Road: A case study assessing the vulnerability of women under the impact of development-induced migration in Western Uganda*. Wageningen University.

Oil In Uganda (2015) *Rwamutonga Evictions: Four Dead, Hundreds Starving, Oil in Uganda*.

Otsuka, K. (2002) 'Land Tenure Systems and Their Impacts on Agricultural Investments and Productivity in Uganda', *The Journal of Development Studies*, 38(6), pp. 105–128.

Republic of Uganda (1995) *The Constitution of the Republic of Uganda 1995 (as amended)*. Entebbe: UPPC [Uganda Printing and Publishing Corporation].

Republic of Uganda (1998) *The Land Act, Cap 277*. Entebbe: UPPC.

Republic of Uganda (2004) *The Land Regulations*. Kampala.

Republic of Uganda (2013) 'Uganda National Land Policy'. Kampala: MoLHUD.

Republic of Uganda (2017) *Commission of Inquiry on Land Matters Sworn in*. Entebbe: State House.

Ssebuyora, M. (2013) 'Banyoro form associations to fight for their land rights', *Daily Monitor*, 18 June. Available at: http://www.monitor.co.ug/artsculture/Reviews/Banyoro-form-associations-to-fight-for-their-land-rights/-/691232/1885814/-/ipc27l/-/index.html, 11 August 2016).

The Observer (2014) 'Evicted Hoima Residents Seek Help as Action Aid Intervenes', September. Available at: http://www.observer.ug/business/38-business/35698--evicted-hoima-residents-seek-help-as-actionaid-intervenes, 15 Sept. 2016).

Tumusiime, R. (2014) 'Thirty houses burnt in Hoima, police deploy to avert violence', *Daily Monitor*, 4 December. Available at: http://www.monitor.co.ug/News/National/Thirty-houses-burnt-in-Hoima--police-deploy-to-avert-violence/688334-2543778-72j4dqz/index.html, 15 July 2017).

Uganda Human Rights Commission (2013) 'Oil in Uganda: Emerging

Human Rights Issues'. Kampala: Uganda Human Rights Commission.

USAID (2010) *Uganda Country Profile, Property Rights and Resource Governance*. Kampala.

UWONET (2017) *Securing Women's Land Rights In Uganda, Submitted to the Uganda Land Inquiry Commission by Uganda Women's Network on behalf of the Women's Movement*. Kampala: Uganda Women's Network.

Watts, M. (2001) 'Petro-Violence: Community, Extraction, and Political Ecology of a Mythic Commodity', in Peluso, N. L. and Watts, M. (eds) *Violent Environments*. Ithaca and London: Cornell University Press, pp. 189–212.

World Bank (2016) *Good Land Governance Policy Paper, Progress to date and the way*.

CHAPTER SEVEN

Civic Engagement Action Plans: A Strategic Social Accountability Methodology

Kiran Cunningham and Arthur Bainomugisha

Introduction

Across the world, researchers, civil society, and communities continue to develop and try out innovative civic engagement strategies for increasing government accountability. Meaningful engagement of the electorate in democratic governance requires transparency in the relationship between government officials and citizens, a sense of obligation among government officials to be responsive to citizens, and an empowered citizenry capable of punishing their government representatives if they fail to do so (Lee, 2011).

In low- and middle-income countries the focus of these accountability initiatives is often connected to service delivery. As a 2011 World Bank publication on social accountability observed:

> In many low- and middle-income countries, dismal failures in the quality of public service delivery are demonstrated by high rates of absenteeism among teachers and doctors; leakages of public funds intended for schools, health clinics, or social assistance benefits; and shortages of stock-outs of pharmaceuticals and textbooks. These failures have driven the agenda for better governance and accountability. Governments, civil society, and donors have become increasingly interested in the idea that citizens can contribute to improved quality of service delivery by holding policy makers and providers of services accountable (Holla, Koziol and Srinivasan, 2011).

Indeed, a subsequent 2016 World Bank report, *Making Politics Work for Development*, focused on harnessing the power of citizen engagement to hold government accountable for the provision of public goods rather than private benefits. The authors of that report are adamant that the solutions to public sector failures lie in direct engagement by citizens with political processes (Devarajan, Khemani and Walton, 2013; World Bank, 2016).

Scholars and practitioners continue to delve into the elements of social accountability initiatives and citizen engagement processes in order to identify the factors that seem to be the key to maximum impact (Asmah-Andoh, 2015; Krawczyk and Sweet-Cushman, 2017; Larreguy and Marshall, 2017). Grandvoinnet, Raha, Kumagai, and Joshi (2015), for example, undertook an analysis of the constitutive elements of social accountability, which they claim has been a fuzzy concept, in an attempt to be able to use and support social accountability initiatives more strategically. Similarly, Grandvoinnet, Aslam and Raha (2015) opened the "black box" of social accountability and explored what is inside. A common finding in all of this work is that effective social accountability processes involve citizens, civil society organizations and government officials.

The involvement of citizens is often referred to as "voice." Citizen voice is a key component of strategic social accountability initiatives. Voice refers to the various ways in which citizens – either as individuals or in organized formations – can express their opinions and concerns, putting pressure on service providers, policy makers and elected leaders to demand better services or to advocate for them (Crawford, 2009). Enhancing voice is part of activating the "demand" side of accountable governance.

Reviews of social accountability initiatives have shown, however, that results from initiatives that rely solely on citizen voice are generally weak (Gaventa and McGee, 2013; Joshi, 2013; Fox, 2014). Many citizen report card initiatives suffer from this problem. Researchers have found, however, that citizen voices can be strengthened with the involvement of so-called interlocutors or intermediators who facilitate two-way communication between governing bodies and citizens, and bridge cultural and power gaps (Fox, 2014).

Even with amplification of citizen voice by interlocutors, effective social accountability initiatives also need "teeth" – i.e. governmental capacity to respond to voice (Fox, 2014). In the language of demand and supply, teeth are about the supply side of accountability, and include the capacity of government to respond positively to citizen voice. Responsiveness involves having the systems and mechanisms in place for providing information to citizens, for receiving citizen input, and for responding to issues and concerns raised by citizens (Kavuma *et al.*, 2017). It also includes governmental capacity to change practices and structures that inhibit transparency through, for example, investigating grievances and changing incentive structures to discourage wasteful, abusive or corrupt practices (Fox, 2014).

These three sets of players – citizens, civil society, and government officials-are all critically important to effective, strategic social accountability processes. It would be a mistake, however, to think of them as in a linear relationship to one another, with citizens using their voice, CSOs amplifying it, and government receiving it. Instead, the relationship must be circular and ongoing. Fox discusses the power of "sandwich strategies" that can create a "pro-accountability power shift" through "state-society synergy." He argues that:

> While initial opportunities for change are necessarily context-driven and can be created either from society or from the state, the main determinant of a subsequent pro-accountability power shift is whether or not pro-change actors in one domain can empower the others – thereby triggering a virtuous circle…of mutual empowerment (Fox, 2014).

Without a sandwich strategy – or attention to strengthening both the demand and supply sides of democratic governance - experiments with social accountability all too often remain experiments. The Civic Engagement Action Plan (CEAP) process described in this chapter is an example of a social accountability tool that incorporates such a sandwich strategy and has resulted in improvements in service delivery and accountability in Uganda.

Developed by ACODE over the course of implementing the Local Government Councils Scorecard Initiative, CEAPs are actions plans developed by citizens, with the support of their elected officials, to use the tools of civic engagement to enforce the social contract and demand improvements in service delivery. The innovation of CEAPs was a response to the glaring policy constraints/challenges that hinder decentralization from delivering effectively on its promises. For example, while a critical analysis of the decentralization process in Uganda reveals significant achievements in most socio-economic and political spheres, there exist enormous challenges and weaknesses that require policy interventions. For instance, many of Uganda's citizens are not aware of their civic rights, civic duties and obligations as citizens. Consequently, they regard service delivery as a favour from government and do not demand for better and efficient services as a right. It is against this background that the CEAP tool was developed in a deliberative and participatory manner to enhance civic education and enable communities to be more effectively involved in holding their leaders accountable for service delivery (clean water, health services, education, roads and agricultural services) at the community level (Bainomugisha *et al.*, 2015).

Overtime, CEAPs have increasingly gained popularity especially among the local communities because of the opportunities that have been gained due to civic empowerment and problem-solving elements of the tool. Through involvement in the CEAPs, local leaders have been able to respond to problem-solving instantly, such as fixing bore holes and drug stock outs. In Gulu district where CEAPs were first piloted before rolling them out to now 35 districts, communities give testimonies where, as a result of the CEAP process, leaders were able to immediately follow up to fix identified problems as citizens continued to follow up on promises by reminding their leaders through radio phone-in programmes (Bainomugisha *et al.*, 2015).

Policy challenges that the CEAPs and other social accountability initiatives under ACODE seek to address are primarily in education, health, roads, water and agricultural sectors. Within the education sector, for example, numerous challenges remain even after the Universal Primary Education programme, introduced in 1997, opened the gates of schools wider for every school going child. Several years down the road, UPE suffers underfunding, staffing, massive dropout rates with most of the graduates unable to read and write. In the health sector, despite significant increase in the levels of funding to the sector many newly constructed health centres are not operational, and, the sector suffers absenteeism, drug stock outs, understaffing and low motivation of staff to the extent that Uganda child mortality rates are still unacceptably high standing at 60 deaths per 1000 birth annually.

The story is not very different in the roads sector, which receives more funding by far than other sectors. While government has prioritized the roads and infrastructure for investment, the sector has not produced roads to trigger development of other sectors as had been anticipated. There has been massive mismanagement and corruption in the sector which prompted government to set up a commission of inquiry into the mismanagement of the public funds and a number of high level politicians and technocrats are facing court charges.

In the environment and natural resources sector, Uganda has witnessed the greatest level of wanton destruction of forests, wetlands and protected reserves largely by the political elites and adjacent communities. This has resulted into adverse climatic conditions including droughts that destroyed food production, flooding and famine.

The civic engagement action plan (CEAP) process can be used in any of these service delivery contexts to trigger the virtuous circle of mutual empowerment that Fox (2014) describes. This chapter describes the methodology behind this process and provides a step by step guide to using CEAPs to create the pro-accountability power shifts necessary for government officials to do the jobs they are mandated to do and for communities to receive the public goods and services to which they are entitled.

What is a CEAP? Explaining the Concept

A Civic Engagement Action Plan (CEAP) is a social accountability strategy that enables citizens to hold their elected local governments accountable for service delivery and enables local governments to respond effectively and efficiently to those demands. Tied to the dissemination of information on, for example, service delivery sector budgets or the performance of local government officials, the CEAPs engage communities in making sense of the information and using it to develop step by step action plans for using civic engagement tools such as petitions, letters, and community meetings to engage with government officials to address specific service delivery issues.

The beneficiaries of the CEAP process are citizens, civil society, and local government leaders. Through the CEAP process, citizens deepen their understanding of the mandated roles and responsibilities of their local elected officials, better understand their own rights and responsibilities as responsibilities as citizens, and gain experience also gain experience using the tools of civic engagement, all of which are essential for holding their leaders accountable and activating the demand side of democratic governance. Because CEAPs are facilitated by civil society organizations, these organizations deepen their roles as important intermediaries between citizens and elected political leaders. In this capacity, they both amplify citizen voice and monitor government response to civic action. Government officials, too, benefit from the CEAP process as they are able to engage with a more informed citizenry and receive demands from citizens in forms they can use. Thus, CEAPs:

- Enhance the effectiveness of citizens and civil society to demand political accountability and effective service delivery.
- Enhance the capacity of civil society to act as mediators between citizens and local government councils to improve service delivery.
- Enhance the capacity of government to respond to citizens demands for better service delivery.

Development of the Methodology and Proof of Concept

The civic engagement action plan methodology was developed in the context of ACODE's Local Government Councils Scorecard Initiative discussed in detail in Chapter 5 of this volume. The methodology was subsequently adopted by ACODE's Centre for Budget and Economic Governance (CBEG). Both LGCSCI and CBEG are strategic social accountability initiatives designed to enhance the capacity of the citizens to hold their local government officials accountable for service delivery and enhance the capacity of local governments to execute their mandates as provided for under the Local Government Act. Both are grounded in a central premise that by regularly monitoring and assessing local government officials and providing information about their performance to the electorate, citizens become well equipped to demand accountability from their local elected officials. This demand, which CSOs and local governments channel upwards to the national level, ultimately results in a more engaged citizenry, a more responsive government, better performing local government officials, and more effective public service delivery. Activating this accountability chain requires building the capacity of citizens and CSOs to demand accountability by their local governments; and enhance the capacity of local governments to respond effectively and efficiently to those demands.

The centrepiece of the LGCSCI project is the local government councils' scorecard. Through the assessment process tied to the scorecard, district councils are scored, using a sophisticated evidence-based methodology, on the extent to which they performed their various responsibilities, and ranked from highest to lowest in terms of their performance. The CEAP methodology was originally designed to be undertaken during the dissemination of score-card results. The goal of dissemination was to help communities understand the roles and functions of their local elected leaders, their duties and obligations as citizens and how their elected leaders are performing in order to make informed decisions about whether or not to re-elect them. At the same time, citizens use the results to develop step by step action plans for using tools such as petitions, memoranda, community meetings, and ACODE's new SMS platform to demand that their elected leaders resolve pressing service delivery problems.

The CEAP process was initially piloted in five districts in March of 2015 and, after showing remarkable results in terms of local government's responsiveness and improvement in service delivery outcomes, it was rolled out to all 35 districts in Uganda covered by the LGCSCI. At that point it was also connected to the work of CBEG, which has expanded the kind of information citizens have access to and brought the technical side of local government more directly into the process. Through CBEG, citizens receive information from the district fiscal profiles and budget monitoring exercises conducted in the districts.

As the case studies later in this chapter suggest, the CEAP process has indeed strengthened citizens' voice, increased the capacity of CSOs to amplify that voice, and increased the ability of local government officials to respond and ensure that services are delivered effectively and efficiently. The CEAPs have also helped clarify the roles of elected local leaders to the electorate, countering prevailing assumptions that their roles were to attend weddings and burials, and provide school fees to children of poor parents. The CEAPs have also motivated the elected leaders who no-longer fear to face the 'begging' electorate now that their roles have been clarified, service delivery is improving and a partnership for problem-solving has developed.

Tools of Civic Engagement

The CEAP process is designed to build the capacity of citizens to use the tools of civic engagement to effectively hold their local government leaders accountable for the work they are supposed to do. As a strategic social accountability tool, it is also designed to enhance the ability of government to respond to citizen demands. Thus, while there are many tools citizens can use to express their demands, the CEAP process focuses on those that have the demand and the supply sides of accountability embedded in the tool.

For example, while a protest or demonstration is a form of civic engagement, as a tool it is focused on the demand side. While communities engaging in a protest might hope for some form of government response in the end, it is not necessarily embedded into the process. By contrast, in Uganda, writing a "petition" is a form of civic engagement that feeds into official government processes. Petitions are formal requests, signed by a number of community members, demanding that a service delivery problem be fixed. Once written, they are submitted to the Speaker of the district Council, who is then mandated to introduce the petition on the floor of the Council during the deliberations in order for the Council to act on it. Moreover, government responsiveness or lack of responsiveness can be easily tracked by citizens' or civil society intermediaries from publically available records such as Council minutes.

Important to note here is the fact that civic engagement tools will vary from country to country, and language about these tools will also vary. For example, in the USA, a "petition" is something quite different than it is used in Uganda, and is not a strategic tool as it does not require government response. Before engaging in a CEAP process it is, therefore, crucial to have a clear understanding of government processes and which kinds of civic engagement tools directly link to those processes. Because this discussion stems from the conducting CEAPs in Uganda, the civic engagement tools focused on here are petitions, letters, and community meetings with local government leaders. The CEAP process, however, is not defined by those specific tools and can be used with any tool that is strategic.

It is also imperative to engage the level of local government that has responsibility for the planning, implementation and oversight of service delivery issue at hand. In Uganda, as a result of decentralization policies, it is the district that is responsible for service delivery. Hence, while it can be useful to invite leaders from lower local government levels to the CEAP process as participants, the CEAPs conducted by ACODE have all targeted district-level officials.

The CEAP Methodology

The CEAP methodology is grounded in a participatory action research framework. Knowledge generation and action are tied together not just in an "application of knowledge" kind of way but in a truly action research way wherein the research itself results in new meanings for all participants and activation of the supply and demand links in the accountability chain. Each of the five steps in CEAP process is designed to increase the ability of participants – whether they are citizens, community-based organizations, or local government officials – to trigger the virtual circle of empowerment that Fox (2014) describes. Citizens become more adept at using the tools of civic engagement to hold government leaders accountable, CSOs and CBOs become more adept at amplifying those voices and acting as intermediaries, and government officials increase their ability to activate the mechanisms of government responsiveness. The five steps in the CEAP process are:

1. Participant mobilization
2. Issue identification
3. Information sharing
4. Action planning
5. Monitoring and support

Ideally, facilitators of this process should come from civil society, especially community based organizations (CBOs) whose missions align with promoting civic engagement and increasing local government accountability. This is important because the CEAP process does not stop with the creation of the action plan; as described below, it involves supporting the communities as they implement their plan and monitoring the response of government officials. When this work aligns with the work of the organization, capacity building occurs and the CBO link in the accountability chain is strengthened. Members of CBOs are also likely to speak the local language, something that is also of utmost importance.

In keeping with the action research framework, the facilitation of each step must be deeply participatory, involving community leaders and local government officials representing the communities in which the CEAPs will be conducted. Below are descriptions of each of the five steps, written in the form of a how-to guide.

Step 1: Mobilizing Participants

The CEAP process begins with identifying and mobilizing communities to engage in the process. Working with local elected officials from the start is important for two reasons. First, they gain a stake in the process. Local government officials have a lot to gain through a more engaged citizenry, and involving them in the mobilization process helps them understand that quickly. Second, elected leaders have tremendous convening power; when they ask their constituents to come to a meeting, people usually show up. Involving male and female leaders is also imperative, as the CEAPs themselves are often best done in gender-specific groups. Indeed, in countries such a Uganda where women, youth and persons with disability (PWDs) have mandated representation in local government district councils, working with these councillors to mobilize their constituents ensures that these various interest groups are represented in the process and enables group-specific action plans to be created.

In addition to working with local government officials to mobilize participants, facilitators and organizers need to reach out to community groups, women's groups, youth organizations, and officials at the lower local government levels. The CEAP process has worked with as few as 30 or as many as 90 people. The key is to have good representation from various interest groups, as the action plans themselves will be developed by sub-groups of 10-15 people.

Step 2: Identifying service delivery issues

The actual CEAP session begins with a facilitated brainstorming discussion of the key service delivery issues in the community. Facilitators should make sure that all constituent groups (e.g. women, youth, and persons with disability) participate in this discussion, anticipating the eventual breaking out into action planning groups. If issues of particular concern to members of these groups are raised at this stage, it will easier for these groups to engage in the action planning later on. Facilitators should encourage participants to talk about service delivery improvements in addition to problems. Asking participants to list improvements is a helpful segue to Step 3, which begins with local government officials talking about their roles in service delivery and a few of their recent accomplishments.

Step 3: Sharing Information

This component of the CEAP methodology focusses on enhancing community knowledge about the roles and responsibilities of local elected officials, and the tools of civic engagement. Having the leaders who are present talk about one or two of their recent accomplishments in the water, roads, and education, health care, or agriculture service delivery sectors is a useful way to kick this off. As participants listen to what they've done, which is often tied to monitoring service delivery points or receiving citizen complaints, they learn about how their elected officials interface with service delivery. For the elected officials, it is an opportunity to engage with their constituents around positive change, which is always appreciated. In terms of the process, this engagement between leaders and communities provides a foundation for engagement grounded in collaboration rather than confrontation or animosity.

Once the leaders have described their work, facilitators pick up the thread and ask participants to name some of the key roles and responsibilities of local government officials. Even if some participants are mistaken in their understanding of these roles, it is likely that others will correct them, thereby building a more accurate understanding within the group as a whole. In the ACODE sessions, for example, is was common for someone to say that attending weddings and funerals was a responsibility of district councillors, an expectation that frustrates many elected officials. In each instance, however, someone else in the group explained that in fact that is not an official responsibility. When possible, it can be useful to incorporate into the discussion a description the official roles of local government as mandated and described in official government documents. In the ACODE context, this is accomplished through disseminating and discussing of the results of the Local Government Councils Score-card, in which each elected official is scored on a set of performance indicators tied their roles and responsibilities as mandated in Uganda's Local Governments Act. The responsibilities of councillors in monitoring service delivery and engaging with their constituents should be emphasized, as these are responsibilities involving community-level connection.

This part of the process is also the point at which other kinds of information could be shared that citizens can use to support their demands and better hold their leaders accountable. For example, information on how government funds should be used, how agricultural inputs should be delivered, what pupil:teacher ratio are supposed to be, and hours that health care facilities are supposed to be open can all help citizens make compelling cases for service delivery improvements and use the tools of civic engagement to hold their leaders accountable for what they are supposed to do.

The information sharing component of the CEAP process concludes with a facilitated discussion about tools of civic engagement that citizens can use to most effectively engage with their government leaders. As with the previous discussion, beginning with eliciting participants' knowledge of these tools works well. The ACODE experience suggests that most of the tools will emerge from the participants if the session is facilitated well. As discussed earlier, the tools of civic engagement include writing petitions, writing letters, using civic tech tools like SMS platforms, organizing community meetings with elected leaders, attending council meetings, and participating in radio call-in programs. While it is important to help the group generate a complete list of ways that citizens can engage with government leaders, the action plans themselves should focus mainly on petitions and letters, as these can be most directly entered into government processes and tracked.

Step 4: Developing the Civic Engagement Action Plans

With pressing service delivery issues identified, understanding of government roles and responsibilities enhanced, and the tools of civic engagement discussed, the foundation is laid for the development of the actual CEAPs, which are step-by-step plans for using a civic engagement tool to request that a service delivery problem be remedied. This step begins with the formation of action planning groups, each of which has a trained facilitator. Recognizing that there are overlaps, it is important to divide participants into constituent groups – i.e. women, men, youth, persons with disabilities, etc. – so that one group's interests do not get subsumed by another's. The ideal size of an action planning group is 12-15 participants, but the process can work with smaller and larger groups if needed. The number of participants may depend on the number of facilitators available and the size of the various constituent groups. Each group should also include a local government official who can provide guidance to the participants on the action plan steps. Not only is this useful in generating the plan, but the interaction builds rapport and establishes a relationship between the community members and their local government officials, which strengthens the accountability chain.

Once action planning groups are formed, each group needs to decide what service delivery issue they want to focus on and which civic engagement tool they want to use. Facilitators should help the group identify a specific problem that can be addressed; for example, a broken bridge, a borehole in need of repair, teacher absenteeism at a primary school, lack of drugs at a health centre, or agricultural inputs not being delivered on time. In terms of the civic engagement tool, ACODE experience has shown that letters and petitions have the most impact and are actually appreciated by council members, as these enable them to be active in council meetings and get results for their constituents.

Figure 7.1 is an example of CEAP that was produced by a group who wanted to write a petition to demand that a broken bridge be fixed. The facilitator's job is to help the group identify the steps in writing a petition to be submitted to the appropriate office of local government, in this case the Speaker to the District Council. For each step, the groups needs to identify a person responsible for ensuring that that particular step is done, a date by which that step should be completed, any challenges they might encounter, and the response they expect from their councillor.

Table 7.1: Example of a Completed Civic Engagement Action Plan

CIVIC ENGAGEMENT ACTION PLAN
Civic Engagement Tool: Petition Issue: Broken Bridge Location: XX Sub-county, XX District Date: July 25, 2016

Action Steps	Person Responsible	Deadline (target date)	Evidence of Completion	Potential challenges	Desired Councillor Response
1. Set a date for a meeting to discuss the petition	(Name)	Aug 1, 2016	Notice of meeting posted on notice boards	none	N/A
2. Invite LCV and LCIII Councillors to the meeting	(Name)	August 1	Record of phone calls made	Unable to reach invitees, lack of airtime	Councillor accepts invitation
3. Draft the petition, using evidence from budget monitoring report	(Name)	August 5	Draft of petition	Low attendance	N/A
4. Discuss the petition at the community meeting	(Name)	August 8	Attendance sheet from the meeting	Low attendance	Councillor attends meeting and offers constructive feedback
5. Revise the petition based on discussion	(Name)	August 10	Revised petition	Lack of stationary	N/A
6. Obtain signatures	(Name)	August 14	Signatures on the petition	Transport to villages	N/A
7. Submit the petition to the Speaker	(Name)	August 17	Receipt of submission	Transport to district headquarters	Petition presented in council

Once each group has completed their action plan, they should present it to the larger group so that the broader community is aware of the actions to come. This is important because planning group members will likely want to obtain signatures for the petitions and letters from community members beyond their planning group. At the close of the session, facilitators should obtain contact information for the persons listed as responsible for each step, and take pictures of the action plans, as they will need to support and monitor the implementation process.

Step 5: Monitoring and Support

With the action plans created, the role of the CBO facilitation team shifts to supporting the implementation and monitoring government response. While the team does not need to micro-manage the process, it is useful to occasionally check in with the persons responsible to see how the process of producing the petition or letter is moving along. As with any implementation process, occasional nudges are useful to those responsible. This is also an opportunity to troubleshoot issues that may have arisen if the person initially identified to lead the process turns out not to have been a good choice. Helping the group get back on track will be much appreciated.

Once the groups have submitted their petitions or letters, the focal persons will monitor the response of those officials to citizen demands. This is a critically important role for CBOs and CSOs in the social accountability process, as they are uniquely placed to be watchdogs of the process and engage local government officials. While community leaders can and should be encouraged to contact their elected officials to find out about the status of their petition or letter, members of civil society can amplify citizen voices in this regard and use their own influence to hold leaders accountable for using the mechanisms of responsiveness that are built into government processes. Keeping track of when the letter or petition was submitted, to whom it was submitted, when it was introduced to Council, when it was deliberated, etc. is also recommended, as this will strengthen both the community's and the CBO's ability to monitor the process and hold appropriate officials accountable.

Case Studies: Demonstrations of the CEAP Methodology

The following case studies of the CEAP process and its outcomes show how the theory and methodology of the CEAPs have played out in practice. Each case study includes a description of the problem, the action steps taken, the service delivery outcome, and lessons learned. These case examples were originally written by facilitators of the CEAP sessions, all of whom are also connected to local CSOs or CBOs in the districts where the CEAPs occurred. While they have been slightly modified for uniformity in structure, much of the original language remains. When this is taken into account, the impact of the CEAPs on all three sets of actors targeted in the methodology's underlying theory of change – citizens, civil society, and government officials – is clearly visible.

Case #1
Moroto District: Addressing the Foot and Mouth Disease Crisis
Civic Engagement Tool: Petition
Group: Men

The Problem

Cattle and the Karamajong are inseparable; hence, a foot and mouth disease outbreak is a crisis that goes to the core of the society. This was the ensuing situation in Rupa sub-county on the afternoon of 22nd August 2016 when the ACODE team organized a CEAP meeting. The team took the community participants through the process of problem identification and the available options for expressing their demands (writing a petition, phone calls, writing letter, meetings). Of these options, the men's group adopted the petition as the strategy they wanted to use to make their voice heard.

Action Steps

As a first step in the petition-writing process, the communities of Rupa called for a community meeting at their "tree of men". With the help of their area councillor, a petition was written to Moroto district demanding immediate attention to the plight of the cattle. The presence of the councillor was helpful in making sure that follow up on the petition was undertaken. In addition to the petition, a team of elders engaged the district chairperson to further articulate their concerns on the livestock disease which had killed many cattle. As a follow up, the district leadership worked hand in hand with the Ministry of Agriculture, Animal, Industry and Fisheries to respond to the emergency.

The Outcome

Subsequently, 30,000 vials of vaccine for foot and mouth disease (FMD) were availed to the district. In the first week of November 2016, vaccination against FMD started at the kraals located near Kobebei dam in Rupa sub-county.

Lessons Learned

From this case, three key learning points can be drawn. First, the involvement of political leaders in the process right from the start is important. With the high illiteracy levels, the area councillor in this case was not only able to facilitate the group in petition writing but also to make follow-up. Second, this case points to the fact that numerous approaches can be used to ensure a quick response if citizens are involved. The elders in Rupa, in addition to writing a petition, also engaged the district chairperson to address the problem. Lastly, the intervention by the responsible ministry points to the fact that some of the solutions for the local challenges can only be addressed by a higher office. This therefore points to the need to engage the line ministries to address some of the challenges at the local government level.

Case #2
Mukono District: Sanitation at a Primary School
Civic Engagement Tool: Petition
Group: Men and Women

The Problem

After a discussion of service delivery issues in the district, the sanitation problem at Wakiso Primary School emerged as one of the most pressing. Despite the school having a population of over 427 pupils (217 girls and 210 boys) all were sharing one pit latrine that was full to the brim. During the CEAP process, the participants developed an action plan for writing a petition to engage their leaders in solving the issue at hand.

Action Steps

A community meeting was organised on the 17th of August 2016 where key resolutions were made. These included, writing a petition to the district councillors (both male and female) representing the sub-county to bring to their attention the plight of the primary school; mobilising the community to provide building materials and manual labour for a new latrine; and following up the process in a timely manner.

Outcome

The area councillor presented the petition to council and it was subsequently discussed in the relevant committee and passed as a council resolution, tasking the technical team to take immediate action to resolve the problem.Construction of a new pit latrine was included in the district work plan and budget for the FY 17/18. In addition, the district employed the services of a cesspool company to drain the old pit latrines for the pupils to use in the interim. Also, in March 2017, the female district councillor, the LC3 chairperson and the school leadership organised a meeting with the district leadership. This meeting was held during the sanitation week in Mukono, and they used that opportunity to further engage the district leadership.

Lessons Learned

The above case exemplifies the power a well informed and empowered citizenry can have over changing their status quo. From this success story, four major lessons can be drawn for citizen engagement and service delivery. First, citizens need to be educated and sensitised about their rights and duty in service delivery. The CEAPs go to a great length to emphasise the citizen role in service delivery. Second, a platform that brings together citizens and leaders needs to be created. In this case, the meetings which brought together the political leaders and citizens forged a way forward by clearly identifying a need and agreed upon course of action. Third, citizens need leadership amongst themselves, someone responsible for follow-up. Most often, citizen initiatives lack proper follow-up because no one is willing to take up the mantle of leadership. In this case, the participants agreed upon key actions with specific people to make follow-up. It was even possible to mobilise the community to contribute to the initiative. Lastly, local governments respond to official documentation and evidence. By putting the demands of the community on record through a petition it was easy for the political leaders to make follow-up and take subsequent action.

Case #3
Amuru District: Broken water source
Civic Engagement Tool: Community meeting
Group: Women

The Problem

Corner Lukung is located in Amuru District and has a population of approximately 400 households. During a CEAP meeting conducted by ACODE on 22nd August 2016, citizens reported that the area was experiencing a severe water crisis. The water crisis in this village reached its peak in 2015 when the single borehole supplying the entire village developed a mechanical problem and broke down completely. The residents were forced to trek 4kms to get water in a neighbouring village, or draw water from a stream in the far east of the village that they shared with livestock. Participants decried failure by their local leaders to take any action despite several pleas from the community. They reported that they, too, had resigned to their fate.

Action Steps

At the CEAP meeting, a group composed of women agreed to organize a community meeting at which they would invite their area councillors and engage them in a bid to address the crisis. They organized a meeting on 21st November 2016, during which residents in attendance openly presented their challenges to the male and female LCV councillors, both of whom were in attendance. The female councillor confirmed during follow up discussion with her that she and her counterpart had duly engaged the district engineer and his team, and also met with the council chairman. She was happy to report the process of repairing the borehole was now in their plan.

Outcome

According to one resident of Corner Lukung, the meeting was so fruitful that not long after the meeting, the borehole was repaired.

Lessons Learned

The CEAPs are critical in guiding decisions on delivery of services. By engaging with citizens, leaders are able to respond to the most pressing service delivery needs that they would otherwise not have paid the needed attention.

Case #4
Gulu District: Child Labour
Civic Engagement Tool: Community meeting
Group: Women

The Problem

Coopil village is located in Unyama Sub-county in Gulu District. The village is home to sand mining and stone quarrying sites from which local residents draw their livelihood. However, the major economic activity in the area had proved to be a hindering children's education as children of primary school age were leaving primary schools in the area to work in the mines and quarries. In Coopil P7 School, 70 children had dropped out of school to take part in the sand mining and stone quarrying; in Ogul, 60 had dropped out; and in Angaya P7, 56 pupils had dropped out. During a CEAP meeting held at Unyama Sub-county Headquarters on August 1, 2016, this was identified as a major issue that was affecting both performance and enrolment of pupils in the Sub-county.

Action Steps

Attempts by local authorities to force parents to abandon the use of children as source of labour in the stone and sand quarry sites at the expense of their education had proved futile, according to the LCIII councillor of Unyama Parish, who was present at the CEAP session. During the meeting, the District Council Chairman, upon learning of this issue, directed the LCIII Chairman to ensure that the sub-county steps up its effort in addressing the issue.

The women who attended the CEAP meeting adopted the strategy of holding a community meeting with government officials to address the issue. According to the LCIII councillor for Angaya Parish, who led the women group, a meeting was held on October 16, 2016 to set the ground for the community meeting whose agenda was to sensitize the communities located around the sand mining and stone quarry sites about the dangers of child labour and the need to send their children to school. The councillor reported during the CEAP follow up on December 17, 2016 that at the meeting with the group members it was agreed to hold a grand meeting at the quarry sites. They also agreed to involve officials from the education department, district political leaders, and the sub-county leaders in the meeting at the quarry.

On January 16, 2017 a meeting involving the LCIII chairman, LCV councillor, Secretary for Education, Unyama police officers, and the Inspector of Schools In-charge was held at Kidere sand mining site in Coopil village. During this meeting it was agreed that all children of school going age be sent to school and that defaulting parents would be arrested by police and local authorities.

Outcome

According to the LCIII chairperson of Unyama, the community-led effort has proved successful. He noted that: since the start of the term, he has observed that many pupils have gone back to school. The chairman's observation was shared by the LCV councillor for Unyama Sub-county who was happy to report that during his routine monitoring visits, there were no more children at the quarry sites.

Lessons Learned

The case is a strong justification for the need for combined effort between the different stakeholders in addressing key service delivery needs without waiting for the district council to take a decision or action on it. It is a demonstration of the effort needed to bring about an attitudinal change in a society. Again it presents the power citizens have to impact development in their communities.

Case #5
Jinja District: Health sector changes
Civic Engagement Tool: Petition
Group: Men and Women

The Problem

Citizens in Buwenge lamented having silently endured poor health services, including persistent drug stock-outs, late arrival by staff for duty, poor sanitation, unavailability of medicines to treat older persons, and lack of care for patients. These concerns were raised by citizens during the CEAP meeting conducted on 11th August, 2016 at the sub-county headquarters, with four health centres named as being particularly problematic.

Action Steps

During the CEAP meeting, one citizen group created an action plan to write a petition to be submitted to council requesting that the council come up with a health ordinance to improve the state and quality of health services in Buwenge Sub-county. The citizens convened three separate meetings to discuss the issues identified and draft the petition. The citizens, under the leadership of one of their group members and with support from ACODE's researcher and local CSO partner based in the district, drafted the petition which was submitted through their group leader to the office of the Speaker of the District Council on December 12th 2016. By January 2017 the speaker confirmed having forwarded the petition to the district council's Education, Health and Community-based Services Committee through the committee chairperson.

By March 2017, significant actions had been taken by the district to address the health concerns raised through this petition: a joint monitoring visit to health facilities in Buwenge Sub-county was conducted by the DEC and technical officers in January. There has been a massive staff reshuffle through transfers involving seven health centre staff. From her follow up visits to some of the health units, the lead petitioner reported noticeable improvement in the staff arrival time in three of the health centres named, especially after the transfers were effected. She also reported that older persons were able to access medicine at the fourth health centre named, which was not the case before the petition.

Lessons Learned

Feedback from the citizens during the process showed an apprehension by citizens to engage in activities that check their leaders, due to fear of being labelled a rebel and being isolated in their communities. The fact that the citizens in this group persisted in their push for change even without the initial support of their local leaders is evidence of their untapped potential to steer local development. This case also highlights the critical role of the local CSO partners in the CEAP process, particularly in providing guidance to citizens given their limited experience in writing petitions. Finally, the joint monitoring exercise undertaken by the district leadership that steered the administrative adjustments in the health units justifies part of the objective of the CEAPs, which is to empower local governments to take effective and efficient actions to address pressing service delivery gaps.

Conclusion

The cases presented here are powerful testimonies to the effectiveness of the CEAP process. To be sure, not every action plan results in a service delivery improvement as there are many points in the process where the process can end or be stymied. Even with the support of the CSOs, designated point persons can fail to fulfil the responsibility they committed to. Civic Engagement Action Plan groups can fail to follow through with the process, and local government officials can be non-responsive. This is the case with any action planning process. However, when the community is committed, and when CSO facilitators are persistent in their provision of support and monitoring, the process is likely to yield results.

The cases above represent a range of ways those results can occur. Sometimes, the action planning process catalyses the community to act on its own, as was the case with the broken borehole in Gulu. Other times, as with the case of the primary school in Mukono and the health centres in Jinja, petitions triggered government processes that led to government's response to service delivery problems. In other instances, as in the case of the children labouring in the stone quarry in Gulu, the CEAP process led to citizens and government officials working together to resolve the issue without a letter or petition being formally submitted.

These outcomes are powerful illustrations of what can happen when citizens become empowered with the knowledge to engage their councillors around issues of service delivery. Citizens are not the only ones who benefit from this process, however. Councillors also benefit when their citizens engage with them using citizen engagement tools. One of the councillors representing Anaka sub-county in Nwoya district reported, for example, that because of the CEAPs, issues affecting the people of Anaka sub-county take precedent at council because when they debate issues in council, the letters from citizens provide evidence of issues raised by the community, leading to their issues being treated with more importance compared to others. The other councillor representing this same sub-county agreed, stating that the CEAPs have made their work in the council much easier, as they have documented demands from citizens to debate.

As communities and civil society members around the world have been developing and trying out social accountability mechanisms, practitioner-scholars have been watching, learning, and gaining clarity about the essential elements of effective social accountability initiatives. The civic engagement action planning methodology described and illustrated here has benefited from this action-learning cycle and adds to it. Drawing on ACODE's experience with the Local Government Councils Score-card Initiative, the methodology emphasizes the importance of attending to both the supply and demand sides of local governance. Effective social accountability initiatives, as Fox (2014) and others have found, strengthen both citizen voice and government teeth. The CEAP methodology does this and takes it a step further by catalysing that virtuous circle of mutual empowerment as citizens engage with their local government leaders in ways that feed directly into the mechanisms of government response. Because the action plans focus on the tools of civic engagement that are directly connected to local government processes, government leaders can be held accountable not only for the delivery of public goods and services, but for acting on citizen demands. One of the responsibilities of local government councils in Uganda, for example, is to present citizen petitions in council for deliberation, but ACODE's research had repeatedly found that councillors often did not receive petitions from their constituents because citizens were not informed about the roles and responsibilities of their local government leaders, nor were they knowledgeable about the tools of civic engagement that mandate government response. The CEAP methodology enhances both and voice and teeth – demand and supply – and connects them so that the virtual circle of mutual empowerment can begin to turn.

The CEAP methodology will no doubt continue to evolve, both within its "home" context at ACODE in Uganda, and as it begins to be taken up in other contexts and other countries. Since its inception, a lot of learning and improvement has taken place. For example, it evolved from a process that looked more like focus groups, where ACODE researchers facilitated community conversations about service delivery, much like what is described in Step 2 of the CEAP process. It gradually became participatory where the target communities became more involved and started facilitating the meetings themselves. Initially, too, the process targeted small numbers of people to fit in the focus groups method of research; this, however, became a limitation in terms of reaching a critical mass of people with civic education based on service delivery standards. The deliberate integration of an action research approach into the methodology was another turning point, as civic action was added onto civic education. Consistent with the iterative action research approach, adjustments will continue, and the CEAPs will evolve as a strategic social accountability tool and enterprise as situations and governing contexts require.

References

Asmah-Andoh, K. (2015) 'Can the reporting of local government performance enhance citizens' engagement? A perspective', *Africa Insight*, 44(4), pp. 169–185.

Bainomugisha, A., Tamale, L. M., Muhwezi, W. W., Cunningham, K., Ssemakula, E. G. and Bogere, G. (2015) *The Local Government Councils Scorecard Assessment 2014/2015: Unlocking Potentials and Amplifying Voices,*. Kampala.

Crawford, S. (2009) *Voice and accountability in the health service of Bangladesh. How-to Note.* London: DfID.

Devarajan, S., Khemani, S. and Walton, M. (2013) 'Can civil society overcome government failure in Africa?', *The World Bank Research Observer*. The World Bank Research Observer, 29(1), pp. 20–47.

Fox, J. (2014) *Social accountability: What does the evidence really say?* No.1.

Gaventa, J. and McGee, R. (2013) 'The impact of transparency and accountability initiatives', *Development Policy Review*, 31(S1), pp. S3–S28.

Grandvoinnet, H., Aslam, G. and Raha, S. (2015) *Opening the black box: The contextual drivers of social accountability.* Washington, D.C.: World Bank.

Grandvoinnet, H., Raha, S., Kumagai, S. and Joshi, A. (2015) *Social accountability: A Popular yet fuzzy concept.* Washington, D.C.

Holla, A., Koziol, M. and Srinivasan, S. (2011) 'Citizens and service delivery', in *Assessing the use of social accountability approaches in human development sectors.* Washington, DC: World Bank.

Joshi, A. (2013) 'Do they work? Assessing the impact of transparency and accountability initiatives in service delivery', *Development Policy Review*, 31(S1), pp. s29–s48.

Kavuma, S. N., Cunningham, K., Bogere, G. and Sebaggala, R. (2017) 'Assessment of public expenditure governance of the universal primary education programme in Uganda', in *ACODE Policy Research Series*. Kampala: Advocates Coalition for Development , and Environment, p. No.17.

Krawczyk, K. A. and Sweet-Cushman, J. (2017) 'Understanding political participation in West Africa: the relationship between good governance and local citizen engagement', *International Review of Administrative Sciences*, 83(1), pp. 136–155.

Larreguy, H. and Marshall, J. (2017) 'The effect of education on civic and political engagement in non-consolidated democracies: Evidence from Nigeria', *Review of Economics and Statistics*.

Lee, T. (2011) *The (im)possibility of mobilizing public opinion, Accountability through public opinion: From inertia to public action*. Edited by S. Odugbemi and T. Lee. Washington, DC: World Bank.

Malena, C., Forster, R. and Singh, J. (2004) 'Social accountability: an introduction to the concept and emerging practice', *Social Development Paper*. Washington, DC: World Bank, p. 76.

World Bank (2016) 'Making politics work for development: harnessing transparency and citizen engagement', in *Policy Research Report*. Washington, DC: World Bank.

CHAPTER EIGHT

The Future of Civic Technology: Amplifying Citizens' Voice in Local Governance

Atukunda Phoebe Kirungyi & Wilson Winstons Muhwezi

Introduction

The rapid rise in the use of digital technology by citizens, governments and civil society organizations offers a contemporary possibility of strengthening citizens' voice in their engagement with duty bearers, carving out new spaces for activism and promoting more government accountability. *"Civic tech, an acronym for Civic Technology"* is gaining popularity and is a hot space for technology investments in the world. Governments are waking up to the need to use technology in the 21st century. It's no longer a best practice to have documents hidden in cabinets and huge volumes of reports printed out. Citizens are increasingly demanding transparency from their elected leaders and too often, governments have no alternative ways of engaging with duty bearers. Citizens are entitled to explanation about how or why taxpayers' money is being spent. Civic technology enables engagement and public participation for purposes of equitable development, enhancing citizen communication, improving government infrastructure and improving the delivery of public goods and services. Technology enables greater participation in governance or otherwise assists governments in delivering citizen services and deepening democratic governance at all levels. Civic leaders, civil society organizations, development partner(s), and citizens increasingly recognize the power of *"civic tech"* to connect people, improve participation and make government more responsive.

Transparency and accountability, on one hand and responsiveness on the other are some of the key aspects critical for good local governance and improving delivery of public goods and services (Rodden and

Wibbels, 2013). Transparency is the government's obligation to avail information on public goods and services to the citizens and involve them in decision-making that affects their communities (Ba, 2011). In addition, it involves leaders in public offices being able to account to the public on policy decisions that have a bearing on their livelihood (Konrad-Adenauer-Stiftung, 2011). Responsiveness as a key aspect of good governance enables governments to bridge the gap between citizens and their leaders. Responsiveness has been defined as effective planning, evaluation, and feedback with regard to particular actions as well as the conduct of a regular review process to ensure that programmes reflect the needs and preferences of stakeholders (Best, 2008). Government's unresponsiveness affects citizens' participation through dampening of their motivation to give feedback on issues affecting their communities (Saunders and Baeck, 2015). The essence of accountability in governance is when elected leaders or public officers respond to the ordinary citizens through their actions and policy decisions during the time they are occupants of the public offices (Konrad-Adenauer-Stiftung, 2011).

Although accountability can take different forms like horizontal, vertical, political, social and legal, this chapter focuses on social accountability as one of the levels (Gyong, 2014). In elucidating more about social accountability, a World Bank report calls it

> an approach towards building accountability that relies on civic engagement. In other words, this is a situation in which ordinary citizens and/or civil society organizations participate directly or indirectly in exacting accountability (Carmen et al, 2004).

According to a UNDP report,

> social accountability is a form of civic engagement that builds accountability through the collective efforts of citizens and civil society organizations to hold public officials, service providers, and governments to account for their obligations with responsive efforts (United Nations Development Programme, 2013).

In his article, (Fox, 2015) goes ahead to discuss some of the positive impacts of social accountability initiatives. Elements of social accountability include access to information from government, civic education, and using different tools to engage government (United Nations Development Programme, 2013). Social accountability mechanisms have been embraced especially in developing countries because they contribute to poverty reduction, give a voice to the marginalized leading to improved public service delivery, empower the public to engage with their leaders and public officers (Carmen et al, 2004). For transparency, accountability and responsiveness to take root in local governments, evidence is clearly emerging to the effect that the involvement of citizens is very crucial (Bhargava, 2014).

In addition, civic engagement as a key aspect in fostering good governance plays a crucial role in amplifying citizens' voice, in as far as participation in decision-making, policy making, improving the quality of public goods and services, holding local leaders accountable are concerned. Citizens' voice also improves government responsiveness in the management of public affairs (LOGIN, 2014). Civic engagement, according to Thomas Ehrlich is defined as:

> working to make a difference in the civic life of our communities and developing the combination of knowledge, skills, values, and motivation to make that difference. It means promoting the quality of life in a community, through both political and non-political processes (Bowen, 2010).

Furthermore, the UNDP Human Development Report 1993 defines civic engagement as *"a process, not an event that closely involves people in the economic social, cultural and political processes that affect their lives"* (United Nations Development Programme, 1993). Civic engagement empowers citizens' ability to identify issues affecting their community livelihoods and demand action from their elected leaders. It also empowers citizens to be agents of social change in communities (Bassler *et al.*, 2008).

This chapter discusses the rise of civic technology or "civic tech" as a facilitator of civic engagement and the role of this technology in amplifying citizens' voice in local governance. Its effectiveness in fostering transparency, accountability and responsiveness of elected leaders and public officers in improving the delivery of public goods and services is presented through looking at different cases around the world as well as ACODE technology initiatives. It also takes a look into the future of "civic tech" as a change agent in deepening democracy at the local level.

The Rise of Civic Tech

Civic tech is defined as the use of Information Technology (IT) to facilitate citizens' engagement with their local leaders on issues of public service delivery. It is becoming the norm instead of an exception (Urban Sustainability Directors Network, 2015). It is also used to refer to the technology that is explicitly leveraged to increase and deepen democratic participation (Gilman, 2015). Civic tech has been embraced by governments, development partner(s) and civil society organizations worldwide to amplify citizens' voice in demanding for better delivery of public goods and services (Peixoto and Fox, 2016). The term *"civic tech"* is related to other concepts such as digital citizen engagement (World Bank Group, 2016). According to the Knight Foundation report, civic technology innovations are grouped into those that support open government such as data access and transparency, data utility, public decision-making, resident feedback, visualization, mapping and voting. Innovations that support community action such as civic cloud-funding, community organizations, information crowdsourcing, neighbourhood forums and peer-to-peer sharing (Patel *et al.*, 2013). Digital tools that are normally used in civic tech include mobile phones (simple and smart), tablets and computers among others (Leocadia, 2013). *Civic tech* innovations are high-tech like crowdsourcing, websites and interactive mapping, medium-tech such as mobile phone-based Short Message Service (SMS) or call centres and low-tech such as community radio (World Bank Group, 2016).

Although the popular opinion in the contemporary world understands how to identify and support the types of citizen participation that contribute to deepening democracy, the exact role and results of "civic tech" used in this process remain less clear. The rise in the use of technology to increase citizens' access to information provides an avenue to bridge the communication gap between the citizens and public officials. It is hoped that this will transform how governance is practiced. However, this seems to be driven by the underlying, yet largely untested, assumptions about technology's ability to increase the quantity, quality, and democratizing influence on citizen participation. In spite of the exuberance for new technologies, there is not enough data available to show how it impacts on political processes and institutions. *Civic tech* is intended to influence emerging democracies which potentially creates additional challenges in designing and implementing programs (National Democratic Institute for International Affairs, 2013).

For close to a decade now, there has been a growing debate concerning civic technology or "civic tech" and its opportunities for leveraging digital tools to benefit the public good. Governments, development partner(s), and civil society organizations are continuing to embrace the use of technology to facilitate civic engagement (National Democratic Institute for International Affairs, 2013). Information and Communication Technology presents an opportunity for citizens to communicate from anywhere and anytime hence leading to the increased involvement (Amelina, 2007). In this digital age, information travels faster to and from anywhere around the world and therefore calls for innovations that adapt quickly to the changing time (Mandarano, Meenar and Steins, 2010). According to the International Telecommunication Union (ITU) report for 2016, seven billion people (about 95 percent of the world's population) live in an area that is covered by a mobile cellular network. Mobile broadband networks reach 84 percent of the global population of which 67 percent of the population is in rural areas and this continues to grow at a rate of 41 percent in developing countries. The report further shows that more than half the world population is not connected to the internet with 75 percent of the people are in Africa and 25 per cent in Europe. The report compares Internet usage by gender and notes that more men use the Internet than women and records this gender gap as being highest in Africa at 23 percent and America at only 2 percent (International Telecommunication Union, 2017).

Technology in governance has been used to improve service delivery, provide a platform to amplify the citizens' voice, data collection, transparency, and accountability in government expenditures, disseminating information, fighting corruption and monitoring human rights (DANIDA, 2012b). It is important to note that citizens, development partner(s) and civil society organizations which are critical pillars of good governance can use technology in outreach and advocacy, monitoring governance, holding political and technical officials accountable and providing a platform for amplifying citizens voice (Ghaus-Pasha, 2004). It's no wonder that most innovations to improve transparency and accountability as well as public service delivery have been initiated by civil society organizations.

Amplifying Citizen's Voice in Local Governance

Over the last decade, there has been a number of innovative tools developed and tested in many countries all aimed at empowering citizens to engage with their leaders at all levels of government. There has been a remarkable increase in the use of Information Communication Technology tools, especially at the local level, to amplifying citizens' voice as an important pillar in empowering citizens, men and women to hold decision-makers accountable. The use of civic technology has helped to ensure that the voices of citizens are heard and that governments have both the capacity and the incentive to listen and respond in a timely manner. This involves bringing together unusual combinations of people – from the arena of technology, development, government, social activism and civil society to work together in unfamiliar ways on new ideas in accountable governance. A number of tools have been developed and used in many countries with varying impacts. In this section, we present some of the tools that have registered positive impacts in promoting transparency, fighting corruption, empowering marginalized communities, vulnerable groups and are harnessing the power of new technologies to make governments more efficient and accountable around the world as discussed below.

• *FixMyStreet* is a web-based innovation that was launched in 2007 by "*mySociety*" a not-for-profit social enterprise based in the United Kingdom. This is an interactive system that enables citizens to report and view physical issues related to infrastructure in their local areas such as bad pavements, potholes, and other public service related issues. The system also allows citizens to track responses from the respective local councils on any issue raised via the same platform (Sjoberg, Jonathan & , 2015). According to the *FixMyStreet* website, this innovation has been embraced in other countries like Uganda, Malaysia, India, Australia, France, Ireland, Norway, Spain,

Switzerland, Chile, and Uruguay among others (FixMyStreet, 2018).

- **WritetoThem** is another web-based civic innovation in the United Kingdom developed by "*mySociety*" whose goal is to provide a platform for citizens to contact their political leaders such as councillors and Members of Parliament. It also facilitates a dialogue between the constituents and their representatives. This innovation has registered a high level of user satisfaction although the rate of responsiveness varied depending on the category of leaders (Escher, 2011).

- **Checkmyschool** is a participatory monitoring initiative specifically developed for the education sector in the Philippines. This initiative seeks to improve the quality of education services by bringing the participation of citizens and communities into the governance of public schools in the country. It was launched by Affiliated Network for Social Accountability East Asia and the Pacific (ANSA-EAP) in 2011 as a partnership project with the government department of education to advocate for better access to information and social accountability. The website allows parents, NGOs, pupils, school authorities and the education department to monitor resources allocated to schools by the government and give feedback when there is misuse of public funds, teacher absenteeism, and lack of scholastic materials such as text books among others. Although the initiative has registered successes, there are still challenges in the implementation of this innovation largely due to limited internet access in the Philippines, lack of technological skills, quality of data received on the website and how it is verified (Shkabatur, 2012).

- **IChangeMyCity** combines a web based platform and a mobile application that enables citizens to communicate with their elected leaders on service delivery issues. The system allows discussions among citizens and this leads to the formation of civic action groups within the communities. This platform is being run by an NGO in Bangalore, India (Dietrich and Myrttinen, 2012). According to *IChangeMyCity* website, common issues raised on the website include, garbage collection, impassable roads, stray dogs, and traffic related issues among others. A number of success stories have been registered for instance potholes and street lighting normally get fixed after such issues are raised on the platform (*ichangemycity*). This innovation has been evaluated to have a medium uptake and a high response rate to issues raised on the system by the authorities in India (Peixoto and Fox, 2016).

- *I Paid a Bribe* (IPAB) was launched in 2010 by Janaagraha Centre for Citizenship and Democracy, a non-profit organization based in Bangalore, India to help citizens report cases of corruption in public service (One World India, 2011). IPAB is an online initiative that focuses on "retail corruption". According to their website, it is the largest online crowd-sourced anti-corruption platform in the world today. IPAB uses a crowd-sourcing model to collect bribe reports and to build a repository of corruption-related data across government departments. Most importantly, it empowers citizens, governments, and advocacy organizations to tackle retail corruption both within India and increasingly throughout the world (ipaidabribe).Innovations like *"I paid a bribe"* have played a vital role in the fight against corruption especially in provision and accessing public services. Available data indicates that by July 2015, twenty five other countries had entered into a partnership with *"I paid a bribe"* to replicate this good innovation for the anti-corruption strategies in those countries.

- *Lungisa* is a South African-based innovation that was launched by Cell-Life in 2012. It enables residents of Cape Town to communicate issues affecting them regarding public service delivery using an online form. The system was developed with an aim of improving service delivery by using low-cost technology. *Lungisa* team has established a good relationship with the city of Cape Town and this has led to a high response to issues that are raised through the platform. Some of the service delivery issues posted on the site are related to roads and transport, drainage, water and sanitation, street lighting and electricity. Though this innovation has a high response rate, it has registered a low uptake according to World Bank evaluation report (Peixoto and Fox, 2016).

- *Action for Transparency (A4T)* is another innovation in the anti-corruption campaigns that allows citizens to expose officials and institutions that are involved in corruption through the media and activist groups to cause governments to act on those cases. Using mobile phones with internet access, citizens are able to check on the amount of government funds that are allocated to social services such as schools and health centres, and the actual amount spent. This contributes to strengthening democratic accountability and transparency through citizen monitoring of government expenditure, in order to expose corruption and mismanagement of public funds where it exists. This innovation is currently being implemented in Uganda, Kenya and Zambia (Action for Transparency, 2017).

- *MajiVoice* is an innovation of the Water Service Regulatory Board in Kenya that was developed to help in improving efficiency, accountability, responsiveness and transparency of urban water service providers in Kenya and ultimately lead to improved service delivery. With this system, one can use a mobile phone or a computer to submit complaints or compliments, and any other information about the water sector. It allows citizens to receive timely updates on the issues raised and actions being taken where necessary (WASREB Kenya, 2011). This innovation has registered medium uptake with a high response rate. Innovations that have a link with the government feedback system mechanism are likely to register a high response rate (Peixoto and Fox, 2016).

- *Hudama Fix my constituency* is an another innovation in Kenya that enables citizens' participation by reporting issues in public service delivery sectors such as education, governance, health, infrastructure, water, justice in their districts. This system allows citizens to use SMS or email to report any service delivery issues. Received issues are mapped on the Huduma website for the public to see and the responsible authority is notified (DANIDA., 2012).

- *SautiZaWananchi* is an innovation that is being implemented by

Twaweza in Tanzania to improve public service delivery. According to its website, "*Sauti za Wananchi* (Voices of Citizens) uses mobile phones to regularly collect information from a broad cross-section of Tanzanian and Kenyan citizens. This innovation informs citizens of what's going on and supports policy-makers to be more responsive to the needs and aspirations of citizens" (Sauti za Wananchi, 2017).

- **U Report** is a free SMS social monitoring tool for community participation designed to address issues that people care about. It relies on community members volunteering as U-Reporters and this allows citizens to speak out on issues in their communities. It also provides a forum to amplify their voices through local, national media, and alerts to key stakeholders. This innovation has been implemented in over 11 countries, including Uganda where it is being run by UNICEF since 2011 (UNICEF, 2014).

From the above examples, it's clear that civic technology provides opportunities, and challenges in improving public service delivery and the quality of life in the communities. It's important to note from these examples that some of these are regarded as "high tech" solutions that require relatively tech-savvy citizens to effectively use them, especially the web-based solutions like *WritetoThem* and *IChangeMyCity.* On the other hand others are regarded as "simple-to-use". SMS platforms such as *U-Report* are relatively easier to learn and simple-to-use technology in a way that facilitates a transformed relationship between citizens and their local leaders. It should also be noted that in these examples, some of the solutions highlighted are designed to address specific service delivery needs while others can be used to address a range of service delivery issues.

For instance, ACODE in Uganda adopted technology innovations to facilitate civic engagement. This includes use of an SMS platform and a mobile application. It is widely believed that both citizens and government have a shared expectation as far as the delivery of public goods and services is concerned. Although governments derive their legitimacy and respect from citizens on the account of effective public service delivery systems, citizens, on the other hand, have a responsibility to hold Governments accountable when delivery systems of those services fail and therefore need platforms that amplifies their voice for positive change. Effective delivery of public goods and services is one way of ensuring that political leaders are elected or re-elected into government. Governments that are perceived by citizens as having failed to deliver public goods and services can easily be voted out of office especially in a democracy. On the other hand, citizens elect their leaders with the expectation that those leaders will represent them and make good policy decisions that ensures access to public goods and services such as healthcare, education, agricultural advisory services, and roads among many others.

For this shared expectation to materialize, citizens and their elected leaders must be able to communicate with each other. In particular, there should be mechanisms by which elected leaders can be held to account by the citizens. During the implementation of ACODE's Local Government Councils Score Card Initiative, it was found out that a key barrier to effective representation of concerns of voters at the local level was lack of clear channels of communicating to elected leaders. Conversely, it was also difficult and expensive for elected leaders to provide feedback on the efforts they add making to ensure that the concerns of their electorate were addressed (Muyomba-Tamale, Luba and Ssempala, 2013). In the majority of cases, local elected leaders used social functions such as weddings and burial ceremonies to report back to their electorate and these channels of communication did not give citizens the opportunity to raise their own issues. Unlike in some of the solutions from the examples discussed above, ACODE's technology-based civic engagement platforms were designed to offer a wide range of functionalities to include various public goods and services that citizens could monitor and report any deficiencies to their leaders in these communities.

ACODE's Technology Based Civic Engagement Platforms

As part of the effort to amplify citizens' voice and bridge the communication gap between citizens and their leaders in government, ACODE designed two major technology-based platforms to expand citizen participation in governance. Under the Local Government Councils Scorecard Initiative, ACODE designed and launched the Local

Government SMS platform in June 2013 to facilitate communication between citizens and their elected local government leaders. The platform allowed citizens to report on public service delivery deficiencies in their communities to their Local Council Five (LC V) councillors. Equipped with this knowledge and information, the councillor would then lobby the appropriate agencies of government to respond to citizens' service delivery reports, raise the concerns in the district council and use the Local Government SMS platform to report back on the actions taken. The Local Government SMS platform was first piloted in 20 local governments (districts) of Uganda randomly selected in 2013. It was later expanded to cover 35 districts across the country.

It should be noted that in Uganda, local governments are public service delivery centres in their respective jurisdictions. Therefore, the Local Government SMS platform was designed to equip communities in these districts with the necessary channels of communication to increase interaction between the citizens and their elected leaders at local government level on issues of quality of service delivery, accountability and governance. Communication between the electorate and their elected district representatives was found to boost government responsiveness to inadequacies in public service delivery, thereby increasing government legitimacy.

As Civic tech, the Local Government SMS Platform enables citizens to send messages about service delivery in their communities to their local government political leaders. The platform works in such a way that a message is sent to a pre-defined short code. The Platform supports different local languages in Uganda and citizens can send thier issues about service delivery in their local language dialects. Once a message is received on the platform, it is routed to the area district councillor who in turn provides a response in real time. Both citizens and councillors are charged a nominal small fee once they send messages to the platform. The platform also contains a database of councillors' names, mobile telephone numbers, the districts, constituents they represent and their mandates (chairperson, directly elected councillor, woman councillor representative, person with disabilities representative, councillor for the elderly and youth councillor). For councillor mandates like youth, elderly and person with disability that have both male and female representatives, both councillors receive the same message when a message is sent to the platform to any of these mandates then councillors can each choose to respond accordingly.

It also contains a database of keywords that represent different service delivery categories such as water, roads, health, agriculture, and education among others. Feedback from different citizens is available on the website through an interactive map that shows issues received from different districts for the public to view (ACODE, 2013) To protect the confidentiality of both the citizens and councillors, mobile phone numbers of both parties are kept confidential and cannot be viewed by the public. The platform also receives anonymous messages from users.

Periodic reports of all messages received per district are compiled and shared with district technical and political leaders including the district councillors at the end of each month. The district chairperson receives a report of all messages received from citizens in that particular district as a means of providing oversight to the follow-up processes. These reports help to deal with different excuses from councillors such as loss of mobile phones, access to network connectivity, and faulty mobile phones that may lead to one not receiving the SMS.

Issues raised on the SMS platform have been taken seriously by political leaders who have gone ahead to make sure that solutions are offered to the citizens. For example, the LC V chairperson of Gulu district local government in Uganda was able to address water issues because of the messages sent to him through the platform. Some political leaders go ahead to act on the issues sent to them though they do not respond through the platform. The Local Government SMS platform has been effective in disseminating information about service delivery standards to citizens. As such citizens are able to compare the standards with the public services they are receiving in their communities and if not, then they are able to inform their leaders through the platform. Political leaders' scorecard results are also disseminated through the platform so that citizens know how the leaders they elected are performing as per their legal mandate.

Although the platform registered quite a low uptake, it should be noted that this problem is not unique. Rather, the low uptake reflects the common problems that face new technologies especially in the developing world that still grapple with structural and accessibility issues. Apart from low responsiveness from councillors, the SMS Platform success has also been hindered by infrastructural issues such as poor or no cellular network coverage in some rural districts of Uganda. The literacy level of citizens especially in rural communities is low and they cannot therefore; effectively use these technology innovations. There is also lack of appreciation of the power of these new technologies both by the leaders and the communities. Citizens are not yet fully exposed to tap into the benefits of these innovations in the tech world. It is important to note that poverty levels in these communities negatively impact the use of this platform since there is a cost incurred in sending a message. Although these challenges exist, ACODE is continuously building the capacity of both citizens and their leaders especially Councillors about the benefits of embracing technology in improving the delivery of public goods and services as well as citizen participation.

In addition to the SMS platform, ACODE developed a mobile application - The Citizen Monitor - to supplement the SMS technology. The Citizen Monitor mobile application was designed to strengthen the demand-side of accountability in Uganda by soliciting feedback on public services provided in the country. With the Application, ACODE provides a voice to share both positive and negative experiences on the quality of public goods and services. Feedback on service delivery from citizens is critical in improving the quality of public goods and services including education, health, roads, agriculture to mention a few. Feedback from citizens through the Citizen Monitor mobile app is sent to the relevant Government Ministries, Departments and Agencies (MDAs) for consideration. Once a response to a particular issue is received, a notification is sent to all members informing them of the issue that has been responded to. Citizens can also view issues raised in other districts on the interactive map between technology and based (ACODE, 2016).

Through the use of technology-based civic engagement platforms, ACODE illustrates how the development of effective civic tech can lead to improvement in the provision of public goods and services especially in local governments as service delivery units in Uganda's administrative structure. These platforms have helped in enhancing local democracy at this level where there are opportunities for citizens to keep in contact with their leaders when campaigns and elections end. These civic engagement platforms are unique tools which ensure that citizens are engaged as they remain in constant communication with their elected leaders.

Furthermore, these innovations have contributed to the deepening of democracy through the participation of citizens in local governance. With such communication platforms, citizens can no longer passively look on as when social services like education and primary healthcare are collapsing due to teachers or health workers absenteeism, among others factors. By constantly seeking answers for these deficiencies in service delivery, citizens are actively engaged in seeking solutions to their problems. The platforms have promoted political accountability of elected leaders to the electorate. When leaders receive information from their electorate about service delivery inadequacies, they usually respond in different ways, such as transmitting the reported failures to the responsible agencies of local governments and then central government for appropriate action. Political leaders also bring up such service delivery issues in the local government council meetings so that they are debated and appropriate resolutions or actions taken hence leading to improvements in political accountability. These technology based civic engagement platforms have both contributed greatly to bridging the communication gap between leaders and the led. As such, citizens are increasingly embracing the use of these new technologies as one way of promoting their participation in the affairs of their communities as a pillar of good governance. See Text Box 8.1 for sample messages as transmitted from both systems.

Text Box 8.1

Messages transmitted through the Local Government SMS platform

- *Lessons paralyzed at Mutir primary school due to teachers absenteeism. This school is found in Mutir village (Nebbi District).*

- *Mahoma bridge swept away by floods this morning (Kabarole District)*

- *Poor quality seeds were given to farmers under NAADS (Lira District)*

- *Honorable, we are requesting for a few bags of cement to complete a teachers' house we have built here in Awoja-bridge primary school. It is only plastering and fixing doors that are remaining (Soroti District).*

- *LC V Chairperson, Lemusui borehole has been broken for quite a year now. The school has no water to date, please help use your position to bail us out of this worse situation (Nakapiripirit District).*

- *There is lack of medical attention to patients in Nebbi hospital in the afternoons (Nebbi District).*

- *Wind has uprooted a very huge tree has made the road impassable at Ndhew trading centre (Nebbi District).*

Messages received from citizen using the Citizen Monitor Mobile Application

- *The road that connects Arapai Sub County to Katine Sub County through Angai and Olwelai parishes is bad, yet it is an important road because it leads to Katine cattle market, a key place for doing business. A lot of accidents are happening because nothing has been done to repair this road (Soroti District).*

- *Loruk road which is just close to the main market and the bus park has been neglected and unrepaired by municipal authorities for more than three months now. Also the bridge that branches to Leslona got blocked making floods to erode the road. There is no action being taken to repair the bridge or the road (Moroto District).*

- *The Health Center has few staff serving many patients as well poor and dangerous dilapidated buildings. It belongs to Moroto Municipality which has failed to take care of it (Moroto District).*

- *Prescribed drugs in our health centers are out of stock, like quinine tablets, Coartem (Agago District).*

- *Sensitisation on Government Policies and programmes is really poor and this needs to be addressed. Otherwise, the future of this nation is at stake (Lira District).*

- *I thank office of the prime minister for providing me with an Irrigation Scheme that is enabling me to grow vegetables. But agriculture extension workers from Moroto district local government have failed to visit and assist in agricultural advisory services (Moroto District).*

Source: Local Government SMS Platform &Citizen Monitor Mobile Application respectively

Looking into the Future of Civic Technology in Amplifying Citizens' Voice

The last ten years have seen an exponential rise in the technology world with terms like "open data," "open government", "civic innovation" among others quickly becoming everyday realities within the public sector, civil society, and the donor community. The use of technology by governments, civil society development partner community is in helping the deepening of the democratic relationship between citizens and their governments by providing tools that are enabling to citizen involvement. Furthermore, transparency, accountability, and responsiveness are normally the guiding elements while these technological innovations are being designed with a major goal of improving public service delivery.

The emerging acceptance of civic tech in the public sector has helped in shaping innovation-driven efficiency and is fuelling economic development especially in developing countries. While it's still emerging, there is evidence of the transformative potential of technology in shaping the future of civic engagement, especially at the local level where government policy most directly impacts the lives of citizens in the delivery of public goods and services. Citizens believe that technology innovations can help to make governments more accountable and transparent. A citizenry that has access to information and is involved leads to good governance. This is where there is the biggest opportunity to use technology to realign the relationship between citizens and elected leaders or public officers.

Civic tech in this "digital age" is becoming the foundation for political and economic exchanges. As technology gains prominence in society and becomes available to the population, many government leaders are beginning to appreciate its use for public outreach and feedback. Specifically, the Internet is being used for communication between citizens, local leaders, and civil society groups. Data collected from these innovations is being utilized by government officials and political leaders in monitoring public services and hence; increasing the notion of accountability, transparency, and responsiveness. Although numerous challenges still exist, such challenges are not unique only to ACODE's technology based civic engagement platforms but rather a

Chapter Eight | Kirungyi & Muhwezi

reflection of common issues in the tech world. Some of the challenging aspects are discussed below.

Socio-economic issues such as illiteracy, language barriers, poverty, access limitations, and low appreciation of information technology are some of the factors that affect civic technology, especially in developing countries. However, designing innovations that support local languages, adopting low-cost technologies such as SMS, continuous training and capacity building can help deal with some of the social economic challenges. ACODE's Local Government SMS Platform has equally incorporated the aspect of citizens sending feedback in their local language. Continuous capacity building and training of both citizens and leaders on how to use the local government SMS platform has helped address some of these challenges like appreciation of technology.

Over 46 percent of the world's population lives in rural areas, especially in developing countries (World Bank, 2017). Infrastructure challenges that lead to poor or no network coverage, limited internet access, lack of electricity, especially in rural and hard to reach areas are some of the issues that hinder the use of these innovations. During the launch of the Local Government SMS platform in 2013, most citizens in hard to reach areas did not have Internet network coverage. However, governments in the developing are increasingly realizing the need to develop the infrastructure sector. For example, the Uganda government is increasingly allocating more resources to Infrastructure, Information and Communication Technology sectors as well as youth Innovation Hubs (MoFPED, 2015).

Low awareness of these new technology innovations which is partly due to limited resources to run promotional campaigns and marketing to attract people to use these innovations is part of the limitations. It is against this background, ACODE's technology based civic engagement platforms invested a lot of resources with promotional materials for example posters, flyers, radio adverts, conducting capacity building sessions for local government leaders and community meetings to train citizens on how these technology innovations work.

Poor responsiveness from both political leaders and other public officials to issues raised through these platforms remains a challenge. While users expect quick and positive feedback from decision makers once their issues are raised, most times no responses are provided or take long to provide feedback. This leads to loss of trust in such innovations from the side of citizens. "This is true in ACODE'S technology-based civic engagement platforms which have registered less or no response at all from both political leaders and civil servants on many occasions. To overcome this issue ACODE avails hard copy reports to political leaders who receive messages to follow up with the issues raised.

Misuse of these innovations by citizens, for instance, to insult government officials and political leaders is another issue. The Local Government SMS Platform was modified to block abusive messages by predetermining restricted phrases. Innovations like ACODE's Local Government SMS Platform and Citizen Monitor mobile application have an anonymous feature to encourage the public to be honest with their reporting. Though it's important for such platforms to protect users, it's crucial that each post is verified in a way.

Sustainability of these innovations especially those driven by donor reliant civil society is also a challenge since the impact of these innovations take long to be realized yet most donors prefer initiatives with quick visible impact. Furthermore, some of these civil society organizations receive funds that are tagged on strict on budget that leave no room to deal with unforeseen eventualities in technology development lines which affects implementation. Citizens also view civil society organizations as charities. For example, during the launch of ACODE's technology innovations; citizens requested the organization to offer free phones to enable them use the innovation. Continuous citizen capacity building helps citizens to appreciate technology. ACODE has engaged with development partners to appreciate the fact that technology innovations require time to show impact.

The political environment in developing countries, especially repressive regimes view civil society as anti-establishment. This is largely because in such regimes, transparency and accountability are weak. Here governments - civil society relationship can best be described as a "love-hate" one. While people in government welcome civil society when they are delivering charitable services, they are reluctant to let CSOs into the policy arena. This is mainly because many people in government doubt the capacity of the people within CSOs to engage meaningfully in public policy discourse without suspicion. Such governments misuse state power to suppress civil society just like political dissent. ACODE has established a good working relationship with government to be able to influence policy. For instance, the promotional materials for ACODE innovations were reviewed by a task group composed of politicians, government officials and people from the academia to make sure that all stakeholders involved are comfortable and also in a way establish a partnership with government.

Despite the challenges facing technology-based civic engagement innovations today, a look at the future is promising. There is evidence of a transformative potential of technology shaping the future of civic engagement. Governments in the developing world are waking up to the realization that technology can no longer be ignored. Governments are allocating funds in their national budgets to spend on technology solutions that can transform the way they operate, serve their citizens better and make decisions based upon data. Citizens are increasingly demanding for accountability from their leaders. Technology is presenting an opportunity for the public to participate in election monitoring, budgeting, communicate with their political leaders and government officials, fighting corruption and improving service delivery. With both online and mobile technology tools facilitating citizens to participate and take part in the decision-making process, identifying and sharing with their leaders' issues concerning public service delivery, there is no doubt that to some extent the aspects of transparency and accountability are being positively improved by technology.

A number of lessons learned from the implementation of *civic tech* in different aspects of citizens' engagement have provided useful insights for the technology world to innovate more and tap into this emerging area. Based on experience with the "ACODE"'s technology-based civic engagement platforms, in the initial conceptualization of these innovations, it's important to factor in the end-users. For example, local communities who don't have access to computers and the internet cannot use web-based technology. Therefore, the SMS technology works best in these situations. Continuous capacity building and training for all users is very important to get users to appreciate technology. In local communities, it is important to identify people who influence community and engage them to be champions of these new technology innovations. Identifying incentives for leaders who interact with citizens through these technology innovations is important. Continuous use of both the traditional and new media to promote the use of these technology innovations in improving governance is beneficial. Finally, the good news is that policymakers are beginning to listen. Although a lot of effort is still needed to win over decision makers in the area of governance, specifically in local governance, there are indications of progress.

References

ACODE (2016) *Citizen Monitor Mobile Application, Citizen Monitor.* Available at: http://citizenmonitor.acode-u.org/reporter/ (Accessed: 9 June 2017).

Action for Transparency (2017) *Information on https://actionfortransparency.org/, Action for Transparency.*

Amelina, M. (2007) 'Information and Communication Technologies for Demand for Good Governance Enabling the Power Shift'. Available at: http://siteresources.worldbank.org/EXTSOCIALDEVELOPM ENT/Resources/244362-1193949504055/4348035-1352736698664/ICT_for_DFGG__final_clean.pdf.

Ba, Y. M. (2011) 'Democratic Deepening and Provision of Public Goods: A Study on Decentralisation and Agricultural Development in 30 Countries in Sub-Saharan Africa.', *Political Science Theses.* Georgia State University, USA, p. Paper 44.

Bassler, A., Kathy, B., Neal, F. and Ron, T. (2008) 'Developing Effective Citizen Engagement: A How-To Guide for Community Leaders.' Harrisburg: Center for Rural Pennsylvania. Available at: http://www.rural.palegislature.us/eff ective_ citizen_engagement.pd f.

Best, E. (2008) *The Assessment of Regional Governance: Principles, Indicators and Potential Pitfalls UNU-CRIS Working Papers.* W-2008/10.

Bhargava, V. (2014) *How do citizens fi ght corruption successfully? Stories and lessons from Asia at Asian Development Bank Headquarters.* Asian Development Bank Headquarters.

Bowen, G. (2010) *Civic Engagement in Higher Education: Resources and References.*

Carmen, M., Forster, R. and Singh, J. (2004) 'Social Accountability: An Introduction to the Concept and Emerging Practice.', *Social Development Papers 76*. Washington, D.C.: World Bank, Participation and Civic Engagement Group.

DANIDA (2012a) *Using ICT to Promote Governance: A DANIDA Study*. Available at: http://um.dk/en/~/media/UM/English site/Docume nts/Danida/Partners/Research-Org/Researchstudies/Using ICT to Promote Governance 2012.ashx..

DANIDA (2012b) *Using ICTs to Promote Governance, A Danida Study*. Available at: http://www.unapcict.org/ecohub/using ict to promote-governance.

Dietrich, D. and Myrttinen, H. (2012) *Data Wrangling: European Public Sector Information Platform Topic Report No. 2012*. Public Sector Information Platform Topic Report. Available at: https://www.euro peandataportal.eu/sites/default/files/2012_data_wrangling_tools.pd f.

Escher, T. (2011) *Analysis of users and usage for UK Citizens*.

FixMyStreet (2018) 'Report, view, or discuss local problems'. Available at: https://www.fixmystreet.com/.

Fox, J. A. (2015) 'Social Accountability: What Does the Evidence Really Say?', *World Development*, 72, pp. 346–361.

Ghaus-Pasha, A. (2004) 'Role of civil society organisations in governance', in *Sixth Global Forum on Reinventing Government Towards Participatory and Transparent Governance*. Seoul, Republic of Korea, pp. 4 27. Available at: http://unpan1.un.org/intradoc/groups/public/do cuments/un/unpan019594.pdf.

Gilman, H. R. (2015) *Hollie Russon Gilman Columbia SIPA Civic Tech Symposium*. Available at: https://sipa.columbia.edu/system/files/expe rience sipa/5 Russon Gilman_Civic Tech for Inclusive Governance. pdf. (Accessed: 5 June 2017).

Gyong, J. E. (2014) 'Good governance and accountability in a democracy', *European Scientific Journal*, 7(26), pp. 71–89. Available at: https://www.ichangemycity.com/ (Accessed: 30 May 2017).

International Telecommunication Union (2017) *ICT Facts and Figures 2017, Geneva Switzerland., International Telecommunication Union*. Available at: https://www.itu.int/en/ITU D/Statistics/Documents/ facts/ICTFactsFigures2017.pdf.

Konrad-Adenauer-Stiftung (2011) 'Concepts and Principles of

Democratic Governance and Accountability', *Action for Strengthening Good Governance and Accountability in Uganda*, pp. 4–24. Available at: http://www.kas.de/wf/doc/kas_29779-1522-2-30.pdf?11121919022.

Leocadia, D. R. (2013) 'Enhancing Civic Engagement in the Digital Age: Global Activism, New Media and the Virtual Public Sphere', *Universidad de Murcia, y. Actas del I Congreso Internacional Comunicación y Sociedad*, pp. 6–49.

LOGIN (2014) *Local Governance Initiative and Network (LOGIN) is a South and East Asia, LOGIN*. Asia. Available at: http://www.loginasia.org/pages/learning_activities.

Mandarano, L., Meenar, M. and Steins, C. (2010) 'Building Social Capital in the Digital Age of Civic Engagement', *Journal of Planning Literature*, 25(2), p. 123–135.

MoFPED Uganda (2015) *National Budget Framework Paper FY 2017/2018-FY 2021/22*. Kampala.

Muyomba-Tamale, L., Luba, D. S. and Ssempala, D. (2013) 'Local Government Councils' Performance and Public Service Delivery in Uganda: Mpigi District Council Score-Card Report 2012/13.', *ACODE Public Service Delivery and Accountability Report*. Kampala, (16).

National Democratic Institute for International Affairs (2013) *Citizen Participation and Technology: An NDI Study*. Massachusetts: National Democratic Institute for International Affair. Available at: www.ndi.org.

One World India (2011) *ICT Facilitated Access to Information Innovations: A Compendium of Case Studies from South Asia*. South Asia.: OneWorld.net.

Patel, M., Sotsky, J., Gourley, S. and D, H. (2013) 'The Emergence of Civic tech: investments in a Growing Field'. Available at: https://www.knightfoundation.org/media/uploads/publication_pdfs/knight-civic-tech.pdf. Accessed 1/8/2018. .

Peixoto, T. and Fox, J. (2016) *Digital Dividends When Does ICT-Enabled Citizen Voice Lead to Government Responsiveness?* Washington, D.C.: World Bank.

Rodden, J. and Wibbels, E. (2013) 'Responsiveness and Accountability in Local Governance and Service Delivery Responsiveness and Accountability, An Agenda for USAID Program Design and

Evaluation Local Governance and Service Delivery', *United States Agency for International Development Center of Excellence on Democracy, Human Rights, and Governance*, pp. 1–17. Available at: https://sites.duke.edu/wibbels/files/2014/10/USAID-Evidence-Review_Responsiveness-and-Accountability-in-Local-Governance_May-2013.pdf.

Saunders, T. and Baeck, P. (2015) *Rethinking Smart Cities from the Ground up*. London, UK: NESTA. Available at: https://ofti.org/wp-content/uploads/2015/06/rethinking_smart_cities_from_the_groun d_up_2015.pdf.

Sauti za Wananchi (2017) *Welcome to Twaweza: Sauti za Wananchi*. Available at: https://www.twaweza.org/go/sauti-za-wananchi-english. (Accessed: 22 May 2017).

Shkabatur, J. (2012) *Check My School: A Case Study on Citizens' Monitoring of the Education Sector in the Philippines*. Washington, D.C. Available at: https://openknowledge.worldbank.org/handle/10986/23031 (Accessed: 6 August 2018).

UNICEF (2014) *U Report*. Available at: https://goodpracticessite.files.wo rdpress.com/2016/03/u-report_unicef.pdf (Accessed: 31 May 2017).

United Nations Development Programme (1993) *Reflections on Social Accountability, Catalyzing democratic governance to accelerate progress towards the Millennium Development Goals*. New York.

United Nations Development Programme (2013) *Reflections on Social Accountability, Catalyzing democratic governance to accelerate progress towards the Millennium Development Goals*.

Urban Sustainability Directors Network (2015) *The Civic Technology Landscape: A Field Analysis and Urban Sustainability Directors Network Recommendation*. Chicago: Urban Sustainability Directors Network. Available at: https://www.saenv.com/wp content/uploads/2015/07 /1.-Civic-Tech-Final-Report.pdf.

WASREB Kenya. (2011) 'Ensuring Access to Quality Water Services for All', *Water Services Regulatory Board, Republic of Kenya*. Available at: https://tikenya.org/wp-content/uploads/2017/06/national-water-integrity-study.pdf.

World Bank (2017) *World Bank Statistic, World Bank*. Available at: http://data.worldbank.org/indicator/SP.RUR.TOTL.ZS (Accessed: 11 June 2017).

World Bank Group (2016) *Evaluating Digital Citizen Engagement: A Practical*

Guide. Washington, D.C., DC: World Bank.

CHAPTER NINE

Conclusions: Local Governance in Uganda

Wilson Winstons Muhwezi, Arthur Bainomugisha,
Kiran Cunningham & Lillian Tamale-Muyomba

In this book, the authors have attempted to examine the rationale and the practical application of decentralization policy in Uganda since it was adopted in 1992. After almost three decades of implementation of decentralization in Uganda, it has been hailed as one of the best far reaching local government reforms in the developing world. Most political observers have described decentralization as a vehicle that has deepened democracy by taking government closer to the people. The very essence of the decentralization concept is that it contributes to development by empowering citizens and institutions at every level of society; improves access to services; increases people's participation in decision making; assists in developing peoples capacities; and enhances governments' responsiveness, transparency and political accountability. Local governance structures are at least in place in Uganda. However, there is widespread recognition that delivery of efficient public services and political accountability remains a challenge. Moving from rhetoric to practice is yet to be fully actualized. The need to invest in enhancing the capacity of local governments to deliver as anticipated is yet to be fully realized. Hopefully, this book has interrogated all facets of the promises and practices of decentralization in the context of Uganda.

The book traces the positioning of fiscal decentralization in Uganda. The devolution of functions and responsibilities to sub-national governments under decentralization in Uganda was accompanied by devolution of funds. A key expectation is that sub-national governments should raise revenues through taxes, fees and levies and spend the generated revenues and grants from the central government. Graduated tax, which used to be a directly collected annually from each able-bodied adult male used to earn local governments significant income but it was abolished in 1997 leaving local governments with very few own-resource revenues (Anywar, 2006). Therefore, local governments depend on central government transfers for over 90 percent of their finances. Uniquely however, is that the biggest chuck of financial resources that local governments appropriate are doled out by the central government. Revenue sharing between the Central and Local Governments is mainly by a grant system because the State does not allow local authorities sufficient tax powers to finance expenditure at their level. On average, the Central Government transfers account for 92 percent of local government budgets followed by donors at 5 percent and locally generated revenue at 3 percent. Although the main aim of decentralization is to bring services closer to the people, improve service delivery and make people's welfare better; evidence on whether decentralization has improved service delivery in Uganda is still inconclusive. Evidence from the regular assessment of performance of local governments in the 30 districts that have been regularly assessed has established that there exists lack of commensurate revenue for service delivery at lower levels of local government. In addition, the shortage of qualified and experienced staff, corruption and unresolved conflicts can also explain inconclusiveness.

It is in the context of a chequered decentralisation that citizen perspectives on service delivery was deliberately assessed, through civic engagement meetings held in 35 districts in Uganda. This book demonstrates that citizens throughout the districts need better and efficient service delivery. As users of the services, the citizens realise that they can influence the decisions of policy makers—through voice—and by influencing the behaviour of service providers—through client power. However, they need access to information about services. When citizens are given a voice, new pathways emerge for local governance (Richardson *et al.*, 2014). Citizens offer valuable perspectives on service outcomes. Citizens do not only have much to say but also about how systems are supposed to work. They also, however, lose hope and stop participating when they feel like their voices aren't listened to, responded to, or even taken seriously. This should be of utmost concern to decision-makers and policy makers at both the local and central government levels because without citizen participation, the promise of decentralisation – and even of democracy itself – cannot be realized.

This book chronicles the concept of 'accountability' and what it means in a decentralized governance system. In essence, accountable governments are supposed to be responsible for what they do and should be able to give satisfactory reasons for their actions. While holding local governments accountable, citizens are fully empowered with knowledge about their leaders' roles, their own rights and obligations, and are fully aware and confident about when and to whom the right questions should be asked. Accountability is more effective when citizens are involved. Accountability goes side-by-side with participation and it imbibes the actions of explaining or justifying what one has or has not done. For this to happen, elected leaders have to feel some sort of pressure to account to citizens. This pressure is related to the periodic elections where citizens may be forced to make decisions based on how best their local priorities were addressed. This makes local government elections a powerful form of accountability. No matter what form of accountability is talked about, it is important to observe that the concept has two key characteristics:

> (i) answerability, which is the right to receive a response and the obligation to provide one, and (ii) enforceability, which is the capacity to enforce action and seek redress when accountability fails. This means that governments accept their obligations to provide adequate, accessible and appropriate basic services, which are of good quality for all their citizens. It also means that citizens need to accept their obligations duties and responsibilities including paying taxes, participating in elections, and readiness to hold their leaders accountable when they fail to deliver on their mandate and promises. One of the powerful tools of accountability that has been applied in Uganda and is well explained in this book volume is use of Scorecard. The Scorecard has been instrumental in delivering service delivery based civic education, community engagement and empowerment of citizens in selected local governments.

Systematic implementation of the Local Government Councils Scorecard (LGCSCI) in Uganda was initiated by Advocates Coalition for Development and Environment (ACODE) in partnership with Uganda Local Government Association in 2009. There are important lessons learnt over time that translate in adaptability with the changing political times. The scorecard initiative focuses on building the capacity of citizens to demand for effective service delivery and the capacity of local governments to meet these demands by providing services effectively and efficiently. While LGCSCI does much to strengthen the *"voice"* – or demand side of social accountability, its centre-piece is focused on the *"teeth"* – or supply side. In contexts such as Uganda, where democratic governance and decentralization are fairly recent phenomenon and local governments have only recently been established as the governing bodies responsible for ensuring effective and efficient delivery of services, focusing on the *"teeth"* side of social accountability cannot be underestimated. Indeed, the LGCSCI experience suggests it may be an essential model for deepening democracy in most of the emerging and fragile democracies in the developing world.

This book volume also demonstrates the fact that notwithstanding any measure that is applied to assess gender, gender inequality still persists globally. Women continue to work more and earn less and have less direct access to productive resources than men. It is argued that much of the value of women's work remains invisible due to the association of *"work"* with income, leading to a lack of recognition of their practical and strategic needs especially, as those differ from men's. In the face of this persistent gender inequality and an increasingly sophisticated understanding of the differing roles, responsibilities and needs of women and men, especially in the global south have focused on increasing women's representation in government as a strategy for ensuring that the specific interests of women are taken into account when policies and programmes are developed and implemented. However, the participation by women in politics is still a relatively new phenomenon, especially in many developing countries like Uganda. Whereas it is generally acknowledged that women have indeed registered substantive political and social outcomes over time with regard to policy and delivery of services, the levels of this achievement evidently vary from country to country. This is mostly so because of the diverse cultures, social structural and internal country political characteristics that impacts the level of response to the global demand for women empowerment and inclusion in public, particularly political spheres.

This book volumes brings to the fore cases that demonstrate how women in politics have sufficient potential to bring about desired policy and service delivery change at the local government level if there is a conducive and supportive environment. Like their male counterparts, the book underscores the limitations that leaders, particularly women persistently grapple with. These range from effects of lower education levels to limited resources, multiple gender roles and responsibilities, a physical material-minded electorate, as well as challenges from a patriarchal mind set. It is no secret that women in much of rural Uganda are increasingly taking on the role of heading households, even though the degree may arguably be dependent on the social and political history of a local government. The cases used in this book volume clearly show that patriarchy still undermines the women's confidence to contest for directly elected positions while at the same time burdening them with domestic roles that fail their ability to balance their family and public roles. The one important message from this book volume is that governments around the world should remain engaged in the advancement of support to women in government, both at national and local levels. Success stories cited have come at a cost with so many sacrifices. One should not lose sight of the fact that these could most likely be cases of individual women who have overcome the structural barriers with great recognition, to the benefit of their societies. The ground is not yet levelled for both men and women. Laws still need to be reviewed to ensure equal representation where inequality exists, women in leadership should be supported to further their academic qualifications and society should be sensitized to support women leaders.

This book volume demonstrates the issue of civic engagement and communal land rights using the case of Rwamutonga internally displaced peoples, in Hoima district. In this case, the use of a variety of civic engagement strategies helped to turn attention to hitherto ignored land rights. The book reveals that effective civic engagement for the promotion and protection of land rights for poor and marginalized communities requires prior understanding of the forces driving land rights violations, key actors, and gaps in existing redress mechanisms. It demands the difficult but important process of overcoming political and bureaucratic corruption that promote impunity, hinder implementation of existing and new land-governance frameworks and reforms, and stymie institutional effectiveness. Documenting actors who enhance communal land rights protections, creating awareness of communities about their land rights, exposing and sanctioning perpetrators of land rights violations, and forging cooperation between communities and local governments are the starting points for local government interventions.

Furthermore, the book interrogates the concept of *Civic Engagement Action Plans* (CEAP). These are powerful strategies that enable citizens to hold their elected local governments accountable for service delivery. They also enable local governments to respond effectively and efficiently to those demands. CEAPs are a social accountability tool developed by ACODE in the course of the implementation of the Local Government Councils Scored that helped to improve service delivery. CEAPs are in essence a kind of a social contract, developed by citizens, with the support of their elected officials, to civically engage and demand for improvements in service delivery. The innovation of CEAPs was a response to the glaring policy constraints that hinder decentralization from delivering effectively on its promises. For instance, many citizens regard service delivery as a favour from government and not a right to demand better and efficient services. The CEAP tool is developed in a deliberative and participatory manner to enhance civic education and enable communities to be more effectively involved in holding their leaders accountable for service delivery (clean water, health services, roads and agricultural services) at the community level (Bainomugisha *et al.*, 2015).

As communities and civil society members around the world develop and try out social accountability mechanisms, practitioner-scholars are challenged to watch, learn, and gain clarity about the essential elements of effective social accountability initiatives. The CEAP methodology described and illustrated in this book has benefited from the action-learning cycle. Drawing on ACODE's experience with the Local Government Councils Score-card Initiative, the methodology emphasizes the importance of attending to both the supply and demand sides of local governance. Effective social accountability initiatives, as Fox and others have found, strengthen both citizen voice and government teeth (Fox, J. 2016; Grandvoinnet et al., 2015). The CEAP methodology does this and takes it a step further by catalysing that virtuous circle of mutual empowerment as citizens engage with their local government leaders in ways that feed directly into the mechanisms of government response. The CEAP methodology enhances both and voice and teeth – demand and supply – and connects them so that the virtual circle of mutual empowerment can begin to turn.

Lastly, this book acknowledges the importance of digital technology to increase options for strengthening citizens' voice in politics, carving out new political spaces for activism and promoting efficient service delivery and political accountability in local governments. *"Civic tech"* is presented as a term gaining popularity to represent the hot space for use of technology in enhancing democratization and good governance. Many Governments are waking up to the need to update their technology. It's no longer good practice to have documents hidden in cabinets and huge volumes of reports printed out. Citizens are increasingly demanding transparency from their elected leaders and too often, governments have no way to provide a clear window into how or why taxpayers' money is being spent. Civic technology enables engagement and participation of the public for equitable development, enhancing citizen communications, improving government infrastructure, and generally improving the delivery of public goods and services. Civic leaders, civil society, donors and citizens increasingly recognize the power of *"civic tech"* to connect people, improve participation and make government more responsive.

Despite the challenges facing technology today, a look at the future is promising. There is evidence that technology is constantly shaping the future of civic engagement the world over. Governments in developing world are waking up to the realization that technology can no longer be ignored. In the last decade, for the first time in years, governments are allocating funds in their national budgets to spend on technology solutions that can transform the way they operate, serve their citizens better and make decisions based upon data. Technology is presenting an opportunity for the public to participate in election monitoring, budgeting, communicate with their political leaders and government officials, fighting corruption and improving service delivery.

Diverse lessons learnt from implementation of civic technology in different aspects of citizens' engagement have provided useful insights for the technology world to innovate more to tap into this emerging area.

Based on experience with the ACODE Local Government SMS platform and the Citizen Monitor Mobile App, it's important to factor in the end-users. For example, local communities who don't have access to computers and internet cannot use web-based technology. In such cases, the SMS technology that is often mounted on simple mobile phones works as the best option. Continuous capacity building and training for all users is very important to enable users to appreciate technology. In local communities it is important to identify people who influence community so that they can be engaged as champions for the new technology innovations. There is need to provide incentives to elected leaders who interact with citizens through these technology innovations. Continuous use of both the traditional and new media to promote the use of these technology innovations in improving governance is beneficial.

In the final analysis, the authors conclude that decentralization has been largely relevant in deepening democracy and improving service delivery in Uganda. While, decentralization in Uganda is still unfinished business as it still faces a lot of constraints including inadequate financing, attempts at recentralization by the central government, a largely disempowered and disengaged citizenry and corruption; its noticeable success qualify it to be replicated elsewhere in emerging democracies. The LGCSCI implemented by ACODE and ULGA with its various innovations such as CEAPs, SMS, Mobile Applications are critical in building citizens engagement and empowerment necessary for democratic consolidation.

Taken together, the chapters in this volume confirm what many other researchers have found to be true of decentralization in Uganda and elsewhere: it is a work in progress. Local governments still struggle with what is many ways an incomplete decentralization process. Local governments need to do the work they have been mandated to do even with the little discretionary authority they have to use the funds that they receive. Citizens, still, experience service delivery that is anchored in an imperfect system decentralization process. While gains have surely been made, the citizen voices presented in Chapter 2 leave no doubt that much remains to be done.

Democracy itself, however, is always a work in progress. It requires citizens and civil society to be constantly engaged and vigilant, and it requires the same of government officials. Decentralization, by moving government closer to the people, was designed to enhance the ability of citizens to hold their elected leaders accountable and lessen the distance between government officials and their constituents. As each of the chapters in this book demonstrates, this system does indeed open space for meaningful civic engagement. However, civic engagement isn't produced simply by the opening of spaces; it must be facilitated by civil society organizations like ACODE. ACODE's relentless efforts to strengthen both the supply and demand sides of governance are at the heart of the work presented here. Through the creation of strategic social accountability initiatives such as the Local Government Councils Scorecard Initiative (LGCSCI), the civic engagement action plans (CEAPs), and ACODE's technology-based civic engagement platforms, ACODE has shown that activating citizen voice in ways that lead to government response strengthens both sides of accountable governance. Local government leaders appreciate engaged citizens who understand the roles and responsibilities of local government. When they receive input in forms they can use, local government leaders' effectiveness is enhanced. Citizens too gain confidence in the workings of democracy when they see evidence of their voices being heard and acted upon. With this confidence, they are more likely to remain engaged, and hold their leaders accountable in ways that enable government responsiveness.

References

Anywar, S. (2006) *Publoc Sector Governance and Accountability Series: Local governance in Developing Countries.* Washington D.C.

Bainomugisha, A., Muyomba-Tamale, L., Muhwezi, W., W., Cunningham, K., Ssemakula, E., G., Bogere, G., Rhoads, R. and Mbabazi, J. (2015) 'Local Government Councils Scorecard Assessment 2014/2015': *Unlocking Potentials And Amplifying Voices*, Kampala, ACODE Policy Research Series No. 70,.

Fox, J. (2016). Scaling accountability through vertically integrated civil society policy monitoring and advocacy. Working Paper, December 2016. Accountability Research Center and Institute of Development Studies.

Grandvoinnet, H., Aslam, G. and Raha, S. (2015). Opening the black box: The contextual drivers of social accountability. Washington, DC: World Bank Publications

Richardson, L., Kingsley, P., Cotterill, S., Rees, J., Squires, G. and Askew, R. (2014) 'Responsible citizens and accountable service providers? Renegotiating the contract between citizen and state', *Environment and Planning*, 46(7), pp. 1716–1731

Index

www.ingramcontent.com/pod-product-compliance
Lightning Source LLC
Chambersburg PA
CBHW050431280326
41932CB00013BA/2076